CRY PALESTINE

Inside the West Bank

Saïd K. Aburish

Routledge
Taylor & Francis Group
LONDON AND NEW YORK

First published 1991, 1993 by Westview Press

Published 2018 by Routledge
52 Vanderbilt Avenue, New York, NY 10017
2 Park Square, Milton Park, Abingdon, Oxon OX14 4RN

Routledge is an imprint of the Taylor & Francis Group, an informa business

Library of Congress Cataloging-in-Publication Data
Aburish, Saïd K.
Cry Palestine : inside the West Bank / by Saïd K. Aburish.
p. cm.
Previously published: London : Bloomsbury Pub., 1991.
ISBN 0-8133-1797-5. — ISBN 0-8133-1798-3 (pbk.)
1. West Bank—Social conditions. 2. Palestinian Arabs—West Bank—Social conditions. 3. Intifada, 1987- —Influence. 4. Jewish-Arab relations—1973- 5. Palestinian Arabs—Government policy—Israel. 6. Israel—Politics and government. I. Title.
DS110.W47 1993
956.95'3044—dc20 92-41651
CIP

ISBN 13: 978-0-367-01087-4 (hbk)

ISBN 13: 978-0-367-16074-6 (pbk)

CRY PALESTINE

To my cousins Amer and Nasser

CONTENTS

ACKNOWLEDGMENTS

Thanks are due to a great number of people who were generous with their time and counsel. Among those who helped during my stay in the West Bank are Yehuda Litani, Lea Tzemel, Othman Halaq, Ziad Abu Zayyad, Ibrahim Karaeen, Daoud Khuttab, Jad Izhaq, Hanna Seniora, David Grossman, Hani Shubeitah, Mahmoud Abu Zuluf, Sari Nusseibeh, Faisal Al Husseini, Zev Barran, Michael Sheridan, Dr Selim Al Husseini, Haidar Al Husseini, Dr Samir Abu Khalaf, Miree Ghoneim, Nadi Farraj, Samir Huleileh, Makram Sa'ad, Saleh Al Khatib and my good friends of Al Rashaidah tribe.

In London, my friends John Bulloch, Charles Glass, Anice Tawil, Khladoun Solh and Maher Othman read parts of the manuscript and provided encouragement and advice.

Lastly, this whole project wouldn't have been possible without the generous help of members of my family in Bethany. To all of them, particularly my cousin Nabil Aburish Hamad, I owe a huge debt of gratitude.

Introduction
WELCOME TO THE MIDDLE EAST

It is 21 August 1990 and all the newspapers I bought at Gatwick Airport tell the same story: the Gulf crisis threatens to turn into war. Perhaps I should be somewhere else reporting the Gulf story, instead of aboard Dan Air flight 4964, London to Tel Aviv. Although my presence on this flight suggests that I have answered this question, it nags me all the same.

From Ben Gurion Airport I intend to travel to the biblical village of Bethany outside Jerusalem, where I will stay for two to three months to research what I hope to be the true story of the *intifada*. In my mind, the story of the forty-month-old children's uprising against the Israelis has not been told properly. Neither the press reports nor books that I have read about the problem demonstrate an understanding of Arab thinking. Only someone who knows the Arabs of the West Bank well can capture this movement's essence by seeing beyond the statistical horror stories that we frequently read, see and hear about. I am on my way to Bethany to see what the *intifada* has done to my people and their aspirations, to their relationships with themselves, with the PLO leadership in exile, and with the Israelis, Palestinians, Arabs and the rest of the world. I am full of both trepidation and resolve. Never mind which story is more important in the long term, what I am trying to write or the Gulf crisis. My decision to come here was made easier by the fact that I can't report the Gulf crisis as a field correspondent, only as a distant observer or analyst. The circumstances that have irreversibly dictated this have to do with my previous books, which have been critical of all Arab governments. They retaliated, and I am banned from all Arab countries except the geographically remote and politically uninvolved ones in North Africa.

On the other hand, my criticism of the Israelis has been uncompromisingly harsh, though purely personal since I do not belong to a political group or subscribe to a particular ideology. Therefore the more immediate question was whether the Israelis would allow me in. There was the danger that they might identify me and ask me to leave and there is also a general standing prejudice against visitors who were born in Palestine. We are unwelcome and are suspected of going home to foment trouble or of being PLO couriers until we prove the innocent nature of our visits.

Inevitably, my problems with the Arabs and Israelis are linked. I realize this when I reflect on the independent stand I have taken over the years and the intellectual and practical problems it has created for me as a journalist and writer. My general unhappiness with the Arabs, and in particular the Arab leadership, is the result of disappointment. I want them to be better and do better and this persistent wish assumes a shrill edge because I am one of them and family quarrels are vicious affairs. To me Arab leaders could do much more to solve the political, economic and social problems of the Middle East. In addition, many are inept, feckless, corrupt and out of touch with their own people and the real world.

At the same time I have come to the conclusion that the Israelis are a merciless people who have lost whatever sense of purpose they once possessed. More recently, with the prospect of peace so near, they have assumed the ridiculous role of modern-day heroes and perpetuate their cruel domination of the West Bank and Gaza. This attitude flies in the face of all that the world in the 1990s stands for and threatens the future of both Israel and Jews everywhere.

I am on my way to Bethany – the once small village where I was born and lived until the age of fourteen, now a Jerusalem suburb of twenty thousand people – to write a book about life in the West Bank in 1990. What I know so far tells me that it will be a status report on the dark at the end of the tunnel that separates Arab from Jew. If this is confirmed, and my previous efforts are anything to go by, the results of my investigation will offend both sides. This pleasing thought allows my mind to wander to the fifty or so members of my family who still live in Bethany. They are, for the purposes of the Israeli immigration authorities, the reason for my visit, but in fact I do look forward to seeing them.

The pretty girl with auburn hair and sparkling black eyes sitting next to me on the plane speaks to me in Hebrew and I answer her in English. She smiles and repeats the question in attractively accented English: does she, as an Israeli citizen, have to fill out a landing card? I don't know the answer and tell her so but I make friendly noises because I am anxious to engage her in conversation.

I tell her that I am an Arab American who lives in London and that I am on my way to visit members of my family in Bethany. Reaction please, my eyes say; please talk to me. She is an Israeli student at the London School of Economics, that great liberal establishment. Instead of telling me more about herself she hurries to say that there is something un-Arab about me and means it as a compliment. I let it drop; I've heard it all before. Forty-one years of exile change one and I don't want to go through the schooling, the American, British and other aspects of exile that have influenced my life. Nevertheless, I tell myself that I need training, a few weeks to attune myself to Israeli attitudes towards the Arabs and Arab thinking about the Israelis. Back to the girl; I want to keep her talking.

'I love coming back here to visit my family but I don't like the way they treat me when I arrive at the airport. It is as if all Arabs are hoodlums and terrorists. Look at me, do I look like a terrorist?' The question is accompanied by my biggest smile. It works: she smiles back. 'I can't tell a terrorist from a horse, but you must understand that they have to be careful.'

My response comes naturally, instinctively. 'It isn't nice to be treated like a criminal when one is going back to the place of one's birth.'

'I guess so, but they still have to be very careful.'

Otherwise my fellow-passenger is friendly, but with nothing new to offer. She speaks the language of most Israelis. She recites a list of Arab atrocities against Israel and its citizens, a couple of true ones, many exaggerated ones and a good number of total fabrications – for example, that Muslim religious leaders tell people they will go to heaven if they kill a Jew. Not a word about the massacres at Sabra and Chatilla camps; not even a hint that Israel ever initiates trouble. The picture she paints is of an Israel wishing to live in peace and an Arab commitment to violence. I fall silent, but she, slightly embarrassed, manages with my tacit consent to divert me into conversation about the various nice places to see during my visit. It comes from the heart, my agreement that her land and mine is a beautiful country with much to see.

Our chumminess comes to an end, however, the moment the plane touches down at Ben Gurion Airport. As the plane taxis towards the terminal, my travelling companion resists my attempts to prolong the conversation. She behaves as if there was an Israeli law against talking to Arabs, even when their manner of behaviour and passport dilute that identity. The plane comes to rest and passengers start to disembark. She leaves without saying goodbye.

The afternoon heat of 31°C and the total lack of organization in the arrivals terminal slow me down. Politely I ask the immigration officer not to stamp my passport, just in case I have to visit an Arab country that frowns on Israeli stamps. When he looks at me and obliges, I smile at the irony of it all. I am given a pink slip of paper to hand over on leaving the immigration area and I note that most other passengers are given blue ones. As I move forward, two security officers eye the slip of paper and stop me; its blatant pink is the colour for suspects.

The pink slip and my US passport bearing Secretary of State Baker's message 'To Whom It May Concern' to facilitate my travel are taken away from me. The security officers tell me to collect my luggage and take it to an office at the end of the terminal, where 'undesirable returnees' are searched and questioned. It takes forty-five minutes to collect my bags and go to the office, where a female security officer is waiting for me. The room is totally bare except for a metal bench on which the suitcases are placed, and she stands opposite me, on the other side of the bench, dumpy and dishevelled in an unattractive way. She begins rudely.

'Why are you coming to Israel?'

'To visit my family in Bethany.'

'Where is that?'

'Two miles east of Jerusalem.'

'When was the last time you visited them?'

'Three years ago.'

'Why do you keep coming back – don't you have family in London where you live?'

Suddenly my face is hot, but I remind myself that I have rehearsed not getting upset. I successfully fight the natural human urge to tell her that my family have been in Bethany for over a thousand years. Instead I settle for, 'My uncle is sick. [True, Uncle Mousa, who was wounded and crippled in the 1967 war, is in bad health.] I would like to see him before he dies. Besides, I like to visit Bethany.'

'What do you do for a living?'

'I write and I do some business consulting work.'

'If you do these things, then why do you take Dan Air? They're cheap flights.'

'To save money. Surely there is nothing wrong with that.'

'I see. You can sit down, you know.'

'But there's nothing to sit on.' To me, this is another sign that my interrogator doesn't know what she is doing. Her questions are unimaginative, unlikely to reveal anything, but they are aimed at offending. Even my two complaints about my back not being able to take the punishment of standing up for a long time produced an invitation to sit on a chair that didn't exist. I look at her angrily until she leaves to get me a chair. While she is gone I look across the hallway at another cubicle waiting for another 'suspect'. She comes back and I sit down.

'Now,' she says, as if we had just begun, 'are you carrying any letters, packages, or anything for anyone?'

'No.'

'What's in your suitcases?'

'Personal belongings.'

'Did you pack them yourself?'

'Yes. They asked me that in London before boarding the plane.'

'Did anyone have a chance to put things in your suitcases without your knowledge?'

'No.'

'Not even your wife?'

'Not even her; she isn't there.'

'Don't give me confusing answers, OK?'

'Yes ma'am.'

'You wait here.'

She struts out of the room unhappily, but I am pleased with myself. If the Israelis are going to subject me to these indignities, then they should use a more intelligent person.

A man with a priest's collar is now in the room across the way. He is also waiting for his interrogator and I wave and he returns the greeting. An immediate sense of solidarity is born of our predicament.

'Where are you from,' I shout to him.

'Originally from Ramallah but now from Chicago.'

'Really? I went to graduate school in Chicago.'

'Where?'

'University of Chicago, Graduate School of Business.'

'That's funny. I taught there during the sixties – School of Near Eastern Studies.'

'I was there before, in the fifties.'

My interrogator returns with a five-foot-ten male Israeli army officer who looks typical: somewhat overweight and dishevelled. They see me talking to the priest and show their disapproval by closing the door. The officer tries his best to wear a ferocious face but I refuse to react.

'OK, open your suitcases one at a time and take things out one by one.'

'You want me to pull things out of the suitcase item by item?'

'Yes, that's what I said.'

I do it, item by item, slowly, and whenever something doesn't speak for itself, he takes it from my hand and squeezes it and does other things to it to determine it is safe. It takes forty-five minutes of this unpleasant routine to go through two suitcases before we eventually set to work on my briefcase. Trouble is suddenly visible, in the form of a battery-operated electronic stimulator that I have to apply to my back nightly to keep it from becoming stiff. I reach for the item but the officer shouts, 'Stop. Don't touch it. What is that?'

'A Mini-Tens to stimulate my back muscles. Let me show you.'

'No don't touch it.'

The atmosphere is charged. The two security people speak to each other animatedly in Hebrew. I stop myself smiling. You can't smile at people's fears even when they are imagined. The two and a half inch square wired Mini-Tens begins to look bigger and more ominous. It sits there with all three of us staring at it until finally the officer pulls it out carefully like a bomb-disposal expert. It lies in the middle of his pudgy hand as he carries it out, leaving me with the female officer.

'Did they see it in London?'

'Yes . . . I told them what it is.'

'Did they take the battery out?'

'No.'

'Why not?'

'I don't know.'

'Was the briefcase with you on the plane?'

'Yes.'

'So you could have put a battery in it even if they had taken it out.'

'Yes.'

'Did you?'

'No, it was already in.'

'Where did you get it?'

'From my physiotherapist. Her name is Alison Kirby and she lives in Devonshire Street.'

'Why?'

'Why what? . . . I have already told you, it's a back relaxer.'

'But you look healthy.'

'Looks are deceiving.'

'OK, don't move out of this room, don't open the door and don't talk to anybody.'

Soon they are back. The Mini-Tens is thrown on the table and I wonder if it is broken. They want to damage it because it frightens them. The rest of what is in my briefcase is visibly innocent. My passport is handed to me and the two officers tell me I can leave while everything is still scattered all over the place. I repack carelessly and run out of the room.

As I push my trolley out of the terminal I remember my travelling companion, the girl from the LSE. I decide that she's probably already at home with her family and I think of the members of my family who are waiting for me. My first cousins Khalil, Zakkaria and Ashraf are there and are pleased to see me in spite of the delay of over two hours. My apology is dismissed and I am told that I have fared better than other visiting members of our widely scattered family.

On the way out of the airport compound Ashraf's car is stopped twice for an identity card check for them and a passport check for me. Eventually we are on the four-lane Tel Aviv to Jerusalem highway. My cousins are telling me how bad things are in the West Bank, but they speak in hushed voices, even in the car. Zakkaria is sitting beside me in the back. He asks, 'Saïd, do you think there is going to be war in the Gulf?'

'Yes.'

They speak of the atmosphere created by the fear of war and how it has deepened the division between the Arabs and the Israelis. They tell stories of people naming their new-born sons Saddam and others adopting the name for grown-up children, and cross-examine me about the horrors of chemical and biological warfare.

The past seven hours of the trip, including this topical conversation, comprise a typical welcome to the Middle East.

Part One
The Brutal Reality

Chapter One
A WEEK IN THE LIFE OF THE WEST BANK

The *intifada* is now more than three years old, and the newsworthiness of everyday happenings in the West Bank is in question. The amount of newspaper and magazine space and radio and television time allocated to them has dwindled. In fact, except for the occasional disaster such as the Temple Mount–Harram Al Sherrif massacre of October 1990, in which twenty-one people were killed and over a hundred and fifty wounded, the press ignores daily happenings and concentrates on abstract diplomatic moves that do very little to alleviate the hideous conditions on the ground.

The story of the *intifada* has repeated itself with a regularity that dulls the senses. For the press, it has become an old story without interest; the atrocious has become run of the mill. How many times can a newspaper run a story that says, for example, that a dozen or more Arab kids have been wounded? I don't intend here to debate what constitutes news, but it is important to note that some of the happenings that are today being ignored as boring would have made the headlines a few years ago. Judging by what I see, hear and read in the local press, the *intifada* continues unchecked; it is just that the media are not treating it as a major news event.

One of the best ways to get a true picture of the state of things in the West Bank is to review a sample of *intifada* events that have taken place in a typical week. For this, one can rely on the reports in the local press, which rightly pays close attention to what is happening to its constituency, and a week is long enough without being too long. For the purposes of my examination, similar incidents are not repeated, so only one case of tree uprooting is used and one house demolition, even when several events of the same type have been reported. I reproduce below news items that appeared in local newspapers and magazines during the week from Monday 24 September 1990, followed in each case by my explanation of what the item means so that it can be understood by readers who are not aware of the background. In some cases it was necessary to contact the people involved to get a clearer view of the story.

> The United Nations Relief and Work Agency (UNRWA) officials say Israeli soldiers are preventing the organization from carrying out its duties in Al Bureij refugee camp. An UNRWA spokesperson said that they have been largely prevented from entering the camp, and that their movements have been restricted by soldiers. The camp and the area around it have been under curfew since 20 September when an Israeli soldier was killed there.
>
> (*Al Sha'ab*, Jerusalem)

The killing of the Israeli soldier took place when he lost his way into the camp. Aware that he was in unfriendly territory, the soldier panicked and ran over two pedestrians. The local people, afraid that he might use his gun, attacked him with sticks and stones and killed him. Unable to apprehend those responsible for the crime, the Israeli authorities placed the whole camp under curfew for an indefinite period. When a refugee camp or a town or a village is placed under curfew, the inhabitants are punished by the prevention of all basic living requirements, including food, from reaching the place.

This camp has been the scene of repeated anti-Israeli riots. Its inhabitants are poor people who were displaced in the Arab–Israeli war of 1948, and their descendants. They rely on UNRWA for food and the most elementary of health and education facilities. To forbid UNRWA officials from entering the camp meant the camp's meagre supples did not reach its twenty thousand inhabitants. After several protests to the relevant Israeli authorities, the curfew was lifted and UNRWA officials were allowed to resume their work. The camp was under curfew for four days.

> The family of prisoner Nasser Yousef Abu Jesh, 24, appealed to humanitarian organizations to help them get permission to visit their son who was arrested two months ago. The Beit Dajan family had already unsuccessfully appealed to the International Red Cross to help them with this matter.
>
> (*Al Itihad*, Jerusalem)

When the Israeli security forces detain a Palestinian, he or she is usually denied visits by members of their family or a lawyer for up to three weeks. The reasons for this vary, but the most common ones have to do with hiding the fact that the prisoner has been beaten or tortured and keeping the prisoner from communicating with anti-Israeli activists outside. When a prisoner is beaten or tortured, the Israelis don't want visitors to see the bruises or scars. Also, relatives or lawyers can carry messages to the prisoner's colleagues advising them of how much the Israelis know about their resistance cells and whether they should go into hiding.

Judging by how long this particular prisoner was denied visitors, this is obviously a very difficult case. The family's appeal for outside help was prompted by fear that the prisoner had been severely tortured.

Appeals to international humanitarian organizations to help families secure visiting rights have become common. The International Red Cross, Amnesty International and the left-wing Israeli Association for Civil Rights are among the most active in this field. In addition to dealing with the Israeli authorities, such organizations have been known to assist the families of detained people to reach a prison or detention camp. Many of the families of the detainees do not have the money for such a journey, even when it is only a few miles.

> The Israeli military government in Nablus informed all printers in the city that it is forbidden to print any text containing the word Palestine regardless of whether the text is political, social, educational or otherwise. Those wishing to be exempted need the approval of the local military authority.
>
> (*Al Sha'ab*, Jerusalem)

What this badly written item refers to is textbooks. Here is a typical example of arbitrary behaviour by local military commanders of the Israeli army. However, the incident has a significant background in that Israeli policy forbids the painting of the Palestinian flag or the use of the words 'Palestinian people', and violation of either decree is a misdemeanour punishable by a prison term or a fine. The punishment differs from place to place, and week to week, but it usually entails a prison sentence of between a week and two months or a fine of about a thousand US dollars.

Further examples of this policy of repressing the Palestinians' wish to assert their separate identity include a military order in the district of Bethlehem forbidding the mention of the 1948 Arab–Israeli war. This policy goes further, for people are not supposed to know or learn about the works of writers and politicians with leftist or liberal leanings. Among the writers, thinkers and politicians whose books are banned in detention camps are Plato, Jean-Paul Sartre, Albert Camus, Mao Tse-tung, Thomas Mann, Hermann Hesse and John Le Carré. Israeli writers whose books are similarly banned include David Grossman and Israel's former Foreign Minister Abba Eban. The list of Arab writers whose books are proscribed includes Saïd Aburish.

The International Commission of Jurists is sponsoring a local associate group, Al Haq (that which is right or righteous), in the town of Ramallah. Al Haq devotes much of its time to investigating Israeli attempts to suppress information. Because no textbooks mentioning Palestine and Palestinian history are available, schoolteachers resort to teaching these subjects orally.

> The administration of Ansar 3 detention camp issued new regulations on what Palestinian lawyers may bring their clients. The management of the camp will allow only blue collarless sweat suits for the purposes of personal wear. White and blue sheets are also allowed as is white and blue underwear. But the prisoners are permitted to receive any kind of shoes. The only food gifts permitted are olive oil and *za'atar* [a spice] and the latter item must be wrapped in plastic bags. The lawyers have been forbidden to meet with their clients without a member of the Israeli security forces being present.
>
> (*Al Sha'ab*, Jerusalem)

The rules and regulations governing what prisoners may receive from outside change frequently, but most books are banned and radios have never been allowed. The restrictions go even further, and often a lawyer is denied visiting rights for several weeks before his client's trial. The International Red Cross and the Israeli humanitarian organization B'tselem try to help families and lawyers communicate with detainees, but with limited success.

> Several cases of typhoid have been diagnosed in Nur Shams refugee camp and the patients were transferred to the Tulkarem hospital. Camp residents appealed to the Israeli authorities to help try to stop the spread of the disease, especially since some of the people stricken were children.
>
> (*Al Quds*, Jerusalem)

There are occasional outbreaks of infectious diseases that could spread to affect the population of Israel proper, as happened with typhoid in 1974. In spite of the obvious health hazard, the Israeli authorities resolutely take no preventive action and little or no remedial action. Among the reasons for the outbreaks of infectious diseases are open sewers and cesspools, the cramped conditions of the camps and lack of proper medical care. According to the Israeli writer David Grossman, the Deheisheh refugee camp has one of the highest population densities in the world.

> Vandals burned or stole the contents of the Beit Hanina home of Zuhair Kathem Al-Muthafar, located next to the Neve Ya'acov Israeli settlement. Muthafar and his family of eight had fled the house in July after attacks from Neve Ya'acov settlers following the killing of two Israelis in the area.
>
> (*Al Quds*, Jerusalem)

Whenever Israelis are attacked or hurt, Israeli settlers have been known to take the law into their hands and retaliate. Driving Arabs from their homes has become one of their better-known activities. Some of their methods to get local Arabs to leave include fencing them in so they can't move, denying them access to wells, and random break-ins and unlawful entry. In the village of Issawiya, two miles north-east of Jerusalem, some of the settlers forced people to leave by exposing themselves to conservative Muslim women whenever they saw them.

The Israeli security forces refrain from interfering with the activities of the settlers; indeed there have been many cases of the army aiding and abetting them. Very few of the Palestinians subjected to harassment and intimidation resort to the law for protection, even when they can afford it personally or with the help of an outside group. Their reluctance to use the law courts derives from the fact that these have consistently sided with the settlers, in one case accepting the testimony of one settler against that of seven Arabs.

> Journalist Najib Farraj, a resident of Deheisheh refugee camp in the Bethlehem area, disappeared from the camp three days ago and has not returned. Eyewitnesses said they saw soldiers patrolling the camp stop the journalist in a street after which he was beaten, tied up and put in a jeep. The family has not received any notice of the journalist's arrest.
>
> Lawyers Mohammad N'Amneh and Ibrahim Nasar and the Centre for Human Rights (Al Hurriyah) were told by the local police that there is no record of Farraj being arrested. Military sources referred the lawyers' inquiries to the Beit El military legal advisor who promised to look into the matter after the Jewish New Year holiday. Journalist Najib Farraj, an employee of the Bethlehem Press Office, has been arrested five times during the *intifada*.
>
> (*Al Itihad*, Jerusalem)

It took four weeks before the lawyers were able to determine the whereabouts of this highly respected journalist. The Israelis finally admitted that a six-month administrative detention order had been issued against him. This is the sixth time Najib Farraj, who is twenty-nine, has been detained. He is a resister, but is totally committed to non-violent means, and has written several articles urging the local population to engage in civil disobedience without resorting to violence.

> Israeli authorities closed a store in Hebron belonging to Anwar Fathi Abu Sakran, 22. Abu Sakran was accused of permitting persons unknown to use the store's roof to throw stones on Israeli patrols.
>
> (*Al Quds*, Jerusalem)

There are about ten similar cases every week. The authorities assume, without proof, that the shop owner knows who the stone-throwers are and that he approves of their action. The response of the security forces depends on the prowess of the stone-throwers and whether they have been successful in hitting the Israeli patrol vehicles. A good marksman who manages to hit a jeep can cause a whole street to be closed.

This is essentially an expression of the Israeli policy of collective punishment. Such punishment and disproportionate responses are also part of Israel's policy in dealing with its neighbours. When a Lebanese Muslim group in southern Lebanon fired a Katyusha rocket at an Israeli settlement, the Israeli Air Force attacked the bases of the group responsible for three consecutive days. Shop closures are so frequent that the law courts refuse to deal with the resulting complaints.

Both in cases of shop closures and of disproportionate military response to armed groups, the Israeli policy of 'massive retaliation' backfires, just as the principle of collective punishment worked against the German occupying forces during the Second World War.

> The Israeli military authorities closed the Al-Safa mosque in Al Bureij refugee camp until further notice. The Israeli authorities alleged that the mosque was a centre for fomenting protests against them. Five streets in Al Bureij were also closed.
>
> (*Al Fajr*, Jerusalem)

Except for the religious aspect, this situation is similar to the preceding one. However, the fact that the Israeli authorities have not shied from closing places of worship is significant, particularly in a part of the world where religious feelings are growing ever stronger. Churches have suffered the same fate.

Mosques are very often raided because Muslims use minarets to broadcast appeals to the faithful and spread appeals against the Israeli authorities' harsh measures. The imam of the mosque is often arrested, and if there is a public-address system, it is dismantled. Muslim and Christian religious leaders have repeatedly protested to the Israeli government about such measures, rightly pointing out their consequences. But it shows no signs of heeding these warnings.

> The Israeli military court in Nablus sentenced Mu'Ayed Abdel Latif Duqa, 26, to life imprisonment. Duqa, a resident of Attil village near Tulkarem, was accused of killing collaborator Ahmad Jaradat, also from Attil, in January 1989.
>
> (*Al Quds*, Jerusalem)

No proof exists that Duqa committed this crime, but it is true that he is a member of Fatah, the largest PLO group, and there is evidence that he is Fatah's local leader.

The Israeli authorities have consistently used the killing of collaborators as an excuse to punish people whom they have earmarked as troublemakers. This Fatah man has been a thorn in their side and they used the pretext of the murder to 'eliminate his troublesome presence'.

Interestingly, ordinary murders are very seldom investigated, as in the case of two in my home town of Bethany. Similarly, the disappearance of Arab activists is seldom investigated and suspicion lurks that members of the Israeli security forces are behind these happenings. Conversely, the murder of an Israeli or a collaborator produces an immediate response with little regard for the due process of law.

> Israeli soldiers bulldozed the house of Yusuf Murshed Rabi', 48, alleging that it was erected without a building permit. In nearby Qattana village, ten miles north of Jerusalem, four more houses were demolished for the same reason. Among the owners are Ahmad Taha and Nasser Taher.
>
> (*Al Quds*, Jerusalem)

The various figures available for the number of buildings demolished in this way do not agree, but at least five thousand houses have been razed during the past three years. It is true that houses are built without proper permits, in most cases because the Israeli policy aimed at making life unbearable and forcing Arabs to leave the West Bank includes refusal to issue building permits. But in the West Bank there are no fewer than thirty thousand structures built without permits. The Israelis know about them and look the other way, except in the case of those whom they suspect of anti-Israeli activity.

However, houses razed because of the lack of a permit are but a small proportion of the five thousand demolished. The rest were demolished for the following reasons: stone throwing from roofs, refusal to pay income tax, the conviction of a member of the household for participation in anti-Israeli acts and even the involvement of a relative overseas in anti-Israeli activity. Often the owners of a house are given an hour to remove their belongings, but on occasion the order is carried out before anything can be removed. There have been several cases of demolition orders being carried out in the middle of winter, resulting in the death from exposure of members of the evicted family. Others have suffered lesser effects of exposure.

> The Israeli authorities notified the *mukhtar* [village headman] of Awarta that 3000 *donums* [710 acres] of Al Sha'Ab quarter of the village will be expropriated. Most of the land in question is planted with olive trees.
>
> (*Al Fajr*, Jerusalem)

This piece of land was expropriated because the land belonging to an Israeli settlement runs through it and there have been cases of Arab children using olive trees as cover when stoning Israeli patrols. But similar confiscation orders take place when Israeli settlers decide to expand the land allocated to them by the authorities, and an expropriation order can be issued against totally innocent local Arabs. Since the Israeli occupation of the West Bank after the 1967 war, most of that land has been expropriated by the Israeli government and much of it has been used to settle Israelis. The government admits to expropriating fifty-two per cent of the land in the West Bank, but the Arabs claim that the real figure is much higher, some estimates being as high as sixty-seven per cent.

No compensation has been paid for the expropriated land. In most cases the Israeli government has claimed it is public land, while in others the owners have refused offers of compensation because that is tantamount to selling the land that was taken without their consent.

The only legal recourse against the expropriation of land is offered by the Military Appeals Court. However, Arabs no longer resort to this court because it has reversed only four out of over five thousand confiscation orders.

> The Israeli military used bulldozers to uproot 500 olive trees in Qattana village north of Jerusalem, alleging that stones were thrown from the olive orchard.
>
> (*Al Fajr*, Jerusalem)

This act of brutality against nature is very common here, and is becoming more frequent. During the past five years the Israelis have uprooted more than two hundred thousand olive trees and countless trees of other types. The olive tree is an important part of the economic life of the West Bank because it provides the olive oil that is used every day, while the olive itself is a staple food. Some of the trees uprooted are hundreds of years old. The reasons used to justify such acts are similar to those used to sanction the razing of houses. The Roman Catholic Church, the Greek Orthodox Church and Wakf (the body that oversees Muslim property) are among the victims of this policy, but repeated appeals to the Israeli government to change it have fallen on deaf ears.

> The Israeli military authorities fined Abdel Karim Ahmad Ghannma Israeli shekels 1000. The Burqin village youth was accused of throwing stones at an Israeli patrol.
>
> (*Al Sha'ab*, Jerusalem)

The fine imposed on this youth is the equivalent of five hundred dollars; the average monthly per capita income in the West Bank is considerably less than two hundred dollars. The reasons vary for imposing a fine rather than imprisoning a stone-thrower. In some cases fines are imposed when there is no place for more children in Israeli detention camps and prisons, while in others fines are imposed summarily because there is not enough evidence to take the accused to court. When a person is unable to pay a fine, a frequent occurrence because of the low standard of living, he is accused of 'refusal to pay monies owed to the Israeli government' and is tried for this misdemeanour without reference to the original crime or his inability to pay. The refusal to pay carries with it a heavier sentence than the simple act of stone throwing.

> The Israeli military court in Ramallah imposed a fine of Israeli shekels 1000 on Said Attalah Salim from the Deheisheh refugee camp because his son Muhammad, 11, threw stones at soldiers.
>
> (*Al Fajr*, Jerusalem)

This boy is too young to imprison because there are no detention facilities for children of his age. The fines imposed on parents are 'substitute punishment'. But as the father lives in a refugee camp, he is undoubtedly poor and it is unlikely that he can afford to pay the fine. This means that the father will be tried for 'refusal to pay monies owed to the Israeli government' and will be imprisoned.

> Soldiers confiscated a television set belonging to Qaddoura refugee camp resident Ziad Al-Rom, 27. The confiscation followed Rom's refusal to pay a fine of Israeli shekels 350 imposed on him after nationalist slogans were written on the outside walls of his house.
>
> (*Al Fajr*, Jerusalem)

I have talked to this man, who claims that he has no knowledge of who was responsible for writing the slogans. He says it took place at night while he was asleep. Furthermore, he claims that the Israeli authorities are trying to make an example of him to frighten other residents of the refugee camp, and make them turn against the children who do the writing. On the question of the fine, it is a simple case of not being able to pay. The value of his television set is four thousand Israeli shekels, but he says that the Israelis sell such confiscated goods at low prices and if they don't get enough money to meet the fine then he will still go to prison.

> The Israeli military government placed Nablus resident Anan Tahseen Makawi under administrative detention for the seventh time. Makawi, 30, was ordered to serve a detention of ten months. His family appealed to the International Red Cross to help obtain his release due to the detainee's deteriorating ill health.
>
> (*Al Quds*, Jerusalem)

The Israeli military authorities have suspected this man of being a local PLO operative without producing corroborative evidence. To stop him carrying out his suspected anti-Israeli activity, the authorities place him under administrative detention every time the tension in this area is high. Administrative detention – in reality a military order imprisoning people for six months without trial, and renewable indefinitely – can be carried out on the basis of unsubstantiated suspicion. The longest consecutive period of administrative detention anyone has served is seven years. The victim was released without trial.

According to lawyers Lea Tzemel and Ziad Abu Zayyad, many people are detained repeatedly. A few weeks after telling me this, the latter was himself placed under administrative detention for six months. Abu Zayyad is a highly educated, Hebrew-speaking Palestinian who devotes his time to defending *intifada* children charged with crimes by the Israelis, and he is totally committed to non-violent means. The Israeli system of justice is diminished without him.

In the case of Anan Makawi repeated detentions have affected his health: a nervous disease has reduced him to barely being able to walk.

> Toubas schoolteacher Bassam Naji Masa'id was fired from his teaching job by the local Israeli military officer because Masa'id had served four months of administrative detention.
>
> (*Al Quds*, Jerusalem)

The Israeli military authorities are empowered to deny the right of employment in a government department to anyone who has suffered administrative detention, even those who have never been charged with a specific crime. This applies to teachers, health officers, municipal employees and all those who hold jobs that come under the general description of civil administration. The same law can also be applied to students, who can be denied the right to attend classes after undergoing administrative detention. The number of students who have suffered administrative detention or prison terms of other varieties is over thirty thousand. However, not all of them have been denied the right to an education, and very often the whole thing is left to the discretion of the local military officer. Israeli laws in this area are not only arbitrary but also selective.

> For the eighth consecutive day, the residents of the Tulkarem refugee camp have suffered from 'water supply problems'. Deheisheh refugee camp residents are also suffering from a water shortage for the sixth consecutive day. The residents of both camps are appealing to the authorities to do something to alleviate the problem.
>
> (*Al Sha'ab*, Jeusalem)

The Tulkarem refugee camp has eight thousand residents, who are maintained by UNRWA. The camp has a long history as a centre of anti-Israeli activity, and many of its residents have suffered fines, detention, long prison sentences and torture. My enquiries into this case reveal that the Israeli authorities cut off the water supply to the camp after other measures failed to stem the anti-Israeli activity of its detainees. Cutting off water and electricity supplies has lately become a prevalent tool of retaliation against local populations. Several UN agencies, the British Medical Aid to the Palestinians (MAP) and Swedish and Italian medical aid groups have warned that stopping the water supply could lead to the spread of disease. The Israeli government nevertheless adheres to this policy.

> The hunger strike by thousands of detainees at Ansar 3 detention camp in the Negev Desert has ended. The strike began because the camp's military administration refused to respond to the detainees' complaints asking for improvements in the camp's conditions.
>
> (*Ha'aretz*, Jerusalem)

The Ansar 3 detention camp houses three thousand Palestinian detainees of fifteen years and older. The conditions against which the detainees protested include the cessation of postal deliveries, denial of visiting rights and appalling sanitary conditions. The UN was refused permission to investigate the authenticity of these complaints. The strike ended after postal deliveries and visiting rights were restored. According to a Swedish Medical Aid officer, the sanitary arrangements within the camp remain 'utterly inhuman'.

> The Israeli newspaper *Hadashout* reported that the government has not made plans for the distribution of anti-chemical warfare gas masks to the Arab population of the West Bank and Gaza. Meanwhile plans to distribute gas masks to the population of Israel are well under way.
>
> (*Al Quds*, Jerusalem)

The decision to distribute gas masks was taken in response to the threat made by the Iraqi President Saddam Hussein to use chemical weapons against Israel. Most military analysts agreed that the threat to the Arab population of the West Bank was the same as the threat to the population of Israel itself.

Hadashout's campaign against this sinister act of discrimination caused the Israeli government to modify its position: it offered instead to sell gas masks to the Arab population for ninety dollars each. (Masks were supplied free to Israeli citizens.) The Arab population could not afford this price, and as a result remained vulnerable.

> The Israeli military government placed Salah Hikmat Al Masri, a member of Al-Najah University Board of Trustees, under administrative

detention for six months. Masri, a resident of Nablus, was arrested early in September.

(*Al Sha'ab*, Jerusalem)

The detainee is a member of a well-known Palestinian family of notables. He is one of the local leaders put forward for membership of a Palestinian delegation that would, when the time came, negotiate autonomy or independence with Israel. His detention means that he now has a criminal record, which disqualifies him from membership of any body that has official dealings with the State of Israel. Most Palestinians who have been chosen to participate in the proposed peace negotiations have been detained at one time or another, or have been disqualified for other reasons. Soon the Palestinians will have no potential peace negotiators left to field – to the Israelis they are all criminals.

The Israeli military used bulldozers to block the southern entrance to the Balata refugee camp near Nablus. Rocks and dirt were used to build a wall to block entry to and exit from the camp.

(*Al Sha-ab*, Jerusalem)

This is another example of collective punishment. In this case access to the camp remains possible, but has been made more difficult by the closure of one entrance. Even in cities, very often a whole street is closed. In Bethlehem the vegetable market was closed for over a month, in Jerusalem the jewellers' market was shut down for two weeks and in Jericho farmers were denied access to their land for four months, during which time most of their plants died.

The aim of this policy is to punish a whole community or a group so that they pressure 'troublemakers' to desist from further anti-Israeli acts. It has the opposite effect.

Two children have been killed and another fifteen wounded when the security forces in Tulkarem and Nablus opened fire on demonstrators who threw stones and Molotov cocktails at members of these forces. The disturbances continued throughout the night.

(*Al Quds*, Jerusalem)

These confrontations between Israeli soldiers and Arab schoolchildren, the accepted symbols of the *intifada*, are an almost daily occurrence. Over the past three years more than twelve hundred Palestinian children have been killed and more than eight thousand have been wounded. In addition to the forty thousand who have been detained, others have been stopped and beaten on the spot, while over three thousand are wanted but remain at large.

The *intifada* shows no signs of abating. People have learned to live with what they call 'sacrifices'. For their part, the Israelis show no willingness to deal with the uprising beyond carrying out punitive acts of the kind reported in this chapter.

Chapter Two
THE LANGUAGE OF FEAR, HATE, VIOLENCE AND DEATH

I have been in the West Bank for a month now and already my contact with the outside world is receding. The atmosphere is overwhelming and the harsh facts of life here bear down on me. I have even adopted the language of the *intifada*, a linguistic transformation necessary in order to avoid cumbersome academic or formal descriptions when talking with people. Such alien terms would only create unease and defeat my purpose: to get a true picture of life in the land where the word 'hope' is conspicuous by its absence.

As a result of this brief stay, people might think I have become somewhat demented, speaking as I do in terms drawn from the morbid realms of criminology. It is a vocabulary of fear, hate, violence and death, but these are the things people talk about in the West Bank and to relate countless tales of misery the *intifada* has developed a language of its own that continues to evolve.

My first cousin, Ali Aburish, now uses the phrase 'administrative detention' almost unconsciously and with unintended frequency. He was among the first people who came to see me after my arrival in Bethany. Calm and gentlemanly in demeanour, this schoolteacher of forty-one tries to suppress his inner pain when talking about the administrative detention of his sons Amer, sixteen, and Nasser, fifteen. They have been held by the Israeli authorities for the last seventeen months, and hope is fading for an early trial date. The latest postponement was last week.

This inhuman act of detaining people for long periods without trial is made possible by the Israeli military laws of occupation, and although my cousins' case is worse than most, it is far from unique. The number of children under administrative detention runs into thousands and others who came to greet me have children suffering an identical fate. They too have the same compulsion to repeat the atrocious combination of words.

The phrase contaminates the soul like an infectious disease, affecting more and more people. I have begun to suffer pain when using it myself and whenever I do I hurry to take refuge in its local modifiers and definers, to talk about where and for how long particular children have been held – just in case there is light at the end of the tunnel.

While the term 'administrative detention' consumes the heart with its pervasive immediacy, the word *t'azeeb* (torture) in its various meanings slowly corrodes the senses. Most often it is heard in its usual sense: the systematic beating of newly arrested detainees to obtain confessions. But *t'azeeb* is also used to describe more subtle forms of punishment, including long periods of solitary confinement and (mostly unfulfilled) threats of direct punishment against a detainee's family unless he or she confesses and cooperates. (Israeli interrogators have been known to put pressure on an uncooperative detainee by telling him that his sister would be raped or his family home would be demolished.)

Then there is the *t'azeeb* of the detainee's family by what has been called bureaucratic torture: the denial of visiting rights, not telling parents where their children are and, on occasion, whether they are alive or dead. To my cousin Randa, the interception of letters to and from her seventeen-year-old son Muhammad is a supreme form of *t'azeeb*.

The population of the West Bank and Gaza is one and a half million and over forty thousand children have suffered some form of arrest and the *t'azeeb* that goes with it. Little wonder that it is on everybody's mind. In spite of promises to myself not to succumb to the local terminology, I have grown accustomed to this living ugliness and use the word without reservation.

Israeli army patrols and their behaviour towards people are a constant topic of conversation not only because the patrols are omnipresent but because the conduct of patrol members is not uniform and much is left to the dubious discretion of patrol leaders. Among other things, as has been demonstrated tragically by the Temple Mount–Harram Al Sherrif massacre of October 1990, the rules that govern conditions under which patrol members may resort to the use of live ammunition are vague or, to the local population, *mish ma'rouf* (unknown). Fear of the unknown, an accepted psychological weapon, is palpable here.

The frightening unknown is any Israeli soldier with a rifle in his hand.

West Bank Arabs are always talking about things being 'thick' and 'thin'. This is a reference to the frequency of Israeli patrols and the number of soldiers in a patrolling unit. From where I am staying, I can look out of my bedroom window and issue my own summary of the 'thickness' or 'thinness' every few minutes if I so choose. They prowl around in jeeps or two-ton lorries or in combinations of both, young soldiers clutching their rifles or sub-machine-guns as if a shooting war were about to break out. Their mates are constantly using the radio to stay in touch with headquarters and its inadequate long-distance instructions. In addition, there are foot patrols of four or six soldiers each who take readiness a step further: their fingers are always on the trigger. They are what the Arabs call *Al Musha*, foot soldiers.

The duties of one of these patrols can involve over ten miles of walking daily in temperatures of 35°C and the records of the local human rights organizations are full of *Al Musha* going berserk at the expense of the local people. Random unexplained beatings are frequent, but they are never investigated unless they cause serious injury or death. This is why the patrols are feared and stories of their presence and the looks of weariness and hate on their faces give constant rise to whispers between locals.

The only Arab opposition to *Al Musha* are the actions associated with the *intifada*: stone throwing and the very occasional crude Molotov cocktail. Both of these methods are hit-and-run tactics. The absence of tools with which to resist more forcefully and the fear of retaliation have driven the Arabs to invent terms of disparagement. For example, a jeep is a sandal and a two-ton lorry is a boot, since any reference to footwear is profoundly insulting in Arab and Muslim legend, the bottom of the foot being profane.

Among those who patrol on foot are black-bereted paratroops despised as *Al Sawda*, the blackheads. The Falashas, the black Jews from the Ethiopian highlands, have been recruited into the Israeli armed forces and since many of them speak neither Hebrew or Arabic, they are referred to as *Ummyeen*, illiterates. Illiterate or not, their understandable sense of frustration shows itself in many disagreeable ways, including rude gestures to women.

Any contact between patrols and the local population is by nature negative, taking place only when the patrols are performing their hostile duties. They stop people to ask about their shopping bags, disperse groups of more than four children even when they are innocently on their way to or from school, and are particularly hard on people whom they suspect of carrying anything that could be used for painting anti-Israeli slogans, including tomato paste. Ironically, Israeli-made aerosol paint sprays are used for graffiti and a local boy told me, 'You have to have Israeli paint to be a read Picasso.'

All Arabs carry identity cards, which they are required to produce on demand. The IDs are colour-coded to show who has been detained and those whose movements are restricted to town or a particular area. In addition, there are unverifiable but believable reports that IDs are coded in a way not known to the average person (probably by numbers). A person with a green ID is restricted to a town denoted *akdar* (green) and so on. Members of Israeli patrols are merciless with anyone with 'a record' and once an ID reveals this the holder is mocked and kicked around, suffering *t'azeeb khafif* (light torture). Often this on-the-spot torture takes the form of taunting the card-holder to do something heroic and foolish so that the patrol has an excuse for *t'azeeb t'eel* (heavy torture) or detention.

Being stopped for an ID check is a very serious business. People who have come to see me have spoken of others who were supposed to have accompanied them as *Mu'af* – that is, held for interrogation by a patrol. Interrogations can last two hours or more and occasionally a person is stopped and made to wait until the patrol finish their routine tour before returning to continue. A sixteen-year-old told me of how he was kept waiting alone at a street corner for three hours without daring to escape because the foot patrol had taken away his identity card as a precautionary measure. There is no way to live without one's ID, and besides they would have been able to trace his address. His only option was to become a *mushared* (escapee) and that means years of detention if you are caught. There are several thousand escapees in the West Bank, mainly teenagers, the majority of whom are innocent but afraid to face Israeli interrogators; most of them live in caves and travel at night. Stories of *musharedeen* appearing in the middle of the night to ask for food are widespread and people do help them.

I asked several people what they thought the Israelis were doing when they kept them waiting while finishing their routine chores and they all answered, '*b'shimou al nasseem*' (smelling the breezes). This quaint old expression for idle leisure, which probably goes back to the *Arabian Nights*, has assumed a new, eerie connotation. But it is not the only case of reversing the meaning of a word for dramatic effect. People used to associate the word '*M'nakked*' with a naughty active child, but it is now used of any Israeli soldier who has a violent nature and takes on the local kids. Literally the word means 'badly behaved', but its present usage smacks of 'tortured' or 'tormented'. I can't help but think it is appropriate to Israeli soldiers, for those on patrol duty look singularly unhappy.

One of the smaller but better known groups of West Bankers are the *matroodeen*, the deportees. They are West Bankers in the public eye: journalists, academics and politicians who openly oppose the Israeli occupation without committing acts for which they could be tried or detained. They are usually deported to Jordan. The UN, USA, Britain and others have protested against this practice, which violates the Geneva Convention, but it continues. Nowadays, when you ask someone where their kids are they often tell you they are *matroodeen* – a new way of saying they have been sent away for misbehaving. If a child is confined to his room for misbehaviour then he is said to be in a *zinzana*, a dark cell where detainees and prisoners are subjected to solitary confinement.

The most hated type of Israeli law-enforcement bodies are the ones comprised of civilians and run by the *Mukhabarat* (Intelligence). When used as patrols, the *Mukhabarat* are Arabic-speaking security officers armed with point forty-five handguns, and like Intelligence officers everywhere they have a tendency to be violent; they certainly show less restraint than the army, particularly in administering summary justice. Very often the whole situation is either provoked or set up by the *Mukhabarat*: they insult people until they respond or they pretend they are locals and make anti-Israeli statements until the victim joins in. To disguise themselves they have been known to drive ice-cream vans or pretend to be electricians or builders. Amazingly, however, most of their disguises are not aimed at real organizers but at simple people who might say something as innocent as 'I don't like the Israelis.'

Whenever someone turns up late to a meeting, the people who have been waiting examine him with mock incredulity and say, 'You're in one piece, so you didn't run into the *Mukhabarat*, so what kept you?' Another example of black humour is to tell women not to talk to strange females because the *Mukhabarat* have taken to pretending to be women. I was dissuaded from fabricating an incident in order to investigate the methods of the *Mukhabarat* by a cousin who told me, 'Saïd, you'll be half dead before you're given a chance to produce your American passport and even that might not help you. Leave it alone.'

The use of tear gas to disperse crowds is an everyday occurrence. The CS bombs used by the Israelis are particularly strong and have caused ninety-three deaths, hundreds of serious injuries and countless minor injuries and irritations. I shed tears myself because they were used in the village of At Tour, a mile and a half from where I was. When the tear gas wafts through the air, irritating the nose, eyes and throat, those affected invariably giggle and speak of *drat* (farts). Those with a sense of smell acute enough to detect it before the others, hurry to announce that the Israelis have just farted and then describe how strong, ripe or tiny the fart is.

Night is a time of inactivity; public places are closed, and people have nowhere to go, so there is very little movement. Even that great traditional institution and male redoubt, the coffee-house, has suffered because the Israelis have something against groups. Their jeeps and trucks on night duty are equipped with powerful revolving searchlights that scan the countryside, alleyways and even houses for troublemakers, mostly stone-throwers. The searchlight is a *kamar Israeli* (Israeli moon) and the people pretend to swoon when it falls on them while they are sitting in their gardens or the supposed security of their homes. People tell black jokes about the Israelis directing their 'moons' at the homes of pretty girls and tease others less fortunate by saying they are *ma btista haleesh*, undeserving. Sadly, another effect of these searchlights is to cause momentary blindness, which leads some to panic or run away. Worse still, Israeli patrols sometimes respond by opening fire and wounding or killing those who panic.

I violated one of the rules governing conduct under these unusual circumstances without knowing it at the time. Walking to my aunt's place at nine o'clock one evening, I turned a street corner and found myself face to face with an Israeli army foot patrol of six soldiers, three on each side of the road, eyes suspiciously examining me and fingers on the triggers of their M16 rifles, which they held horizontal. There was nobody else around and my body tensed with fear, but I moved forward pretending otherwise. Our eyes stayed on each other and when I was finally parallel with them I made a peace offering by saying good evening in English. I got no response and kept walking – at least I didn't become a *mu'af*.

My innocent greeting was considered a big mistake here. When it comes to encounters with Israeli authority, men follow a policy of leave well enough alone, in local parlance *ibid an ash shar wa ghanelou* (stay well out of harm's way and sing for it). Their avoidance of the Israelis takes elaborate forms, including taking their wives with them on their brief walks because the Israelis for the most part shy away from harassing women. I have heard men announce their intention to visit people nearby and say to their wives, 'Come along my protector.' The term *hamiatee* (my protectress) is part of the local language and some women are pleased with this sudden elevation to equality, while others find it a chore – they would rather follow tradition and stay at home.

The special words, the extension of ordinary meaning to give a word extra scope and the corruption of old phrases to describe situations that are the exact opposite of the original meaning are not confined to talk about the Israelis. They are also used of other Arabs. For example, corruption in the PLO is a major topic of conversation and people keep track of the wealth of many members of the Palestinian National Council, the PLO's parliamentary parent. They preface the mention of names of such people by saying 'The Mendicant Muhammad Abdullah [a fictional name] of our national command'. Everybody here appreciates the reasons for this bitterness about local poverty.

An even more popular word among West Bank Arabs is *'ameel*. Simply translated, it means 'agent'. Understandably, locally it means a collaborator with the Israeli authorities, but it goes beyond this sense and has assumed an uncouth ugliness. It is now used very loosely of someone whose behaviour does not strictly adhere to the official PLO line (this organization, with all its faults, is all the people here have). Certainly it is applied to those who deserve it, cases of open collaboration (alienation and disillusionment do exist and so do informers), but it is also used to describe anyone who does not follow the orders of the United National Leadership (UNL), which is the pro- or crypto-PLO political committee comprising members of the organizations that make up the *intifada*.

Among other things, the UNL regularly orders protest strikes. People have taken to attaching the word *'ameel* to those who do not shut up shop or refrain from work at such times. Often, though, the reason for their compliance is simply a reflection of real financial need. The term's meaning goes further to embrace all those who have genuine political differences with the policies and the ways of the UNL. This is extremely dangerous because the consequences of being dubbed an *'ameel* can be brutal, providing a living reminder that revolutions are blind and do indeed devour their infants.

Regardless of the original reason for the label, the serious local *'ameels* are handled by *Al Mutalathimoon* (the wrapped or masked ones, so called because they use the Arab head-dress to disguise their identity in the manner of the stone-throwers seen on television). *Al Mutalathimoon*, as might be expected, operate at night. They are everywhere and their job is to keep local people in line. Since the *intifada*, the masked ones have eliminated over three hundred people, and lately the rate has accelerated. Because there are no arms or silencers or sophisticated equipment to be had (the possession of a handgun can earn fifteen years in an Israeli jail), the killings are truly sordid affairs, most of them involving the use of axes, knives, chains, sticks, stones and burning.

As if this were not enough, Arab belief in tribe and family often takes over and an *'ameel*'s family is eliminated with him. The blind horror of this act is justified as getting rid of *al dam al wisikh* (dirty blood). Often it is a consequence of the belief that treason runs along family lines, as do, to the Arab way of thinking, other character deficiencies. In some cases elimination is carried out because the masked ones fear identification by members of the victim's family.

Minor offenders not accused of outright treason or damaging disagreement with accepted policies, for example people who open shops and coffee-houses on strike days, are initially subject to *tahtheeb* (discipline). Sometimes they are telephoned and a warning is issued in which they are told not to repeat the offence. I have heard people tease others about being *munthareen* (warned ones), but this is no joke because if the unpopular activity is continued the warning is taken further and the offender can suffer a beating or a broken limb or can have his car or business torched. (Statistics are hard to come by, but there have been at least five thousand such incidents.) If this is not enough to dissuade the *'ameel*, the axe and the knife come into play.

In fairness, it should be stated that the UNL leadership is disturbed by some of the acts of *Al Mutalathimoon* against people when a serious violation of Arab solidarity has not been proven. The PLO Chairman, Yasser Arafat, has spoken out strongly against the methods employed, but neither misgivings nor outright condemnation has put an end to misjudgement and in the absence of courts of law the abuse is inherent in the act.

The word *'ameel* is applied equally liberally to Arabs outside the West Bank. For example, because West Bankers are strongly pro-Saddam Hussein, all the Arab leaders who opposed his seizure of Kuwait are considered *'ameels*. In this case the condemnation means an agent of the United States and the West, who are seen as sympathetic to Israel. In talking about Arab leaders, I can no longer use the inclusive term '*Zumaat Al Arab*' and must divide them into *'ameels* and *shurafa* (the honest ones who have supported Saddam). Because there are no masked ones to administer justice to the *'ameels* among Arab leaders, the word is reinforced by other pejoratives born of anger and frustration such as *'ameel kalb* ('agent-dog', for to Muslims a dog is profane). This new epithet threatens to become an established term of abuse for those kings, presidents and other hated Arabs that the masked ones cannot discipline.

The Israeli authorities, like resented occupiers throughout history, exacerbate local violence by behaving stupidly. The masked ones are hunted and when captured a surprisingly high number of them die mysteriously. They are beaten mercilessly, deprived of legal protection and receive prison sentences of up to twenty years or more. On the other hand, Israeli encouragement of those who violate orders is open and naïve to the point of absurdity. The expression used to describe this activity is *bedal 'oohum* (the Israelis pamper the violators, who are then called 'the pampered ones'). An example of this is the hated *Mukhabarat* standing in front of the shop of a transgressor with their guns sticking out from under their belts. (Who in his right mind would shop there?) There have been cases of the Israelis issuing guns to informers, who are simple enough to brandish them openly and in the process cancel their own effectiveness, for nobody talks to them. Besides, a community is always able to isolate and eliminate an individual who works against it.

There is not a single sign to indicate a more intelligent Israeli effort, such as alleviating the difficult local economic conditions that exacerbate frustrations (see Chapter Sixteen). The Israelis are seen as simply not caring. Oddly, the late Israeli Chief of Staff and Defence Minister, Moshe Dayan, the man who led the Israeli occupation of the West Bank and Gaza, is remembered kindly. With some success, Dayan tried to introduce modern farming methods to Arabs in the Jordan valley and is remembered as a *bani adam* (human being), but the rest of the Israelis are *mish bani admeen* (not human).

The local language continues to evolve. For example, until recently the term widely used to describe Israelis was *Iwlad amna* (our cousins), a reference to the fact that Arabs and Jews are both Semites. The increasing stresses within Israeli society and the consequent divisions have led to a need to amend this time-honoured phrase. The result is several different names to describe distinct Israeli groups.

Al Rous (the Russians) are the newly arrived Jewish immigrants from the Soviet Union and parts of Eastern Europe. *Al Sharkiyeen* (the orientals) are eastern Jews who came to Israel from the Arab countries, mostly Iraq, Yemen and Morocco. *Al Sharkiyeen* is a name that strikes fear in the hearts of West Bankers. They tend to treat Arabs harshly because, shamefully, they themselves are not accepted by European Jews and are at the bottom of Israel's social scale. They derive a sinister sense of superiority from mistreating the Arabs and it gives them a sense of belonging that they otherwise lack and separates them from those – the Arabs – who are culturally closer to them.

On the other hand, the Arabs like the attitude of the *Yassaryeen* (the leftists), most of whom are intellectual Israelis who favour granting the Palestinians the right of self-determination and who disapprove of their government's policies of occupation and the resultant hardship for the Arabs. The last name in this short list of Israeli groups is that of the *Mustamereen* (the colonists or settlers), the Israelis who live on land expropriated from Arabs after the 1967 war. Many of those people are religious fanatics armed by the Israeli government and do not hesitate to use their weapons. Indeed, the settlers live up to their name of colonists and conduct armed raids against their Arab neighbours on the flimsiest of excuses, such as a stray goat grazing on 'their land'.

I note the names given to the various Israeli groups and, despite the prevailing mood of hopelessness, I glimpse a silver lining. For perhaps the existence of good and bad Israelis is a healthy sign that augurs well for the future. To me it is preferable to lumping all Israelis together as objects of hate.

Al Rous are an unknown quantity, but their inevitable development of a political identity will assume great importance because of their large and growing numbers and Israel's possible use of Arab territory to accommodate them. By 1992 they will represent over twenty per cent of the voting population. But for now this is less important than what the Israeli government intends to do with this influx of immigrants. The pressing question is, what are the Israelis going to do with *Al Rous*? Are they going to give them Arab land? I don't know the answer, but there are signs that the Israeli government intends to turn *Al Rous* into colonists. Widespread Arab hope that this frightening transformation will not occur is based on the fact that *Al Rous* are city people who would not readily take to life in isolated settlements.

While Arabs are preoccupied with the influx of *Al Rous*, little is said about the outflow of the *Mugtarbeen* (Arabs who emigrate to non-Arab countries). There are *Mugtarbeen utuk* (old emigrants) and *Mugtarbeen al nakba* (the ones who left since the Arab defeat of 1948). I am one of the latter. The number of people leaving is increasing and the rate is likely to accelerate. I hear of more and more families encouraging their young people to leave to avoid potential political trouble and because of the lack of economic opportunity. Sadly, those who leave are of above average ability; they are the ones who are aware and capable enough to take advantage of opportunities in other countries. I left in 1960 after King Hussein's henchmen threatened to kill me for exposing the demented ways of his younger brother. But it must also be said that of the sixty-six holders of college degrees among the Aburish family, not a single one lives in Bethany.

Amazingly, there is no local term for the hundreds of thousands who have emigrated to other Arab countries, mostly the oil-producing states. The remittances sent by groups of these people to their relatives in the West Bank help keep the place going, however inadequately. Now that the Palestinians have sided with Saddam Hussein against the oil sheikhs, the future of these groups, and hence their contributions, is threatened; the West Bank's already shattered economy might sink still further, becoming like that of Ethiopia. There are words for the worse things to come: *al karitha al jai* (the impending disaster). The signs are already apparent: several thousand Palestinians who used to work in Kuwait have already returned to the West Bank and the jobs of others in Saudi Arabia and other oil-rich countries are threatened. *Al Rajaeen* (the returnees) are a new phenomenon and the fact must be reckoned with that their political thinking is likely to be influenced by what the policies of Yasser Arafat have done to them.

Although this situation has not prompted the local wordsmiths to invent a word for their kin in Arab countries, it has added to the local vocabulary by furnishing new descriptions of the putative enemy. The Gulf people are *'oohoosh* (beasts) and their increasingly bad treatment of Palestinians leaves a great deal to be desired – in short, *b'htikrouna* (they despise us). This leads to the accusation that the Gulf Arabs hate educated superior people and naturally the Palestinians think of themselves as such.

Still amazed at the lack of names or nicknames for the oil-rich ordinary Arabs, I visited a professor of agriculture at Bethlehem University. On the way there the taxi driver was determined to engage me in conversation about the Gulf crisis and spoke about the 'Jews of the Gulf', clearly a current description of the Kuwaitis. This attempt to reduce them to merciless money-grabbers was the latest entry in the local dictionary of despair until my meeting ended and I took another taxi back home. The second taxi driver was a talkative young man who wanted to demonstrate his hipness by talking about *Al Kimawiya* (the chemical, meaning Saddam Hussein's chemical weapons). He concluded his monologue by saying, 'I am not worried about Israeli torture or death by natural causes – I am concerned about *Al Kimawiya*. They say your limbs come off one at a time. Also, do you realize that the Israelis gave their citizens gas masks and sold us ones which don't work? If Saddam starts lobbing *kimawiyas* this way then we're all finished. Why, *Al Akhra jai* (the end is coming), and *fi tari'na la nshouf rabna* (we're on our way to meet God).'

The heat of the Gulf crisis is felt intensely in the West Bank and identification with Saddam Hussein is nearly complete. There is no shortage of words to describe the Iraqi leader, but the one most often used is *gada*' (tough). Saddam's much admired toughness is the result of his ability to stand up to the West, which is still waging a *harb salibiya* (crusade) against Arabs and Muslims everywhere. And yet the choicest pejoratives are directed at his Arab enemies, particularly the Egyptians. In the Egyptians' case, the name-calling is historically inclusive, embracing their inglorious military performances in the 1948 and 1967 wars as well as the fact that Egypt signed the Camp David Peace Accord with Israel and now supports the USA against a fellow Muslim country. The behaviour of the Egyptians reduces them to *bsas* (cats), for the cat is supposed to be cowardly, and occasionally *araneb* (rabbits – both cowardly and good at procreating). The abuse goes further and the Egyptians' racial origins are brought into play (unlike the rest of the Arabs, who are Semites, the Egyptians are Hamites, and are darker) and so the Egyptians are *abeed* (meaning both black and slave in Arabic).

The West Banker accords the other Arabs better treatment than he bestows on the Egyptians – except for their leaders. Little is heard against the Syrians, Saudis or others, but their leaders are *'ameels* and *khawana* (outright traitors). In fact, the local language is not kind in general to those who occupy office and they are accused of having only one concern, the *ḳursi* (chair) – that is to say, their position as leaders. Whenever an Arab leader behaves in a way that is difficult to understand, he is acting to protect the *kursi*. The maladies that allegedly infect Arab leaders, making them unresponsive to ordinary people's wishes, are often summed up in one amusing gesture: people rub their thumb and index finger together and speak of the *'ameels'* attachment to *kursis* because of *imlah* (cash).

In contrast, everyday corruption in the ordinary local Arab, perhaps because it is endemic, is treated differently. People accept it as a way of life, perhaps as a reflection of need, and whatever objections to corruption exist tend to focus on its degree rather than the act itself. Someone who makes a bit of money on the side is absolved, but not those who amass fortunes. Whatever profit people realize locally is *barrani* (from outside). When people talk about a person holding a job, they discuss the salary and benefits received and then the amount of *barrani* the position produces. Even when a college graduate gets his first job, his relatives and friends will ask him how much *barrani* there is.

Barrani is so widespread and intrinsic that I am tempted to view it as self-cancelling, in that when everybody makes money on the side things are likely to even out as if corruption did not exist. However, this view is unfair to the brave few individuals and institutions who do not participate, the ones who insist on seeing *barrani* for what it really is.

Often, when listening to everyday conversation for more clues to what life here is all about, I uncover strange linguistic nuances that undoubtedly elude outsiders. After days of hearing the word *Al za'ama* (collective leadership) repeated to describe leaders of the *intifada*, I managed to ask people whether they thought *Al za'ama* were the beneficiaries of *barrani*. Did they think the leadership of the *intifada* is on the take? A pleasant and encouraging surprise awaited me: the two best-known members of *Al za'ama*, Faisal Husseini and Sari Nusseibeh, are considered clean and above suspicion, representatives of an new class of ideologue, or *zaim*. But sadly this honesty stops there, for the rest of *Al za'ama* are roundly condemned for being corrupt, and their lavish lifestyle, like that of the PLO leadership abroad, is seen as attesting to their excesses. Nevertheless, the existence of the *indaf* (clean ones) is a faint glimmer of hope in a situation that cries out for improvement.

Despite such promising signs, there is one word that summarizes life in the land hope forgot: *al ham* (misery). Life expectancy is higher now than it was when I grew up in the thirties and forties, but it is still low and there are too few health facilities. Many people die from easily curable diseases, but a high proportion of the overall death rate is attributed to *al ham* and I would agree that it seems to be the number one killer. Medical authorities confirm that the incidence here of stress-related diseases (diabetes, hypertension and heart disorders) is proportionately the highest in the world. In the grim local lexicon, a lot of other words will have to fall into disuse before *al ham* is alleviated. A first step would be to eliminate administrative detention.

Chapter Three
THE UNKNOWN

The sixth of September 1990 was a strike day, but it differed from other strike days. The organization that called on West Bankers to strike in protest was a hitherto unknown group with the ominous name of Islamic Jihad (Jihad meaning 'holy war'). The leaflets asking people to protest on that day were issued the day before and distributed throughout the West Bank. The reactions to the leaflets by the Arab population and the Israeli authorities were one and the same: both sides behaved as if they were afraid of this organization they knew nothing about.

This was the first time this underground religious group had advocated any overt protest, and the Arab population could not decide whether to take the leaflets seriously and obey them or dismiss them as the work of a crank organization and ignore them. The locals waited for signs to help them assess the situation, but even their best-known source of direction, the United National Command (the pro-PLO local political group in charge of the West Bank) said nothing, and there were no indications of what might happen to people if they disobeyed Islamic Jihad. It was a confusing situation that inspired fear in everyone.

The Israelis were equally directionless. My telephone calls to the office of the Mayor of Jerusalem, Teddy Kollek, and the office of the regional military governor in Bethlehem, produced no helpful answers. Both said that they knew nothing of the Islamic Jihad, but were taking 'precautionary measures' against all eventualities, because strikes are usually accompanied by outbreaks of anti-Israeli violence.

I heard about the proposed strike on the evening of 5 September, hours before it was supposed to start, during the semi-ritualistic nightly gathering of relatives in aunt Mirriam's garden. It was normally at such gatherings that I tried out my ideas on my unsuspecting cousins and aunts. I had already come to accept the *intifada* as a children's crusade and on hearing of the Islamic Jihad's call, I asked my fourteen-year-old cousin Mahmoud Khalil whether he intended to strike by not going to school. He professed to have no feelings on the subject, nor any idea whether his school, Ar Rashedieh, would shut for the day. He added that Islamic Jihad was unknown to him and his friends, and that their leaflet calling for a strike 'against the Israeli occupation forces' had said nothing that might be construed as justification for such an action.

I turned to the elders and asked whether they knew anything about Islamic Jihad. Nobody did. My question as to their feelings about the call to strike was more to the point, and everybody admitted that they would rather not yet did not wish to run foul of an unknown group that might resort to violence. For, according to them, most of the Islamic movements in the West Bank advocated such measures. As a result my relatives were going to follow the lead of other people. At this point I came clean and told the six people enjoying the family evening that Islamic Jihad was the name of an organization that rose to fame in Lebanon for kidnapping Westerners and holding them hostage. They all seemed to know this, but they added that they had no idea whether the two Islamic Jihads were one and the same, or even related. So Islamic Jihad didn't frighten people because it had a specific history or identity, but because it was an unknown quantity with an implicit commitment to violence.

This fascinating situation led me to wake up at six a.m. on the day of the strike to witness the earliest response to Islamic Jihad's call, but even at this early hour I was already late. A new leaflet, threatening reprisals against those who refused to heed the call to strike, had been distributed during the night, and the walls of houses and shops were covered with graffiti repeating the threat. The Israeli patrols that roam villages and towns at night had obviously failed to stop Islamic Jihad from reinforcing its original demand.

It had worked. The shops were shut, traffic was light and fewer people than usual were moving about at that hour. Meanwhile the number of Israeli patrols had noticeably increased, and the soldiers in the jeeps and four-ton lorries were a little more alert, if not exactly agitated, than usual. There was nothing else to notice.

I went back to the house I had rented to finish an article about the background to the Gulf crisis for the London *Independent* and resurfaced at nine to go to Jerusalem to fax the background piece. I had another look around only to discover how contagious fear is: whatever movement had existed earlier had come to an end; the observance of the strike was total.

I stood at my regular 'service stop' to take one of the shared taxis that carry passengers from Bethany to Jerusalem, not knowing whether the taxi drivers too were afraid of unknown powers. Opposite my stop stood an Israeli army jeep (licence number 6034) with a full contingent of six soldiers. Why they had decided to position themselves in the centre of town, I still don't understand, for that particular spot was a most unlikely place to watch stone or Molotov cocktail throwing or other manifestations of anti-Israeli feeling. But regardless of the reason for the presence of the Israeli patrol, the behaviour of its members merits description.

Except for the regulation haircut of four of them, the soldiers were most untidy. Two of them had their shirts hanging out, five were smoking cigarettes and the beret-type caps they wore at an angle were neither soldierly nor attractive. They took turns sitting in the jeep and standing beside it, but there was no pattern to their behaviour. They kicked stones, laughed long and loud at jokes I couldn't hear and wouldn't have understood, spoke into their walkie-talkies in a relaxed, near insolent way but never strayed too far from the jeep. In addition to those moves aimed at easing the tension surrounding them, the one thing common to all of them was their relationship to their rifles. They never lost touch with their weapons, and for a moment seemed to be very close to using them.

Five minutes passed without a taxi appearing while I stood a mere twenty-five feet away from the soldiers, making them as uneasily aware of me as I was of them. An unplanned staring match began. Two of them eyed me suspiciously and spoke to the others in Hebrew, and the others took turns in giving me dirty looks. Something in me frightened them. Despite my large American-style sunglasses and Ivy League button-down shirt, they probably thought I was an Islamic Jihad suicide bomber or at the very least an ordinary terrorist in disguise.

I considered aborting the trip to Jerusalem but decided against it for fear that it might provoke the soldiers to interrogate me; they would have wanted to know why I faced them for so long then decided to turn tail, potentially to brief another suicide bomber. So there was nothing for me to do except continue to wait, to persist in looking as if I was going to Jerusalem. Suddenly five of them formed a circle, presumably to discuss what to do about my unwelcome presence. I was so convinced they were about to question me that I instinctively felt my back pocket to reassure myself that my American passport was there. But would there be time to produce it? After all, the patrol members and I had already decided we didn't like each other – a situation that usually produces unfriendly behaviour on their part. What would have happened if they had walked over to me and talked to me in the rude way they address most Arabs? I asked myself what I would do if they arrested me – after all, suspicion is grounds enough for them. I imagined that they might even do more, perhaps kick me and beat me up, and as I wiped the sweat off my brow I hoped for a way out of my predicament.

Mercifully, about twenty minutes into our silent confrontation, a taxi appeared out of nowhere and stopped to pick me up. I jumped in so fast that the soldiers had no time to reconsider things. My only concession was to shout, 'American Colony Hotel, please' loudly so they would hear me. Once in the cab, I told the driver not to pick up any other passengers, again in English, and he answered me in Hebrew.

In no time at all my fear of the soldiers was replaced by another. Inadvertently in my state of controlled inner panic, I had jumped into an Israeli taxi. This violated a basic rule of unfriendly conduct whereby Arabs and Jews don't use each other's taxis, and because their licence plates differ it is an easy rule to follow. No wonder this taxi driver wasn't on strike; in fact he was obviously trying to undermine the strikers by working on a run where the regular drivers were Arabs who had decided to stop work. We looked at each other, telling each other many things without saying a word, and I decided that he was harmless and probably thought the same about me.

No sooner had my fear of the taxi driver disappeared than it was succeeded by yet another, in this case of Arab kids who might be hiding behind the many turns in the road ready to pelt any strike-breaker with stones. A car with Israeli licence plates was always game, but a strike spelled open season.

The driver looked at me and decided his uneasy rider deserved sympathy, if only because it was a genuine mistake. It was three and a half miles to the American Colony Hotel, and both he and I knew how fraught the journey was. He stepped on the accelerator and looked at me to tell me that he was aware of the danger confronting both of us and was trying to help. I looked ahead in resignation while he drove at nearly a hundred miles an hour.

As it was, we reached the American Colony safely and in a very short time because there were no cars on the road. The only two cars we saw had smashed windscreens, but the stone-throwers had disappeared for fear of Israeli army patrols. When I paid the driver his fare, he thanked me in Arabic and I smiled back. Apart from our implicit communication, which I will remember forever, that was the only exchange between us that both of us understood.

I faxed my article and walked to Jerusalem's Zahra Gate to face the problem of a ride back to Bethany. When there are no taxis private cars have been known to offer passengers lifts to their destinations. Ar Rashedieh School, the one cousin Mahmoud attends, is across the street from Zahra Gate, and it looked as if it were shut for the day. Once again, by accident, I stood near an Israeli army jeep and though I paid little attention to it I did notice that only the driver was inside.

Suddenly four Israeli soldiers materialized from across the street with an Arab teenager in their midst. He wore jeans, a light red shirt and tennis shoes and was carrying three books. They stopped behind the jeep and began interrogating him. They questioned him in Arabic and I moved a few yards closer, to listen.

Nothing was said to allow me to figure out why he had been stopped by the soldiers, but they were asking him about the drawings in his notebook, and they made it abundantly clear that what they had seen had displeased them. They insisted that the drawings were symbols, and had a meaning, but failed to identify the symbols or what they meant, while the boy swore they were nothing but doodles and invited the soldiers to his house to prove that he doodled all the time.

Far from satisfying the soldiers, the boy's consistent answers seemed to heighten their suspicion. They asked him whether he belonged to a subversive organization and recited the names of several groups. He said no. They accused him of having come to school when it was closed deliberately to foment trouble and throw stones at Israeli soldiers. He gave them the same answer cousin Mahmoud had given me the night before, that he had come because he had no idea whether the school was open or shut.

The boy was exceptionally polite, and I envied his serenity. He didn't plead or beg but answered every question in a straightforward manner. But the more he stood his ground, the more the soldiers kept returning to his notebook and the symbols of fear it contained, trying to cow him into admitting their sinister secret.

The soldiers conferred in Hebrew and I felt that the boy's fate was in the balance. I wished that I could do something to help, but no easy solution came to mind. Suddenly they became aware of my presence and interest in what they were doing and ordered me to move away and I obeyed. Just then, a private car stopped and offered me a lift back to Bethany.

When I left the scene the soldiers were still interrogating the boy, with his dark eyes, perfect set of teeth and small ears, and that rare sense of grace and dignity; the boy that I should perhaps have tried openly to defend, the only person I had seen in the last twenty-four hours who had not shown fear, and, as a result, the one who would give me a sleepless night. That boy was the same one I went to Ar Rashedieh school to enquire about first thing the following morning.

Waiting for dawn to come, I thought of a whole population afraid of an unknown underground group threatening violence; of an Israeli patrol of six soldiers in fear of someone just because they could not figure him out; of the taxi driver and I at first afraid of each other then transferring our common fear to the unseen stone-throwers hiding around every bend in the road; and lastly of another Israeli patrol in a state of fear because a child who couldn't have been a day over fifteen was carrying drawings that they didn't understand and that stirred up the irrational, racist fear lying dormant in their minds.

At seven-thirty the next morning I went to Ar Rashedieh school to investigate the case of my young friend whom I had never formally met. The visit was in violation of a promise I had made to myself when I undertook to write this book. I had told myself that I would behave coolly, but reminders and self-admonishment hadn't worked the night before; the tense atmosphere of the West Bank was claiming me. A part of me refused to give up and wanted to help the kid, but I also detected a personal desire to get involved. Perhaps I felt guilty because of my cowardly behaviour, or perhaps it was bigger, perhaps it was a feeling of guilt born of seeing so much suffering and yet remaining untouched.

On the way to the school my heart had thumped so hard I could hear it and I was so preoccupied with my mission I couldn't read the morning newspapers. When I got to the school I wondered whether my sports shirt, khaki trousers and sandals were the proper attire for what I intended to do. I told myself that the situation I was pursuing transcended etiquette, that nobody had ever told me how to dress to check on the fate of a young man who could have spent the night suffering torture. Still, to go through a symbolic gesture of reverence I took off my large, ostentatious sunglasses.

The students were in their classes and the atmosphere in the school administration building suggested that of a monastery; I didn't see or hear people, but I knew they were there. The two secretaries in the headmaster's office looked up and something told me they had somehow detected I was a stranger.

'My name is Saïd Aburish. I am a Palestinian-American writer living in London. This is my card. I am sorry I have no appointment, but I would like to see the headmaster.'

'I am sorry, but he is not here and he won't be here until the afternoon.' The young lady who answered continued to stare at me, to assess me.

'Is there anybody else who could help me?'

'What is it you want, sir?'

'I saw an Israeli patrol interrogating one of your students yesterday. I should like to find out more about the incident and what happened to him. Whether he has been released.'

The two secretaries looked alike: by Western standards they were relatively short with curly black hair, black eyes, black skirts, white blouses and very little make-up. They behaved the same, both holding on to pencils to allay the nervousness caused by my intrusion. They looked at each other and communicated wordlessly, and I decided that this was a special talent of those who live in an atmosphere where the use of words is a potential source of trouble. They were agreed that they were facing an obvious case of lunacy; at least someone who was totally ignorant of what life in Jerusalem was all about.

At a loss as to what to do with me, one of them asked me to sit down. 'I will see if Mr ----- ------ is here,' she said, and disappeared into the adjacent office, my calling card in her hand. I could hear an exchange taking place but I couldn't tell what was being said. A minute later I was face to face with a mustachioed, thin and unusually tall man in a light-grey suit.

'*Ahlan*, Mr Aburish, come in please.'

We exchanged introductions and I thanked him for seeing me. His office contained a big metal desk with an executive chair behind it and three smaller chairs in front. The walls were bare except for a framed Koranic *sura* (extract) and a crude picture of the Dome of the Rock. In the corner were metal shelves with folders on them.

The tiled floor was clean and bare. My host ordered two Turkish coffees.

'What can I do for you, Mr Aburish? I know your family, knew your late uncles.'

I told the gentleman (whose name and title I withhold to protect him) what I had seen the day before. He listened attentively but without emotion. His reaction neither encouraged nor discouraged me, but I began to feel a little foolish. His calm attitude stood in sharp contrast to my obvious inner agitation, but I continued because I felt I had to.

'Mr Aburish, things like this happen all the time here, ugly incidents which offend the sensibilities of the unaccustomed. Not a day passes without several of our students being arrested, perhaps detained.'

He went on to tell me that the case I had witnessed was 'under control' and that any interference on my part was likely to be counter-productive. His matter-of-factness added to my inner anger, but I held back because the man was obviously genuine and I knew that I was rocking the boat by reacting to a 'small incident'. I accepted his advice and tried to sound dispassionate and intelligent.

'Are you talking about abuse in general or similar attempts to intimidate students into admitting false crimes?' I asked.

'Well, abuse is rampant. But I did mean attempts to intimidate students. Specifically, close to your area of concern, the security forces are in the habit of going through students' books looking for anti-Israeli slogans and suspicious drawings – pictures of Arafat, the Palestinian flag, Muslim emblems and caricatures.'

'But they have to justify searching students and going through their books, don't they? They just don't stop students because they feel like it?'

The man shook his head. 'No, they don't have to justify searching students, going through their books or anything else they do to them, particularly when there is a strike or when the general atmosphere is tense. They just pull them off the street for no reason whatsoever.'

'That's stupid. If the students know about this then the Israelis won't find anything in their books.'

The school official drank what was left of his coffee and smiled.

'On the contrary, it is because the students know that the Israelis find a great deal of what they are looking for.'

He wanted me to ask him to elaborate and I did. 'But why?'

'Defiance, that's why. The students refuse to accept the Israeli decision to interfere between them and their books. Furthermore, they will not allow the prospect of punishment to deter them from expressing their feelings. The whole thing backfires.'

I was taken aback by how little I knew about local attitudes. I understood the wish to express their nationalist feelings, but what did getting between them and their books mean?

This time he smiled in a way that told me he liked the question. 'In Arab tradition, learning is an idea which carries with it a considerable amount of reverence; it's an Islamic tradition which goes back to the time when the Koran was the only book around. It's not dogma; it's an attitude: a person's books are near holy and touching them without the proper respect is almost sacrilegious.'

'I see, I see, so the Israelis are administering to tradition an insult which is not acceptable. But what happens in the latter case, when someone is caught with drawings in his or her notebook that the Israelis don't like?'

'Anything or nothing. It depends on the soldiers' personal reaction to the drawings, how they feel about the Palestinian flag or Arafat's beard – it depends on how much this stuff frightens them. There are occasions when officers don't take these things seriously. Sometimes a book is ripped to pieces and that's the end of it but often a kid gets a kick in the ass or he loses the book and gets a kick in the ass as well. Sometimes the soldiers are so afraid they detain a student or number of students and accuse them of belonging to an illegal organization or a terrorist organization. If the soldiers in the street decide to detain someone, then it's for a minimum of two weeks, sometimes with beatings, sometimes without. It all depends on how frightened the soldiers become, when they see what's in the books.'

'Who decides what happens to the kids when the doodles are deemed suspicious?'

'As I said, the first decision is up to the officer and if he decides to arrest someone then that means two weeks' detention, then the interrogating officer at headquarters takes over and it depends how serious or ridiculous what the books contain is. It's all got to do with what the particular drawing does to the psyche of the officers handling the case. There's no specific enforceable punishment – we are talking about interpretation, about an unknown.'

'Yes, it's fear of the unknown, isn't it?'

He nodded.

Islamic Jihad has since carried out a number of armed attacks, including a suicide mission against Israeli soldiers and now nobody questions its right to call protest strikes. I have no doubt that the fear of young Israeli soldiers on patrol duties is nearer the surface and undoubtedly it occasionally manifests itself in the abuse of Arab schoolchildren. This is the way the cycle of violence perpetuates itself.

Chapter Four
RAMPANT BLIND INJUSTICE

Of all the questions asked about Israel's behaviour in the occupied territories those concerning Israeli justice are most likely to provide the most telling answers. Both detractors and supporters of the Jewish state accept that examining this area reveals the inner workings of the state as it affects its citizens and the people of the occupied Arab territories, and throws light on outsiders' arguments about whether Israel is a true democracy. But dry legalistic arguments, particularly in the grey area of international law and its supremacy over local law, have been rehashed time and time again and still miss the point. By contrast, a case-study is likely to tell us more about the administration of Israeli justice, for it is as much the spirit as the letter of the law that matters. Here once again the human factor comes into play.

Today, 12 September 1990, is the date set for sentencing my first cousins once-removed, Amer and Nasser Aburish. Amer has been under administrative detention for sixteen months and ten days and Nasser was detained two days after his elder brother. They were fifteen and fourteen when they were arrested.

The boys are charged with several crimes. The Israeli authorities allege that they were 'organizers' of a resistance movement against Israeli rule, that they belonged to a terrorist organization (the PLO) and that they personally participated in attacks against Israeli army patrols, using stones and Molotov cocktails. The last allegation does not state the time or place of the attacks or whether they caused any injury. Three other Bethanites were arrested at the same time as Amer and Nasser and accused of the same crimes and they too remain in detention.

Amer and Nasser are the sons of my first cousin Ali and his wife

Hala Irekat Aburish. Ali was born in 1949, five months after his father, also called Ali, died fighting during the 1948 Arab–Israeli battle for Jerusalem, the first round of the unceasing interracial conflict. Two of Hala's relatives, an uncle and a cousin, were killed at the same time as my Uncle Ali. Hala and Ali are both schoolteachers who lead a quiet life and although they are hardly activists themselves, it is reasonable to assume that they grew up with strong anti-Israeli feelings and that these feelings were transmitted to their children. In other words, Amer and Nasser belong to the third generation of Arab resistance to Israel.

I have known Amer and Nasser for five years and have grown extremely fond of them. In Bethany they are local heroes, brave perpetrators of non-acceptance of Israeli rule, a symbol of Arab perseverance. Awareness of the special position the boys occupy among family, friends and fellow-villagers dictated that I speak to outsiders for a more accurate assessment of their character. I have talked to ten of them, including two lawyers and some of the boys' teachers.

The facts about the two boys are simple and engaging, and universally accepted. Both were outstanding students, first in their class, and both were active, popular children who behaved older than their years. They were obedient and happy at home, and remain very close to each other, their parents and their two other brothers and sister. They appear also to have been exceptionally popular with members of the wider Aburish family and the rest of the village. Physically, they are tall, graceful and very handsome, a darker shade of those fine specimens of northern Italy. They have always been the envy of all who know them.

So the simple question of the character of the accused is clear. But were they involved in anti-Israeli activity? Yes. They themselves proudly admit that they belonged to a local young people's group whose aim was to resist Israeli occupation. But they deny ever having thrown stones or Molotov cocktails at the Israelis and view as stupid and simplistic the accusation that they are PLO members. They explain that they themselves do not belong to the PLO or any of its branches, although they are aware that most local groups have PLO connections, and if sympathy or indirect contact with the PLO is a crime then Israel will have to place all the people of the West Bank under arrest.

Their defence lawyer Abid Assali agrees with me that the case against Amer and Nasser is essentially one of belonging to a resistance group, and, considering the boys' character, there is good reason to believe that they were organizers, inasmuch as fourteen- and fifteen-year-olds can organize resistance against a nation state.

On this day of sentencing it is already hot at seven a.m. and I am getting ready to accompany my cousin Hala to the Military Court of Ramallah, thirteen miles away. Each prisoner is usually allowed one visitor and this rule holds for trials. Because cousin Ali is teaching today, I am standing in for him. I am tired because I didn't sleep well waiting for the day to come and for my journey into torment to begin, but my tiredness takes second place when I think of Ali and Hala and the night they must have spent thinking of their children and their fate.

At eight o'clock Hala and I are waiting to share a taxi to Jerusalem, from where we will switch to another to take us to Ramallah. Hala is clad in a simple grey skirt and a lighter grey blouse and refuses my offer to take our own taxi to Ramallah. She tells me that some of the parents of children on trial might be resentful of someone arriving in a private taxi and she wouldn't want to offend their sensibilities. We talk about the harsh economic realities of the West Bank and the more I hear the more I agree with her decision.

We join four other passengers who are already in the service taxi, a diesel Mercedes. Halfway through the two-mile trip to Jerusalem the taxi has to stop at an improvised Israeli road block. These appear and disappear at random at different places and their purpose is to stop cars to ascertain that the driver and passengers aren't tax evaders and that they have paid their licence fees. There are four cars ahead of us and the driver of the first car and the Israeli sergeant conducting the check are having a ferocious argument. The disorganization is typical of the Middle East; the argument holds up everything and everybody. For Hala and me, precious time is being wasted, an agonizingly long ten minutes that threaten to delay us for the court proceedings in Ramallah, scheduled to begin at nine. In panic we leave our taxi, flash our ID for the sergeant to see and start to walk in the direction of Jerusalem. Luckily, in five minutes we are picked up by another service taxi.

Once in Jerusalem, we run two blocks and jump into the taxi for Ramallah. Hala is extremely agitated and her incoherent rambling is born of the fear that being late might have a psychological effect on the children and their behaviour in court. In order to get to the court in time, she appeals to the other passengers in the taxi to forgo their stops until we have been dropped off. They all sympathize with her request and so does the taxi driver, who, in a further gesture of solidarity, refuses to accept the money for the fare. Suddenly we are in a car hurtling towards Ramallah and negotiating winding roads at over eighty miles an hour. Hala is still thanking everybody for their kindness and stating that aiding a just cause is a Koranic command while the other passengers say nothing. The bumpers rattle, the wheels screech lack of care at every turn and the engine makes suspect noises. I am seized by the fear of what might happen to all of us. My only consolation is to draw a comparison between us in the car and the Palestinian situation; each is a just cause hurtling along at full speed with the threat of destruction present every mile of the way.

Finally we reach Ramallah or, more accurately, we are dropped off on the outskirts, a hundred yards or so from a huge stone building surrounded by barbed wire and sentry cabins. In many ways the scene is not unlike pictures of the buildings used to hold important Nazi criminals pending trial after the Second World War: the victor fears an attack on the building that never materializes.

We go up to what looks like the main entrance, an imposing chest-high gate nearly twelve feet across, but we are still fifty yards from the court-house itself. The gate is closed, but in front of it is a yard where court attendees are waiting. I count a hundred and sixty-two people, and, remembering the one visitor to one defendant rule, wonder how many people are being sentenced or tried. Belatedly I am struck by the fact that all the people waiting are villagers, the women are in their national dress of *thoubs* and the men wear *kufiyas* and *egals*. This tells me that there are no townspeople among those about to be tried, and I am annoyed. I ask Hala if this is true and she confirms my deduction. So it is villagers and their children who are the backbone of the *intifada*, just as villagers have been the backbone of every Palestinian nationalist movement since the 1920s. Town-dwellers have always viewed actually fighting for the Palestinian cause as being beneath their dignity. This stupid attitude has vitiated Palestinian effectiveness, and sadly, decades of misery have not changed it. I make a mental note to take up this matter with members of the *intifada*'s command.

The temperature is rising and the dust is thick. There is weariness in the eyes of people waiting to enter the building to hear the fate of loved ones. They talk to each other as if they were friends, people with a great deal in common, and exchange the names, ages of their children and how and when they were arrested, as well as horror stories of torture. They always conclude by wishing each other and the children well. Hala is the centre of attention, even by *intifada* standards, for her case is more dramatic than most. When people wish her well she answers equally sympathetically but I notice that no words of regret or excuse pass anyone's lips, no complaints and no denial that the children were involved or that they shouldn't have done what they are accused of. There is a tacit approval by everybody of what their children have done, and they are proud.

'Hala,' I whisper, 'what are we doing here, why aren't we in court?' She tells me that we have to wait for the gate to open and an Israeli officer to show up and call one by one the names of the day's defendants, at which time the attendee for each defendant will produce an identity document and be allowed in. She repeats the one attendee per defendant limit and tells me that she will go when they announce Amer's name and I am to go for Nasser. Soon an Arabic-speaking Israeli first lieutenant addresses the waiting crowd and Aburish is alphabetically top of the list. Hala goes ahead and I follow her. The officer records our names on his list, next to the names of the defendants, and points us towards the court-house.

We march together through the big gate towards the army post between it and the building. The sergeant commanding the post shouts at Hala to stop. When she does, he tells her that ladies have to wait until later. Then he motions to me to move forward and leave her behind. A soldier leads me into a square room of cement blocks with one rickety metal table in the corner, nothing else.

He speaks gruffly. 'Identity card?'

I give him my American passport without a word.

'Who are you here to see?'

'Nasser Aburish.'

'What is he to you?'

'My cousin.'

'Are you carrying any weapons?'

'No.'

'Raise your arms.'

'Whatever for?'

'Body search.'

I do and his dust-covered hands go up and down my sides, leaving marks, and then he touches my back and is satisfied.

'Pull your trouser leg up.'

I do this and he notices that I wear knee socks.

'Roll down your socks.'

I do, still silently.

'Roll up your socks.'

'Don't you like my pretty legs.'

I know it isn't funny, but I can't help it. The soldier's face is red with rage. He is not accustomed to humour, not even to people talking back to him and he feels that my flippancy is a challenge to his authority. His index finger is less than an inch from my face and he is wagging it. 'I don't need stupid answers. You think your American passport is protection, but remember this is Israel and the only protection is to behave yourself, otherwise you will not be allowed into court. This is an Israeli military court, not an American circus, do you understand?'

Shaken, I nod. For ten seconds we stare at each other without words but with considerable hate. 'OK, give me your passport and go now.'

'I can't give you my passport.'

'I must have it here or you will not enter.'

'How do I get it back?'

'It will be here on the table when you leave.'

'What if somebody takes it?'

'Then your American Embassy will give you another one.'

I notice how my Americanness has offended the soldier, how he behaved as if America shouldn't have allowed me to become a citizen but I give in and move towards the big, four-storey formless building that must have served as a school or government administrative centre years ago. I run into one of the many soldiers moving around and ask, 'Where is the serious cases court please?' I am corrected: 'The serious crimes court is the first door on the right, the first floor.'

I get there after a slow, unhappy walk full of thoughts but the door is blocked by three soldiers wielding M16 rifles, their fingers on the trigger. Four other people, all villagers, are also waiting, hardly enough to justify the ready-to-shoot posture of the guards. I wait for Hala without asking any questions and she appears ten minutes later.

'I am sorry I kept you waiting – not my choice.'

'Never mind, thank God it's a once in a lifetime happening, this idiocy. It will soon be over. I'm sure the sentence will be light.'

'What do you mean?'

'We'll get a verdict today, won't we?'

'It is supposed to be sentencing day but it is very often delayed.

This is the fourth time they schedule the boys to be sentenced – the first three times it was postponed. They always postpone things.'

'You're joking. They can't keep telling you and the boys that it's sentencing day then delay it – that's soul-destroying.'

She shakes her head. 'I know, I know. And they never give us a reason why they postpone it. Didn't Ali tell you?'

'No.'

'We suspect they postpone the sentencing to keep the boys from studying. You can't study, not even read a book, when you're under administrative detention. But after you're sentenced you're allowed to read, to study. It's a well-known fact – they don't want our boys to be educated. Keeping kids from their studies has an evil effect on them – it breaks their spirit. Sometimes they keep them in that state for years and years.'

An inner rage renders me speechless. I can't muster the words of anger or sympathy to express myself. The delays are enough to shatter Hala's spirit, but the reasons for them are even more treacherous. As it is, I make a note to check this allegation. (Lawyers Lea Tzemel, Ziad Abu Zayyad and Abid Assali later confirmed that the Israelis occasionally resort to this practice to intimidate difficult cases.) Hala saves me from my sinking depression by telling me that the female sergeant who had body-searched her told her things wouldn't get started until after ten.

The courtroom is no bigger than the size of a large living room. In front, facing the two entrance doors, on a raised platform, are chairs for the three members of the court. The judge's chair in the centre has a lectern in front of it, while the Israeli flag and emblems of the Israeli army and the civil administration of the occupied territories act as a backdrop. Between the platform and benches for forty people facing it is a small desk with a chair on either side. On the left side is a desk within a wooden partition, from where the advocate-general (the equivalent of a crown counsel or prosecuting attorney) operates, and opposite it across the room is the same arrangement for the lawyers. The place where the defendants sit or stand is an area to the right of the audience and to the left of the judge, and it contains two benches. There is a small bench perpendicular to the benches of the spectators and its purpose eludes me. In the background an old-fashioned ceiling fan whirs away to ease the heat of the day.

'Where's the kids' lawyer, Hala? I understand he's a good one and I am anxious to meet him.'

'He's coming. Good? I don't know, but people say that he's good. He'll be here in a moment, I guess.'

We sit on the front spectators' bench and as my eyes continue to examine the shabby surroundings, Hala opens a miniature Koran and begins to read silently. My first reaction is to cynically tell her that her act of devotion isn't likely to produce results, but then I remember her pain, the psychological dislocation caused by repeated delays, the fear that another postponement is imminent, and the overall situation, and I whisper in Arabic 'May Allah accept'. She acknowledges my good wish and continues.

Abid Assali, the lawyer, appears, a stocky man with long, bushy hair and an impertinent sneer. He shakes Hala's hand and we are introduced. Something tells me that he resents my presence. He views the whole thing as a situation where outsiders ask the wrong questions because they have not yet been ground down so that they accept the unacceptable, whereas the locals have been subdued and have come to view the most unreasonable things in life as normal. What follows confirms the instantaneous antipathy the lawyer and I feel for each other. He tells Hala perfunctorily that Amer is not in Ramallah but in Bethlehem and hence he will not appear to hear the indictment and the court's sentence. In other words, he is to be sentenced *in absentia*. The lawyer tells the distraught mother this the way you say hello to an acquaintance, without the courtesy of an explanation of why her son is not present, and as he moves away I reach for him angrily.

'One minute, please.'

When he doesn't stop, I take two steps after him and my hand grabs the old-fashioned padded shoulders of his jacket. 'I said, "One minute", Mr Lawyer. In the absence of the child's father, I am the patrilineal next of kin.' (Sadly, women still occupy a back seat socially, even in the relatively advanced West Bank.)

'Yes?'

'I would like you to tell me how the hell you can accept Amer's being sentenced *in absentia*. He's in their custody – why isn't he here? Also, doesn't he have to answer when they read out the indictment? This is absurd.'

'What's absurd?'

'Among other things, you're absurd. I don't know how you talk to people here, but don't turn your back to me and talk to me as if I'm a moron.'

When he stares at me without saying anything, I continue. 'The charges against Amer are very serious; I understand he could go to prison for eight years. Why isn't he here?'

Hala is next to me, touching my arm, trying to calm me, but I sense she is not totally opposed to the way I am handling the lawyer. She intercedes. 'They judge them on evidence obtained under duress and they are guilty until proven otherwise. In fact the whole trial and sentencing is a wasteful routine. What the accused says is of no interest to them.'

I shout, 'Their sister's ass [*kus okhthum*]!' I notice one of the Israeli soldiers at the back of the courtroom watching me and I lower my voice.

'Mr Assali, am I crazy or have I heard or read loads of stories that children are tortured into confessing?'

Assali's expression of annoyance with my ways takes the form of answering me in a very slow manner, as one would talk to an idiot. 'Yes that's true, children are tortured.'

'Were Amer and Nasser tortured?'

'Not badly.'

My voice goes up again. 'Were they?'

He looks at Hala. 'Yes, but they still wouldn't confess to certain of the accusations against them.'

'Why can't Amer be here to state these two things: that he was tortured and that he didn't confess to certain elements of the indictment?'

'Ask them.'

'Ask who, Mr Assali?'

'Ask the Israelis – they make the rules.'

'That's your god-damned job.'

'Mr Aburish, please try to be polite. Look at your cousin. She isn't raising a fuss, because she knows how things work here, how difficult things are.'

'OK, I am sorry, please educate me in how things work here.'

At the lawyer's suggestion, we move to the corridor outside the courtroom. Slowly, Abid Assali explains three things to me. First, the burden of proof is not observed by an Israeli court and the accused is guilty until proven innocent. Second, the statements of unnamed witnesses are used as evidence against the accused without them or their lawyer being able to examine the witness. The Israelis invoke a law protecting informers and most of the time these witnesses are in the pay of the Israeli security forces. Third, the people who torture prisoners are never the people who take their confessions. When a prisoner agrees to confess as a result of torture he is handed over to an officer from another department to take the confession. This allows the confession-taker to swear that he never tortured the prisoners and indeed hampers the victim's ability to identify the torturer.

These rules eliminate the need for a court procedure concerned with the admissibility of evidence. What goes on between the advocate-general and the lawyer is no more than an exchange of documents purporting to deal with their assessments of the case. The accused has no role to play beyond talking to his lawyer, who judges his input in the light of what the court would permit. Apart from a foolproof alibi such as mistaken identity, the court is not interested in anything else. Hala tries to help Assali with this explanation by telling me that in one murder case three unconnected people admitted – under torture – to committing the same crime and that the court was ready to sentence all three of them until the error was discovered by the court clerk. Until then the pleas of the lawyers had fallen on deaf ears.

Assali concludes his lecture by telling me that all cases under consideration are settled through a plea-bargaining procedure, not based on the merits of the case but simply aimed at giving the whole transaction a semblance of legality. All Amer's presence would do is confirm that Abid Assali speaks for him, nothing else.

'But this cannot be. If the Israelis destroy their legal system then they will destroy themselves.'

'Mr Aburish, do you know how many cases they're going to try or sentence in this court today? A minimum of thirty. That's only one of the reasons why – they can't cope with the numbers.'

I lower my head in despair and Assali decides that we've argued enough, and the time has come to offer me sympathy, to say that our confrontation is over.

'Mr Aburish, there are nine courts in the entire West Bank and eight thousand people awaiting trial. People are being detained faster than they are being tried. The system can't cope and has moved from protecting the democratic nature of the state to punishing those who oppose it – I'm sure you understand that. If we do not accept the way they sentence people then the same system can keep a child under detention for years and years and years – there's no limit to how long, perhaps forever.'

I have nothing to say and Assali pats me on the shoulder. 'Ask around, if you don't like what I am doing then get another lawyer. I can't do more than plead, not with the court, but with the advocate-general to be generous.'

Assali, Hala and I exchange a few more words then Hala and I sit down while the lawyer moves about.

'Do you always read your Koran when you visit the boys, Hala?'

'Yes, visiting or seeing them in a criminal's cage is very difficult for me. They have moved them from one prison to another four times, three times without informing us or informing Assali. I never know what to expect when I visit them; I never know whether they're there or not. One time we went to visit them in the Hebron prison but they weren't there and it took them three days to tell us where they were. The boys are good: they don't tell us what they do to them because they don't want us upset, but when I don't find them, or I am not allowed to see them, then the Koran keeps me company.'

'So they stop you from seeing them sometimes?'

'Oh yes, and they never tell us why.'

I refrain from asking any more questions and Hala goes back to her Koran, leaving me to think alone. I am enveloped by a loneliness I have never experienced before. Except for the occasional attendance at Quaker meetings, religious worship is not part of my make-up. I consider what to do and I am seized by a fit of inner anger that wants me to attack one of the guards with my bare fists. Eventually, I silently appeal to Him to grant me strength and to remove the thorn of hate that has been implanted in my heart. I look straight ahead and everything is misty and vague. I tell myself that I must not cry, no matter what happens, that I, Saïd Aburish, fifty-five, supposedly a hardened man of the world, certainly a man who has suffered more than his share of physical and mental pain, must not cry, if only because there is a devout woman sitting on my right, and I must set an example by fighting my tears of frustration no matter how helpless I feel and how hopeless the situation is. And when, in spite of all the silent talking to myself, a big tear rolls down my cheek, I wipe it away with my handkerchief and utter a muffled 'fuck', and the down-to-earth woman with me, the brave, God-fearing woman reading her Koran asks what I am saying and I tell her truthfully that I am angry with myself because I can't pray.

A female soldier carries a sweating pitcher of cold water and places it in front of the judge's chair. Everybody is running to occupy their positions, including the advocate-general and the lawyers. Hala tells me the court is about to go into session. There are more soldiers with rifles blocking the entrances and I notice that a rifle rests next to the advocate-general's desk. There are folders everywhere: at least twenty on top of the advocate-general's desk and each lawyer has about five in front of him. The lone bench to the left is occupied by a man and a woman. The man's blazer bears the emblem of the International Red Cross and the woman wears a black skirt and blue blouse. The man loosens his tie, the women opens her satchel and pulls out a note pad and a pencil. I remember what someone had told me about the role of the Red Cross observers: they record what happens but they never publish, nor do they try to interfere with Israeli 'justice'.

The two clerks of court, a male soldier and a female soldier, occupy their places opposite each other beneath the judge's perch. A bespectacled sergeant, one of the soldiers who was until now guarding the door, moves to the front of the courtroom and addresses the spectators in Arabic.

'Quiet, I said, quiet, all of you.' He shouts so loud the forty male and female fellahin present are jarred into frightened silence. He is embarrassed by his own unnecessary volume.

'First, good morning. Two things you must observe. When the judge enters you stand – understand?' He waits for this to register. 'Then, when the defendants are brought in, you are not to speak to them, let alone touch them. Also, if anyone here makes any noise, then I will personally eject them from the courtroom and they will never be allowed here again. You have been warned.'

The sergeant marches back to his position at the back of the room, rifle on shoulder. The judge and the two other members of the court enter and everybody stands up together, out of fear, and then we sit down one by unhappy one. It is ten-forty.

The judge and the advocate-general are conversing in Hebrew. The Arab audience is at a loss; they don't know what is happening but the Red Cross lady is taking copious notes and her colleague is looking over her shoulder. Obviously it is something important because the lawyers too are paying close attention. The exchange is informal: the judge, a short, dark-haired brigadier-general in summer army uniform wears thick glasses and a yarmulka and gives the colonels on his right and left passing glances. The advocate-general is nearly ten years younger than the judge. In his early thirties, he is red-headed, with a yarmulka and a ready smile. But it is the judge's face and his expression that interest me: the blankness, the utter detachment from the human tragedy in which he is participating, amount to a pre-emptive denial, an attempt to say that he will not become humanly involved in the proceedings. After finishing with the advocate-general, clerks and lawyers in that order, the judge looks towards the back of the room and nods and six prisoners are brought in. Hala and I strain our necks but Nasser is not among them.

When the prisoners are finally in the dock an old man of nearly seventy shouts 'Ahmad' and leaps from the edge of the third bench behind us towards the prisoners and holds one of them in a close embrace that charges the atmosphere. The old man is shaking like a leaf, but the object of his affection, though moved, stands erect and defiant. For ten or so seconds time stands still. The judge watches passively, almost inertly, the advocate-general plays with the pencil in his hand, the clerks look at each other then lower their heads and the Red Cross couple are so rigid you would think they had stopped breathing. The Arab spectators do not move, but they emit empathy. The embrace between father and son is tantamount to a challenge to Israeli authority. As they continue to hold hands and look at each other, the same sergeant who had warned against human contact moves forward, seemingly a little awed, but he manages to separate love. The father is not asked to leave the courtroom but to return to his seat, and he does, his face streaked with silent tears. My eyes wander around the room once more and I conclude that love has triumphed and that we are all weak in its presence, for even those who disapproved have been touched. A higher law governing man's relationship to man has been invoked.

The emotional interruption over, the judge motions to the advocate-general to proceed, and he stands up and speaks. One of the clerks is attempting a simultaneous translation but no one is interested; they behave as if they have heard it all before. Ahmad, his name having been called, is standing, but he is not interested either. As each accusation is repeated to him in Arabic he answers, in a bored manner: 'not correct' or 'totally false'. He speaks abstractedly, not to either the judge or the advocate-general and the words 'sir', 'my lord' or 'your honour' never pass his lips. When it is all over he sits down as if regretting that he had stood up, his only concession of respect.

The routine is about to be repeated. This time it is Muhammad Ali Nadar who is called, and he faces the court on his feet. They repeat his name and he acknowledges that he is the defendant in question, but when the advocate-general is about to read the indictment, Muhammad Ali interrupts, 'The accusations against me are a load of rubbish which I deny, so please save your energy. I wasn't even in the village when the incident took place.' The Arab audience breaks into laughter and so do the Red Cross observers. The advocate-general is looking at the judge for direction, but the judge is defeated; the sniggers from the guards at the back of the courtroom grow louder, turning into laughter, particularly from a female soldier with an infectious giggle. Eventually the judge orders the indictment to be read out properly and Muhammad, enjoying his role of entertainer, denies all charges. No interest is shown in his claim that he was away when the incident took place.

The judge makes a relatively long statement that is not translated. When he finishes, the loud sergeant orders us to stand up and we do as the three members of the court march out. I rush over to Abid Assali and ask what has happened.

'The court is adjourned.'

'But they have been in session a mere forty minutes.'

'I know. The judge feels tired.'

'What's happened to Ahmad and Muhammad?'

'The judge says he needs time to study their files; their cases are postponed.'

'Until when?'

'We don't know.'

'How long have they been in detention?'

'Ten and eleven months.'

Walking out of the court back to prison, Ahmad throws his father a kiss. The old man's face is fractured by joy and pain, but he makes no overt gestures.

Hala and I join the milling crowd outside the court-house. I excuse myself and take a walk to look at the military aspects of the place. There are ten Israeli lorries and two police vans with strong mesh wire on the windows to keep passengers from escaping. Male and female soldiers are everywhere, walking to and from offices and I am struck by their flouting of regulations. Some of the men wear tennis shoes, others brown boots, and the women wear sandals or shoes. Their uniforms are dirty and some are torn. I wonder if this apparent lack of discipline reflects a more serious situation.

The soldiers behave as if the Arab crowd didn't exist, and the Arabs return the compliment; each side is in its own world, acting as if the other side weren't there. I notice that a group of Arab parents have gathered around a short lady with brown hair and sparkling blue eyes, an outsider dressed in a trouser suit. I ask Hala who she is and she tells me that it is Lea Tzemel, the liberal Israeli lawyer who defends many of the *intifada*'s children (see Chapter Ten).

Hala accepts my suggestion to visit other courts, the appeal court and one called the minor crimes court. The appeal court's function is self-explanatory but the second court tells another story. My brief visit and later investigation reveal that 'minor crimes' include making the V for victory sign, depicting the Palestinian flag, singing songs in praise of PLO Chairman Yasser Arafat and arguing with a soldier or a policeman. Each of these 'crimes' is punishable by up to two years in prison. We walk out of the minor crimes court and I ask Hala if it is appropriate to engage people in conversation and she says yes. I approach a comely middle-aged lady wearing an attractive green *thoub*.

'Allah be with you, *Haja*.' (This is an honorific form of address originally used to those who have made the pilgrimage to Mecca but now simply to convey respect.)

'Allah keep you, my brother.'

'I hope your troubles are light.'

'With Allah's mercy they are.'

'Is it your son who's being tried or sentenced today?'

'Yes, it is Ibrahim, my sixteen-year-old.'

'What did he do?'

'What does any of our children do? They arrest them for the simplest things.'

'What did they accuse him of doing?'

'Burning tyres in the middle of the street to keep their army patrols from driving through our village.'

'How long has he been detained, may Allah be with him?'

'He has been detained for three months and six days. May Allah never show them happy days.'

'But that's very long for this minor crime!'

Hala flinches and the lady in the green *thoub* is trying to hold back her anger. 'A crime, you call burning tyres to tell the world that we want to be independent a crime? Burning tyres is a duty, my brother; it is not a crime. Everybody in the world is independent except us Palestinians. That's a crime that has been going on for ages.'

I apologize and tell her, untruthfully, that I used the word 'crime' just in case an Israeli military person was eavesdropping and though she sees through my lie she becomes a little calmer. 'Opposing the Israelis is not a crime, my brother, may Allah keep you – opposing them and paying for it is a source of honour. My son is a loyal Palestinian. I never told him not to burn tyres or throw stones, I never admonished him even after he got arrested and beaten up, and he is the only boy among four girls. I hope you don't tell children it's a crime to oppose the Israelis. We should be brave and should sacrifice and sooner or later, probably not in my lifetime, we will win.'

The *Haja* and I talk while Hala wanders around. I tell her that she has good reason to be proud and she tells me how proud Ibrahim's sisters are of him and that she's a widow who lives off two small plots of land and the earnings of her two older daughters, who work as maids. I tell her that I have one daughter called Rasheda (in fact she has two names, the Western one being Charla Josephine) who lives and works in New York and I get a look accusing me of non-Arab behaviour. I dismiss this and explain Rasheda's management consultancy job by telling her my daughter works in an office. Slowly, through telling her how much my family has suffered for Palestine since the 1930s, the *Haja* and I become friends. With a sisterly smile on her face, she tells me that I am still young and that I should marry and produce male heirs to participate in our national struggle, which is likely to last a long time. My mumbled refrain doesn't stop her and she offers to find me a bride and we both laugh as if the world around us didn't exist.

My conversation with the *Haja* ends on this high note. I find Hala sitting in a waiting shed outside one of the courtrooms reading her Koran and decide not to disturb her but move around and talk to other people. Their stories are variations on a theme: teenage children detained and beaten up and occasionally tortured after detention. But not a single parent expresses regret or remorse over a child's activities. On the contrary, I have the feeling that the children are doing what the parents would like to do but cannot because they're older and the punishment would be more severe. I ask one parent why he himself doesn't throw stones at Israeli army or police patrols and he says that stone throwing is for children, that if he got involved he would have to do something more drastic and that would produce enough of an unequal Israeli response to make the activity counter-productive. Still, I am amazed by the sense of oneness, which suggests more anti-Israeli activity is on the way, and by the simplicity of motivation behind it: the fact that most children don't appear to belong to a political movement or organization. According to their parents, the children's anti-Israeli actions are motivated by a wish to be equal and free, a generic state of mind.

At twelve-thirty the bellowing sergeant stands on the outside steps of the serious crimes court to announce that proceedings are about to restart. Hala and I hurry inside and this time we are in the second row, right next to the dock. Everybody is in their place except the judge, but a new pitcher of water is in place, denoting his imminent appearance. Inexplicably the order of things is reversed and the prisoners are brought in before the judge appears. Among them is my young cousin Nasser.

Hala leaps on her son with open arms and they hug and hug and hug, but there are no tears. I am standing behind her; my legs are weak and I don't know what to do. Hala turns to me. 'It's Nasser . . .'

My arms reach out: I am transformed and transported. His strong, manly hand grabs mine and we embrace, only to pull back and embrace again. I am unaccustomed and weak and he is a veteran who takes things remarkably calmly and notices my inability to cope.

'They told me you were coming. How are you?'

His voice is steady, it echoes an inner strength that I cannot match. My words are faint. 'I'm all right. More to the point is how you are.'

'Well, well. I am sorry I haven't read the last book but we are not allowed to read under detention.'

'Don't worry, I'll send you ten copies when you come, which is soon, Allah willing.'

Then the sergeant interrupts again. 'Everybody back to your seats. Staaand up.' We obey and I whisper to Hala, 'I thought we were not supposed to talk to them.'

'Only when the judge is in the courtroom,' she answers.

His Excellency the Brigadier General looks rested. He speaks back and forth to the advocate-general and the lawyer Abid Assali. The three-way conversation lasts five minutes, with the defendants and the audience totally in the dark for lack of an interpreter. The defence lawyer turns to Nasser and his two co-defendants.

'The advocate-general and I have agreed on the outline of a bargain to settle your case. In return for your acceptance – admission – of two charges: throwing stones and Molotov cocktails at a unit of the Israeli security forces and participating in organizing activities against the welfare of the State of Israel, the advocate-general is willing to drop the charge of belonging to a terrorist organization. Furthermore, the advocate-general is willing to allow the sentencing to be a function of the court; he will neither ask for nor recommend a specific prison term. The prison sentence you will receive will take into account the amount of time you have already served, but whatever the prison term there will be a fine, also to be determined by the court. If this is acceptable to you then you will be sentenced today, along with the two absent members of your group. If this bargain is not acceptable to you then your case will be postponed until Tuesday 18 September to give the judge a chance to study your file. Please confer among yourselves and give us your answer.'

Nasser speaks for the group, confirming that the lawyer's statement is understood. I am struck by the fact that the judge was ready to sentence them without being on top of the case and by the blatant admission of this vital fact, but I watch Nasser. Given the circumstances, his physical neatness is startling. He is wearing a regulation blue shirt and loose blue trousers that remind me of the garb worn in an operating theatre, but he looks graceful in spite of that. He is not agitated but he is telling his co-defendants something forcefully, with gestures and in a low voice. He radiates solidity and elegance; certainly there isn't the slightest hint of fear, and its natural by-product, whispering, is absent. All eyes in the court are on my fifteen-year-old cousin, and even the judge and the advocate-general appear to be aware of a rare presence of spirit, of challenge. When Nasser finishes, his two co-defendants, who though older accept his leadership, say a few words then nod approval. He stands up. Silence reigns.

'The bargain struck by the advocate-general and Mr Assali is not acceptable to us. We deny participating in attacks against Israeli patrols. We do not consider belonging to a Palestinian nationalist group to be a conspiracy against anyone – all we want is the right of self-determination. Furthermore, there are no circumstances under which we would pay a fine to the Israeli government or any of its branches or organizations. We are ready to have the court sentence us on the basis of the false accusations of the advocate-general. We are innocent.'

Nasser sits down and I turn to look at the judge. He and his colleagues are unhappy. The advocate-general shakes his head. The Red Cross people's eyes are fixed on Nasser. There is a hint of a murmur among the audience. Abid Assali speaks in Hebrew. The prisoners are ushered out but there is no chance to say goodbye.

I am numb. It is as if my body isn't there, but my mind is totally engaged. Oh God, how I want to talk to him. I want them to bring my cousin back so I can tell him how much I love him. I want him to come back to tell me the meaning of courage. I want to give him one big, all-embracing hug that will tell him how I feel, how proud I am. But of course they don't bring him back and Hala is beside me, Koran in hand, looking at the judge and I don't dare ask her how she feels and she says nothing. She just looks at the judge.

Hala and I stop at the entrance guard post to pick up her identity card and my passport. Cousin Ali, who had hurried to Ramallah after his teaching duties were over, is waiting outside.

'What happened?'

'It's postponed until Tuesday,' I say.

'Damn them to hell. They're determined to break the kids. That's what the delays and bargains are all about. They could have sentenced them but that's too easy; they want to break their spirits and have them confess.'

We confirm Ali's statement by telling him the details of what happened in the courtroom. He is neither surprised nor overtly angry; I think that he has grown accustomed to pain. I insist that we take a taxi directly to Bethany.

In the taxi Ali turns to me and asks, 'How did you find Nasser, Saïd?'

'Ali, the question is, how do the Israelis expect to win when there are Nassers around?'

'Yes. They are not clever, you know. All the arrests, beatings, methodical torture, imprisonment and other abuses do is produce two types of people. One group, like Nasser, challenge them openly. The rest go through nominal confessions so they can get out to work against them again. The number of kids who have been imprisoned twice and three times is staggering and the Israelis still don't see it.'

'Tell me, Ali, do the Israelis try to rehabilitate prisoners or convert them to agree with them?'

'No. No. Their only interest is in punishing people. On occasion they try to turn people into informers in return for a short prison sentence, but that's all.'

'Do they succeed?'

'Rarely. Their methods are crude. The only ones who agree to work with them are people who are willing to accept the principle of racial superiority. It is like a Jew cooperating with the Germans during the Second World War – it's a difficult one to swallow. Everything they do points to the fact that they consider the Arabs inferior.'

'So, they have no long-term solution in mind – just prison terms and torture?'

'Yes. But they do use other things. They intercept letters, stop visits, rotate prisoners so they don't have friends and then there is solitary confinement for difficult cases, one and two months at a time. One guy was kept in solitary for nine months for insulting one of his guards. I think he told the guard that he was an asshole.'

'What about this business of not allowing them to read until they're sentenced. Is this a way to put more pressure on them to confess?'

'Oh yes. Stifling education is part of Israeli policy. Detainees are not allowed to read and study unless they are sentenced, which most of the time means that they have confessed. After sentencing they are only allowed to read certain books . . . yes, education is a target because they know how strongly the kids and the parents feel about it.'

'What are prisoners allowed to read?'

'I don't know really and it is different from place to place, prison to prison. All the prison management gets is an order to keep the prisoners ignorant and they interpret it their own individual way. It's easier to tell you what is banned.'

'Do. What is banned?'

'In Ansar 3 [the largest detention camp in the Negev desert, holding three thousand prisoners] the *Dialogues* of Plato are banned and the whole works of Jean-Paul Sartre.' Ali chuckles and continues, 'The writings of Abba Eban are banned.'

Hala, who has been immersed in her Koran, is startled by my raised voice.

'The writings of their god-damned former Foreign Minister are banned?'

'Yes. Definitely.'

'Wait until I tell this to those who still believe that Israel is the only functioning democracy in the Middle East. They are mad.'

'Yes, the fellow you mentioned the other day is banned as well.'

'David Grossman, *The Yellow Wind*?'

'Yes, *The Yellow Wind*.'

Back in Ali's house in Bethany we have a simple late lunch prepared by his fourteen-year-old daughter Shorouk. We eat slowly, refusing to admit that the events of the day affected our appetites. I make a reference to Amer's absence and all of them say that the Israelis' actions are unpredictable and that sentencing people *in absentia* is a common practice. Then Hala can't help herself and she tells me something that Ali's family probably had decided not to share with me, to spare me pain.

'When the detainees are not there for a hearing or they fail to produce them, the fear is that something ugly is happening. Our fear is that they have given them a bad beating and they don't want anybody, including the court, to know what they have done. Why else would they fail to produce them?'

'Does the lawyer know?'

'Of course. But there isn't much he can do. They try to suppress the whole thing.'

'The world should know this.'

'The world knows. The Palestinian Human Rights Centre, Amnesty and other organizations have documented thousands of cases of torture, but who cares?'

'The world will know more if you permit me to report what happened today.'

I am not allowed to finish. They all tell me to go ahead. Hala continues, 'One time, soon after his arrest, they beat up Amer so badly they shredded the sweater on his back. Another time they beat them in front of each other because they know how close to each other they are. But the boys are brave; they are not afraid. I'll show you some of their letters; their only concern is how we feel. We never know what to expect; we can't predict what they will do next. Then there are the delays, constant delays, every week a sentencing date then another and another and another and we can't do anything . . .'

Hala, Ali and Shorouk are crying and so am I. We cry our hearts out for ten minutes without anybody saying a word; only the muffled sound of despair is heard.

My cousins Amer Ali Aburish and Nasser Ali Aburish are still waiting to be sentenced. Now the advocate-general is asking for a maximum sentence of nine years' imprisonment and a fine of three thousand shekels each. If the fine is not paid then they will have to serve an additional year in prison.

Chapter Five
INDIRECT TERROR

A bad situation got worse on Saturday 17 February 1990 with the first meeting between the Israeli military authorities and the Mayor of Bethany, Abu Munther, in over a year and a half. The only reason for the Israelis to meet with the sole symbol of local authority was to expose an escalation of the pressure on the village people aimed at breaking their will to resist and demonstrating Israel's determination to stop all support for the *intifada*.

Ever since the *intifada* began, life in the West Bank village has seen a gradual, methodical erosion of the villagers' ability to run their own affairs. Villagers are now confronting Israeli rule in a way long familiar to the townspeople. Because elected officials in both towns and villages have solidly sided with their own people and supported the *intifada*, there is an official Israeli desire to reduce them to bearers of bad news, mouthpieces of policies they oppose. As the Israelis are committed to paying the costs of their attempts to contain and destroy the *intifada* militarily through taxing the people of the West Bank and Gaza, the most obvious way to undermine local officials was to make them collect the hated and unaffordable taxes.

The news of the Israeli diktat to the mayor reached me by word of mouth and I telephoned him and asked for an on-the-record meeting. As I walked to his house the day after his unusual meeting with the Israelis I saw the first signs confirming Bethany's position as a centre of *intifada* activity: many jeeps full of soldiers driving around the place – by the look of things a heavier military presence than was needed in other places. In all cases the soldiers were heavily armed and wore the uncomfortable expression of those who don't know what to expect. On the other hand, the local people, old and young, avoided looking at the soldiers and moved about in a separateness full of fear; they wore the weary look of the downtrodden.

At the mayor's residence, a six-room stone house a mile and a half from my temporary living quarters, Arab niceties were still observed. We sat on wicker chairs and drank Turkish coffee and mint tea while he admonished me for needing a special reason to see him. In spite of what occupied our minds, we still took time out to talk about family and friends and remember happenings of yesteryear. The mayor is sixty-three, eight years older than me.

Our recollections included a résumé of his life. He had finished school in 1945, when Palestine was under British rule. Most of his working life had been with the Justice Department, first under the British then, after they withdrew in 1948, under the Jordanians, who governed the West Bank until the Israeli occupation of 1967. After leaving the Justice Department, he had devoted his time to tending a few acres of land that he had inherited until he became mayor four years ago, a position he secured through having a clean record and a large family (he is my second cousin).

We eased gently into the real reason for my visit. He opened the official part of our conversation by saying, 'They shut off the water supply to the village late yesterday, after they came to see me. It's because we're unable to pay our water taxes, or so they say. I say this is what they say because the use of water to punish people is a very complicated matter. There is an overall shortage of water – we've had a drought for three years, and there isn't enough water to go around. So it isn't a simple matter of punishing people, it is also a disguise for diverting whatever water is available to their people.'

'So using water as a weapon came about as a result of the water shortage?'

'Essentially, yes. Before the water shortage they used other methods, nothing as drastic as this.'

'I must say I hadn't heard of it, Abu Munther, but surely they will restore it soon.'

'No, they won't restore it until we pay and then they will take their time, especially if the water we use is needed by them. But the municipality [of Bethany] has no money to pay them anyway, so the whole thing is a blessing in disguise as far as they're concerned.'

'But this means that a health disaster is in the making.'

'Of course, but they don't care. Our disasters don't touch them. I asked them for an extension so I might try to get the money. In the past they gave extensions to other places, but not to Bethany. Bethany is an *intifada* village, so cutting off the supply is handy.'

I smiled. 'Yes, I heard about the special treatment you get, the message they're trying to deliver to get you to change, but they can't turn their back on a health hazard that threatens up to twenty thousand people.'

'You're like all western journalists, Saïd, though you were born here. You think this is a gentlemen's game. It isn't. The kids [of the *intifada*] have been active lately and this is the Israeli answer. But even before the health problem develops, there's the immediate problem of drinking water. In some poor households they don't have utensils to store water, and I was given a four-hour notice altogether – then no water.'

'Surely you aren't telling me that some people will die of thirst?'

'To be honest, no. There are a number of wells in the village, and their owners will share what they have – for drinking purposes. This suits the Israelis: most of the time they will do anything short of having people die. Some of our people will always try to charge for drinking water, but I can stop that.'

'So we're back to the health hazard.'

'Yes.'

'How did it reach this point? Why haven't you paid the water tax and why don't you have the money to pay it now?'

'There are several reasons. The biggest is that many people don't have the money to pay, especially after taxes have been going up and up. A lot of our people are unemployed, tourism is down and what work existed in the cities has dried up. This group who can't afford to pay represents about one third of the people. Then there's a small group who won't pay for political reasons – they consider paying taxes to Israel an act of treason. Of course there are the usual non-payers. Well over half of the people aren't paying.'

'What about the municipal treasury?'

'It's empty. We have no money. People can't pay their other taxes either, and there will be more elaborate punishment in the future because the Israelis do depend on what we pay in taxes to continue their hideous policies.'

'So on the question of water it's a deadlock, unless the Israelis change their mind.'

'They won't. You keep ignoring what I said about this suiting their purposes – they need the water. In the past they gave us several warnings before they did anything, now you hear about water supplies being cutting off on a regular basis. Many villages suffer.'

'But that's mad.'

'Yes, the whole place and everybody in it is mad. But mad people with guns are dangerous – they do things which can kill and wound others.'

My conversation with the mayor lasted two hours. He was full of resigned despair, mercilessly caught between Arab poverty and Israeli insensitivity. He saw the poverty of his people and their political inclinations for what they were, components of an inevitable tragedy, and harshly condemned the Israeli attitude, which didn't see beyond the moment and which, against all historical precedent, sought to break the spirit of a resisting population through unreasonable pressure and intimidation. I told the mayor that I wanted to look into the situation further.

The following day, Monday, I saw the part-time treasurer of the municipality of Bethany, a teacher in the girls' school. He wryly told me that keeping the books of the village took less and less of his time because there was no money to worry about. Though this man's attitude towards the Israelis was one of quiet but open defiance, I shall say nothing of his identity except that he is a tall, handsome man who cares about his appearance. His family has suffered drastically since the 1948 war.

The treasurer was more forthright than the mayor, and saw the bigger picture more clearly. He insisted, and cited convincing but unverifiable examples to support his contentions, that the Israelis' taxation – indirect, personal, business property, and for water and other services – was the most abusive in the whole world. To him, it seemed to have got worse since the *intifada* began: taxes were supposed to have gone up by sixty per cent since then. He viewed this situation in a more dramatic way than the mayor. To him, cutting off the water supply was one more way the Israelis applied pressure to make life in the West Bank so uncomfortable that most people would eventually leave to live in other Arab countries.

It took a few more questions to determine that the opinions of the treasurer were his own, that he didn't belong to any political organization. This and the obvious care he employed in using words prompted me to question him about other aspects of life in the village.

The next day, with the help of knowledgeable Israeli contacts, I easily verified three of the treasurer's more serious allegations. The allegation that the Israeli government, as a matter of policy, refused to grant Arabs building permits and that this policy has led to inhumane crowded conditions was correct. A related allegation, purporting to show how the Israelis were trying to force the Arabs out of the West Bank, had to do with visits by West Bankers to other Arab countries. All males under thirty-nine who undertook such visits were required to stay away for a minimum of seven months, which meant that many got jobs, never came back and eventually sent for other members of their families to join them.

On Wednesday I returned to the immediate problem of the interception of the water supply to Bethany inclined to see it more as a political than a fiscal question. Mayor Teddy Kollek of Jerusalem, whose city supplies Bethany's water, was too busy to see me to discuss this. I settled for a meeting with one of his assistants, a man who spoke Iraqi Arabic but who, with arrogance aimed at insulting, refused to go beyond identifying himself as Maurice.

To Maurice, both the mayor and treasurer of Bethany were liars, and he didn't mince his words, though he claimed he knew both men. He said that it was Bethany and its people who had declared war on the State of Israel. By not paying their taxes they were trying to break the Israeli economy. When I told him that many Bethanites didn't have the money to pay their taxes, he insisted, while refusing to answer any questions about evidence, that Bethany receives huge sums of money from the PLO, so it was 'Bethany's choice whether to use it to pay taxes or foment trouble'. When I resorted to arguing the human and hygiene aspects of the case, he brutally stated that water wasn't essential to Arabs because they didn't bathe all that often. Finally, he had no time whatsoever to discuss the general shortage of water, hardly a state secret since newspapers often reported it.

There were two more days without water. Sharing, saving and savouring water become the main topic of conversation in Bethany, and people convinced themselves that electricity supplies were going to be cut off. The treasurer, mayor and others worked hard and no one went thirsty, nor did anybody benefit from the situation. But people began to smell; they walked slowly and the clothes they wore became dirty because often they were the only ones they had. This was the one aspect of the tragedy that no one discussed.

The water was turned on after Bethany's richest citizens, in fact people with moderate incomes, donated the money owed for water taxes. The Municipality of Jerusalem issued a warning that it would no longer tolerate a delay in the payment of water taxes and that such a delay would lead to a lengthy interruption in the water supply. Unsurprisingly, the restoration of water supplies to Bethany coincided with its being cut off from two neighbouring villages.

The actual act of withholding water from Bethany, shockingly revealing as it was, told me considerably less than Maurice's attitude. This man, an assistant to the supposedly moderate Mayor of Jerusalem, on whom the Western press heaps praise for his efforts to improve Arab–Israeli relations, was in charge of Arab relations, and told me that the Arabs were a dirty people. A man holding such an important post might be expected to know that the Koran equates cleanliness with holiness and to refrain from making statements that do nothing but emphasize and perpetuate the divide between the two sides.

The withholding of water described above took place during an earlier visit to the West Bank. Nevertheless, it typifies the use of water as a tool of intimidation. This practice is on the increase.

Part Two
Self-Appraisal

Chapter Six
TREASON

I have known a number of famous traitors, among them Kim Philby, a highly placed International Red Cross official and the head of a poor Arab state who was salaried by the CIA and on occasion misled and stole from them. I have also known whole groups of people, including Lebanese journalists, who are traitors for hire, who knowingly worked against their country for the highest bidder, regardless of political inclinations and the potential scale of damage.

All this has led me to devote a considerable amount of time to studying what makes traitors turn against their countries and peoples. My fascination with the subject has led me to treat it fictionally in two novels, *One Day I Will Tell You* and *Between Mossad and Mohamad.*

Despite this lifelong fascination with the roots of treason, a single explanation for it, if one exists, continues to elude me. During my stay in the West Bank the questions of what makes a traitor and what a traitor really is confronted me in a more immediate way than during my earlier, theoretical investigations.

In the West Bank the word for traitor, *ameel* (literally, agent) is used liberally, most of the time as a synonym for a collaborator with the Israeli forces of occupation. And although the actual number of such traitors is undoubtedly smaller than the frequent use of the word suggests, Arabs and Israelis agree that there is a substantial number of them. They are the product of the inevitably unhealthy relationship that comes to exist between an occupier and a conquered people.

Sadly, there is treason here, and, like treason under similar historical circumstances, it is a matter of average people turning against neighbour and friend because of deficiencies in their make-up, short-sightedness and for a combination of other minor reasons. In the West Bank and Gaza, three hundred and sixty Arabs have been killed by their own people for 'collaboration with the Israeli authorities' and the cars, houses and places of business of several thousand more have been damaged or torched. An even greater number of people have been earmarked by their communities as possible targets for punishment. Whatever the margin of error, these figures attest to the existence of a major social and political problem that demands consideration.

The problem of treason in the West Bank may lack the romance or ramifications of what Kim Philby and George Blake did, but examining the problem tells us a great deal about the character of those involved and through that we see the workings of the community that produced them, and often eventually punished them.

What is behind the act of treason? Alienation? Yes. Disillusionment? Very often. Ideological commitment? Rarely. Financial need? Occasionally. Blackmail? Very rarely. Combinations of these obviously overlapping reasons? More often than not. We know what financial need means, but alienation could simply result from chronic insecurity: the protagonist's inability to claim a public position drives him to get back at society through becoming a secret hero, if an alienated one. And disillusionment is very often the result of the persistent anger and frustration of someone who does not get what he thinks he deserves, regardless of what it is. The underlying motivation is often this simple, and it is worth recalling Kim Philby's remark about spying as portrayed in the books of John Le Carré, probably the foremost spy novelist of our times: 'The reason is seldom as complex as he makes it out to be.'

It is also important to remember that traitors, collaborators and the like are individuals and individual motivation has the habit of defying the broadest of definitions. Nevertheless, what I found myself pursuing in the West Bank was the common thread that often exists and helps explain a certain activity. Just as scientists, teachers and tractor salesmen differ individually but have something in common, so do traitors.

If a traitor in the West Bank is someone who, in order to live from day to day, cooperates with the Israeli authorities, then everybody in the place is a traitor. They have all cooperated with the Israelis for this reason. Paying income tax and obeying Israeli traffic lights imply an acceptance of Israeli rule, of cooperation. This definition can be broadened to include the use of the Israeli legal system to defend the children of the *intifada* or talking to Jerusalem's Mayor Teddy Kollek about municipal waste. Undoubtedly these acts of cooperation are not treason, and, mercifully, very few people see them as such.

So our concern with treason among West Bankers is not with the circumstantial acts of cooperation by all who deal with the Israelis, but a narrower type of cooperation, the activities of those who, most willingly, aid and abet the continued Israeli occupation of the West Bank against the will of the majority of its people. Nevertheless, it is safe to assume that most people remain opposed to the Israeli presence.

But even when the definition is narrowed, as above, there is no universal means by which to determine what a traitor is, nor yardstick by which to measure what his presence does to the community. For this reason case-studies, two brief and one in depth, will have to suffice, but hopefully these will reveal something of the broader picture.

N.O. is sixty-six and has been the headman of his village for forty-four years; he inherited the position from his father in 1946. During his tenure he served under the British, the Jordanians and since 1967 the Israelis. His position as village headman is secure because the Israelis haven't held an election for over ten years and fear of a victory by pro-PLO elements makes it unlikely that there will be one in the near future.

But if N.O.'s position as headman seems safe, his life isn't. It is threatened by the people of his village who resent and reject his work as a decorator-contractor working for the Israelis. His house has already been torched by PLO supporters, or *intifada* sympathizers, and the likelihood of a more direct attempt on his life is real – all because he is considered a traitor, an accommodator of the Israelis.

But N.O. refutes the accusation of treason by stating that he has been undertaking similar work for the Israelis since 1967 and that nobody has objected to it until recently. His detractors don't contradict his statement of defence; neither do they accept it, because to them 'things have changed'.

This is a most interesting situation. It isn't what N.O. does that has changed but the conditions under which he is performing his work. Objections to his work followed the outbreak of the *intifada* and it is true that things were different before then, and while

N.O.'s work had not been condoned, it had been tolerated. Now, with the *intifada* as a catalyst, his type of work with the Israelis is tantamount to a crime against the national uprising.

Meanwhile, N.O. angrily states that nothing has changed and that some of his accusers have done similar work for the Israelis in the past. 'But why continue with the work if the community where you live is against it?' I asked N.O. after verifying that his counter-accusation was correct. His answer was to state that bowing to the will of the community would do nothing except invite mob rule and that what he does is simple work that isn't likely to influence the political outcome of the situation in the West Bank. He goes further, describing himself as a misunderstood *intifada* supporter.

Having failed to unearth anything that might implicate N.O. beyond the simple act of decorating Israeli homes I decided that his case is an excellent example of the endless conflict between individual and communal responsibility. For him, this man's commitment to his family and their livelihood overrides all others.

If N.O. represents the individual who refuses to accept the constraints of the society in which he lives, then A.K. is the social outcast taking revenge on those responsible for his rejection.

A former owner of a hardware store, a handsome, strapping six-footer, A.K. had the security of a lucrative business and nothing else. The man was and is antipathetic, lacking in social graces in a community that attaches considerable importance to everyday niceties and tact. This had forced him into the position of a loner, a role that reinforced itself and confirmed his separateness from the small community north of Jerusalem where he lives.

In 1967 A.K. saw the arrival of the first Israeli soldier in the West Bank as a godsend. He immediately adopted a pro-Israeli attitude, which manifested itself through open friendliness towards individual Israelis and the stocking of Israeli goods at a time when the Arabs shunned the Israelis and Arab-made products were as good and cheaper. Even now, I am told, he consciously inserts Hebrew words into his conversation with fellow-Arabs when Arabic words would do, just to annoy them.

The whispers and accusations of treason against A.K. include what the villagers might do to him. According to my informants he senses that, but his only response is to sink deeper and deeper into a totally pro-Israeli and anti-Arab attitude. His hatred of the community that had caused his initial alienation is too rooted for him to recant, though his elimination is only a matter of time.

I was advised not to make a direct approach to A.K. My contacts told me that he was an unfriendly man whose behaviour was likely to offend me and endanger my stay in the West Bank. I was deterred by the prospect of his telling the Israelis that I was questioning his friendly attitude towards them. But I did manage to watch him from a distance and can verify the accusations against him.

Clearly this is a simple case of alienation. The man cared more about his lack of acceptance by his fellow-Arabs than he ever admitted and saw in the Israeli presence a way out of his predicament. The Israelis, anxious as they are to befriend any Arab who will reciprocate, play along with him. A.K.'s motivation is akin to that underlying the treason of major spies, who likewise found sordid spiritual refuge in turning against their own society.

My simple probing of the cases of N.O. and A.K. led me to look deeper into a third one about which I had heard a great deal. I was not able to find a single person among Bethany's population of some twenty thousand who had anything good to say about Abu Firaz, the owner of a grocery shop on the western edge of town. Bethanites are all agreed that Abu Firaz is a collaborator, hence a traitor. It is a rare unanimity of judgement against a member of the community. But agreement stops at this broad accusation, for there is no common view as to why this man is a traitor nor a consensus as to how he should be treated. In fact, it all reflects the Arab malaise of not knowing what to do about a problem, let alone how to do it.

There are a few universally accepted facts about Abu Firaz beyond his ownership of the grocery store. He is a new Bethanite, having arrived in the village six years ago, and is still considered an outsider. He has a wife and six children. And he refuses to close shop on the days of protest strikes against Israeli occupation.

This last fact, which I confirmed through personal observation, has led the followers of the *intifada* to torch his shop twice during the past year. He was able quickly to reopen shop after both fires. The fact that he was able to do so dramatizes his contrary behaviour and is responsible for the belief that he is an Israeli agent who receives substantial financial support from his employers. Naturally, others return to the original point and say confirmation of his status begins with opening shop on strike days. A third group says that it matters neither that he trades on strike days nor that he was able to reopen so soon after his shop was destroyed. They speak instead of the information he gathers about the village and thc fact that he owns an Israeli-supplied handgun.

Most other accusations against Abu Firaz, and there are many, are not only impossible to confirm, even circumstantially, but are personal in nature and do not constitute traitorous behaviour even if verified, or they are charges subsidiary to the main one. But in both cases they tell something about his position within the community.

Some locals said that Abu Firaz has another wife who lives in Amman with another brood of kids whom he neglects. Others whispered that he was formerly a PLO fighter who is now wanted by the organization for having been an Israeli plant. A third allegation had to do with the fact that he spoke fluent Hebrew. Lastly, many believed that Abu Firaz was an alias the Israelis had given him and that his true name is Muhammad Tahoul.

I used the excuse of buying a bottle of whisky to visit Abu Firaz in his shop; I wanted to see for myself the man who provokes so much talk. In a Muslim community becoming ever more religious, the act of selling and buying alcoholic beverages is a trespass and Abu Firaz is the only Bethany grocer insensitive enough to stock the forbidden goods, let alone display them openly. A bottle of whisky was therefore a good reason to engage him in conversation.

Abu Firaz was of medium height and stocky, with thick black hair and a heavy moustache. He had roving black eyes whose natural attractiveness was neutralized by the fear they betrayed; they were on the lookout for unfriendly acts every time someone entered or passed the shop. Having geared myself up to observe the unusual, perhaps even the unimportant, I noted the straightness of his hair, in a land of curly or kinky hair regardless of colour.

In manner, Abu Firaz was full of himself in a very shallow way that exposed his fear, particularly of whom and what he didn't know – in this case, me. He compensated for his nervousness by resorting to ignorant bragging. Even by inflated Arab standards, this trait was extreme. (He claimed to have written a number of books, but couldn't remember a single title, and that Israel had over five hundred nuclear weapons.) His boasting confirmed a vital aspect of his character: there was no nobility in the man. In fact he lacked the traditional Arab gentility and welcoming friendliness to such an extent that I concluded that he was the worst brought up Arab I had ever met. What confronted me was a man so ignorant he had no idea that he didn't know.

Slowly I became more amused and intrigued by Abu Firaz than afraid of him. If this was the local source of fear, I told myself, then I could solve Bethany's problem. It was so simple: I wanted him to stop being a jackass and close his shop on strike days and do other things that would please the community around him. But I didn't; instead I settled for asking him why he did those unpopular things.

His eyes evaded mine. Obviously he wasn't accustomed to direct questions, to someone transcending the atmosphere of fear generated by his activity and dealing with what he did as neither frightening nor significant. So startled was he by my approach that he faltered for a minute, before cleverly promising to tell me 'the whole story' before I left Bethany. His apparent wish to rehearse an answer strengthened my determination to continue my probing.

I used the bottle of whisky as the focal point for a small meeting of Bethanites to discuss Abu Firaz and his position in the community. There was no agreement among my five guests as to how Abu Firaz had come to live in Bethany. Because everybody agreed that he was a collaborator, the people who introduced him to Bethany denied responsibility and accused others of having done it, and the latter group, angry and insulted, stopped talking to their accusers and pointed the finger at a third party, who professed total innocence while naming others.

I asked how Abu Firaz came to open his grocery store and this too was the subject of unverified allegations and enfolded in mystery, though there was agreement that he did it on arrival. His success was attributed to his policy of extending credit to his clientele and having a greater variety of products. My friends were adamant that the popularity of the shop didn't extend to the owner.

My next question was harder: why, in spite of all I had heard, did people do business with a traitor? Initially everybody insisted that it was because credit was available. But pressed harder, they refined this answer to mean that that need influenced the behaviour of a lot of people. So need made excusable what is normally reprehensible, and we left unanswered whether need is a good enough excuse for treason, indirect or otherwise.

'What about dealing with the man as a person, not as a shopkeeper? Is he ostracized?' I then asked.

Everybody said that Abu Firaz wasn't ostracized. They justified their relative acceptance of him as a reflection of a tolerant society. They cited examples of how welcoming and generous with outsiders Bethany people were and that unfriendliness was frowned upon. But they emphasized that the outward show of friendliness to Abu Firaz fell short of total social acceptance, which would have meant inviting him to weddings and funerals. There was no recollection of anybody inviting him to a wedding, and when he appeared at funerals, where invitations are not needed, the other mourners kept their distance. So the man was barred from being a full member of the community, but not ostracized.

My impatience surfaced, and I asked the group to repeat in the simplest and most direct terms why they considered Abu Firaz a traitor. After much insubstantial discussion, what I was eventually told confirmed what I had heard before and what I knew about the whole genre: a traitor is someone who knowingly acts against the generally accepted wishes of the community. By way of qualification it was stated that someone who accidentally helped the Israeli authorities was not a traitor, nor was anyone who did it out of need or under pressure. My question about whether communal feeling was a substitute for the law in judging a man accused of treason produced agreement that a community is an acceptable judge of these matters.

'Do the people who don't need credit facilities boycott him?' My question was unwelcome, caused confusion and produced contradictory answers. It was clear that people didn't boycott him under any circumstances. They went to his shop not out of need but for convenience, because it had better products and was closer to their homes. Not only did the community fail to match their words with deeds, but their excuses for not boycotting a traitor were getting thinner and thinner.

One of the more discerning members of my small panel read my mind and tried to amend my implied accusation that a sense of community was lacking. He admitted that while a developed communal sense was missing, it still didn't invalidate the accusation against Abu Firaz. The people of the community may have been lazy and lax, but Abu Firaz's activity must still be judged as indefensible. The speaker contended, probably rightly, that Abu Firaz would have made the same amount of money while observing protest-strike closures. We concluded by agreeing that a considerable difference existed between 'direct acts of treason' and acts of omission.

Another of those present elaborated on the last point. 'I don't know what it is, but he is different; he aims to damage. We talk to Israelis – we have to – but he goes further. His intentions are what matters; he isn't one of us.'

'What,' I asked, 'does his presence in Bethany do to the community?'

All agreed that people were afraid of him; after all, the man was identified with the power that was making their lives miserable.

The more they talked the more it became apparent that their fear resembled anxiety over diseases about which people talk a lot and know very little. Abu Firaz's capabilities were exaggerated and the mystery surrounding him intrigued the local population. Then there was the fear that the disease that he carried might infect the rest of the community and there was an implicit admission that the community lacked an immune system, that it was vulnerable. After all, it was the same place that lacked the wherewithal to boycott him and, lacking the authority of a judicial or governmental system, could only confront him secretly.

The following day I went back to Abu Firaz and told him that the time had come for him to tell me why he didn't close on protest-strike days. He was prepared. 'They're clowns. They're all ignorant. Look, they come and shop at my place, all of them, then they accuse me of being a traitor. Years ago, I wanted to fight the Israelis and I did. I did more than most people would ever think of doing. But the people I fought with, joined – well, they were interested in their own benefit and so we produced no results. In this town they all say they want to boycott Israeli goods, but they do nothing about it – only when they're together, they talk, lip service. Nobody ever faced me to tell me that I was a traitor, nobody dared, but behind my back, oh yes, I am a traitor. The Jews are better organized, much better. The Jews treat me like an equal.'

The shopkeeper went on condemning his own people for fifteen minutes. The man was both alienated and disillusioned. He was leading a disconnected life in a place where people didn't like him; he was an outsider. Regardless of whether it is an inherent part of his character or something he developed to cope with conditions in Bethany, his behaviour was that of someone determined to pay back his 'tormentors' or 'rejectors'. This analysis accords with the results of various attempts to psychoanalyse major spies. Perhaps he had belonged to the PLO and become disillusioned or turned against them because they rejected him. He was simple enough to have adopted a punitive tribal response to personal hurt and become contrary. In spite of attempts to hide it, he was painfully shy and unsure of himself and his simple arrogance wouldn't work outside a provincial place like Bethany. Finally, money was important to him, however small the amounts involved might appear to outsiders. Ultimately, though, all these understandable human reactions still fall short of explaining treason itself, of illuminating the mysterious element that makes someone commit this totally reprehensible act.

Much more important than the diverse character traits Abu Firaz possesses is what his presence reveals about Bethany. Its people can't organize a simple boycott and instead resort to violence and torching. They are sufficiently afraid to excuse their own behaviour and exaggerate the source of their fear. In a way this has played into the hands of Firaz and hundreds of alienated people like him: it has made them celebrities, if hated ones, and their sordid minds cling to the status they have attained, cherishing their 'heroic' stance.

Abu Firaz remains a loathsome little man regardless of what triggered his perversion and what sustains it. He is a traitor because he deliberately acts against the wishes of his community without any ideological justification. He represents the class of Arabs on whom Israel depends to undermine the general refusal by the great majority to accept its policies.

Chapter Seven
THE SMALL LANDOWNER'S STORY

If cutting off water and blocking other essential supplies are the latest tactics of the Israeli occupation, the expropriation of land was the earliest and remains the most controversial. Land seizure began soon after the Israeli occupation of the West Bank in 1967. The most blatant form was official expropriation of public land by military order. This began in 1967 and went on for ten years. Having completed the expropriation of most of the land that qualified as public land, the Israeli government resorted to annexing more land for 'security reasons'. This provoked former Israeli Chief of Staff Haim Bar Lev and other military and civilian authorities on the subject to challenge this policy. They claimed that much of the land being expropriated was not needed for security reasons, and this challenge was upheld by the Israeli courts, forcing the government to adopt a third approach of redefining what was private or public land.

As a result the government declared all the land not tended for five years *mishaa* (neglected), and relabelled it government land subject to expropriation. The burden of proof of ownership now fell on the landowner, who seldom had the means to meet the legal costs of challenging the government order and who faced prohibitive property taxes if his claim to the land was upheld by the courts.

All the Israeli laws sanctioning or facilitating the expropriation of Arab land are in blatant violation of the Geneva Convention, which requires the maintenance of the status quo in conquered territories. The occupied territories of the West Bank and Gaza qualify as conquered territories because the Israeli government has never annexed them, an act that would be illegal in itself.

So, what is public land is not clear, and the Israeli government continues to use different definitions to facilitate its expropriation policy, so that the whole issue is a constant source of conflict. To justify their constant redefinitions of public land, the Israelis selectively use the laws of Turkey, Britain and Jordan because the West Bank has been ruled by these powers in this century and international law demands that an occupying power adhere to the 'laws existing therein'. In short, when the Israelis want a piece of land they examine the laws these countries have used and apply those that afford them the most leverage, either unchanged or amended by them to suit the situation. This is particularly true where the Arabs do not own the land outright but have been entitled to use it for hundreds of years.

Much of the land subject to this redefinition is strategically located and needed for building military camps or settlements. Usually the Israelis make a perfunctory offer to buy the land and resort to expropriation if their offer is refused. My own family refused to sell a piece of land east of Bethany. When we wouldn't sell, the Israeli government seized the land and built the largest settlement in the West Bank, Maale Adumin, on it and land belonging to others.

The combined effect of these policies was to allow the Israeli government to expropriate most of the land of the West Bank: fifty-two per cent according to Israeli government figures and sixty-seven per cent if the figures of the Arab Land Office are used. But the problem is still with us because the expropriation policy continues.

The principal causes of current land problems arise when the Israelis need improved access to land they have already taken, or when the land they have taken isn't enough to built a settlement of reasonable size or when the settlers wish to expand what they already have or decide against having Arab neighbours. These constant sources of local friction are the domain of the Israeli law courts; they are subsidiary to the overall international issue of the legality of land seizure.

If there is one case that exemplifies the Palestinians' determination not to be pushed out of their land and Israel's commitment to taking it away from them, it is that of Sabri Garib, a small landowner in the village of Beit Igza', near Ramallah, north of Jerusalem.

Garib looks and talks like a typical Palestinian villager. He is a shortish, mustachioed man with a dark complexion and a ready smile. At forty-nine he heads a family of fourteen people who depend on the land in question for their livelihood. Garib's troubles began in 1978 when the Israelis built the settlement of Givon Haddashah on land adjacent to his. Garib's land clearly occupies a strategic position as far as the settlement is concerned. He owns thirty acres of land occupying the top of a hill that overlooks the settlement, which lies in the fold of two hills to the south. In a war, occupation of this land would render the settlement vulnerable, and though there is no war, a warlike mentality exists among the settlers.

Technically, Garib's land is part of Beit Igza', a village of over four hundred inhabitants, and the plot has a house with a few trees surrounding it. Furthermore, the history of its use leaves no doubt that it is a piece of private property that has belonged to the Garib family for many generations. With this background, the issue becomes purely one of strategic location.

Garib received offers for the land immediately after the establishment of Givon Haddashah settlement, but refused to sell. The price offered was increased time and again, through ordinary land brokers and occasionally through army officers whose involvement was supposed to signal the importance of the deal and the fact that the military looked with favour upon Garib's acceptance. But he still refused to sell.

All attempts to make Garib change his mind having failed, in 1981 a military order was issued under which the land was to be confiscated. However, proper notification was not served on Garib because the service of such a notice would in itself be an admission that the land belonged to him. Instead the order claimed that the land was fallow and forsaken and therefore qualified as public land subject to expropriation.

Having confirmed the existence of this order – and it took a considerable amount of work – Garib wisely retained the Israeli lawyers Haim Cohen and Yussaf Announ to contest it. They lodged an appeal with the High Court of Justice seeking to declare the confiscation order null and void. After all, the various purchase offers amounted to an admission that the land belonged to Garib. The High Court refused to consider the case and referred it instead to an appeals committee, a branch of the same military who issued the confiscation order.

A series of presentations to the appeals committee continued until 1984, but yielded no results. The record of the purchase offers was deemed inadmissible evidence and Garib's failure to produce an original ownership document worked against him. Furthermore, the confiscation order was expanded to include all the land instead of the major part of it covered by the original order. Meanwhile, Israeli extremists went to work: Garib's lawyers received several telephone threats and were subjected to harassment that included the painting of threatening slogans on their cars. The lawyers, afraid for their lives, eventually resigned from the case late in 1984.

To replace his Israeli lawyers, Garib hired the Palestinian lawyer Jonathan Khoutab of the Al Haq Foundation of Human Rights (an associate organization of the International Association of Jurists). Khoutab began by relodging an appeal with the High Court. His spirited efforts appear to have been directed at forestalling the settlers' use of the confiscated land to stop them from creating a *de facto* situation. He succeeded. A High Court order was obtained preventing the settlers' interfering with Garib's use of the land, except for a tiny part of it, but it fell short of settling the overall issue of ownership. However, the order amounted to a tacit recognition of Garib's right to use it.

But it did not stop the settlers. Determined to have their way, at the beginning of 1986 they bulldozed a road to the Givon Haddashah settlement through the land whose usage was granted to Garib. They went further, fencing in his house and so denying him the use of the only well in existence and access to the outhouse. The settlers' only excuse was that the High Court order's lack of clarity implied public ownership and gave them as much right to use the land as anybody else.

The activities of the settlers forced the court to deal with the real issue of ownership. Garib was able to provide proof that his family had farmed the land for five generations, but he failed to produce a land deed. Under laws governing land ownership of Palestine's previous occupiers a tenancy of thirty years is tantamount to ownership. Nevertheless, all precedents were ignored in favour of the *de facto* situation imposed by the settlers' illegal action. Not only was the land confiscated but Garib was ordered to pay US$1335 in court costs.

Yet another appeal was lodged to uphold Garib's right to use the land without determining actual ownership. But the court, which, according to Garib and Khoutab, had by then been apprised of the strategic importance of the land, turned it down and ordered the imprisonment of Garib for an unspecified period of time. He served twenty-one days and was released.

At this point it is useful to hear Garib himself relate some of what happened. He is clear on the human aspect of the case but misses many vital points because, preoccupied as he is with his own situation, he takes it for granted that others are aware of his history. Again, because of his limited education he is less clear on the legal aspects of the case than on the personal implications. Also, it should be remembered that Garib has little appreciation of the nature of the individuals or groups with whom he is dealing.

'The Israeli iron fist was trying to crush me. All these lawyers couldn't protect me, protect my rights. Lawyer Khoutab and the Land Office [a Palestinian organization that helps people defend their land rights] formed a committee to help me while I was in prison.

'The committee was composed of good people. Good Arabs and good Israelis and good foreigners. Allah bless them. They raised money to help me do things, like put plants in the land to show that it was being used and it was mine. They sent volunteers to help me and they were from many nationalities. But the settlers came and threatened the volunteers; the settlers are not afraid of anything or anybody.

'To stop more trouble from breaking out, horrible things were happening all the time. A military man came to settle the confrontation between the volunteers and the settlers. He asked to talk to me, but this was when I was in prison and he knew that. He didn't try to see me in prison. He asked to talk to my father but he knew my father was dead. My wife said she would talk to him, but he said he didn't deal with Arab women.

'After I was released from prison trouble continued. I was accused of building fences illegally and I said I didn't, but they still fined me five thousand Israeli shekels [US$2500]. I didn't have the money to pay the fine. So they summonsed me to court.

'Another thing happened then. My two sons and I and my wife were accused of throwing stones at settlers' cars. We all know that if you throw stones at Israelis you can be removed from your property. I swear I never did, but they insisted that I did.

'They didn't remove us from the land, but they put me in prison again for planting trees or throwing stones – I really don't know why. But I still refused to leave my house and my family stayed there.

'Then Mr Khoutab, Allah bless him, he contacted the company which had originally built the settlement because they know more about land and its ownership in that area. He questioned them as to why the land wasn't taken away from me before the settlement was built and whether it was because they knew the land belonged to me. The company [Nahalt Israel Company] produced papers which supported me. On their maps, my land was indicated as private property.

'We're back in court now, and they will decide soon. We're using the company's papers to show that the land is mine. This should produce a final decision by the court.

'It has taken a long time and I have suffered a lot – things I don't want to talk about, but the committee [an *ad hoc* group without a name] are helping me and my family. I don't want to move. Where would we go? We've been on the land for generations. We are farmers and we don't want to be refugees.'

The record of the court proceedings limited itself to the question of the land's ownership and subsidiary issues. Neither that record nor Garib's narrative addresses itself to the various attacks on him by settlers and others unknown but suspected of being militant branches of the military. Following is an abbreviated list of these attacks as obtained from Sabri Garib's lawyers and defenders:

1 On 22 October 1984 a group of Israeli settlers attacked Sabri and his son while they were working their land. They were beaten up badly, Sabri was injured in his chest and hand while his son suffered bruises to his back.

2 A month after the attack on Sabri and his son, one of Sabri's daughters was attacked. The eleven-year-old girl was violated by several settlers. One of Sabri's children was lightly injured while trying to come to his sister's aid.

3 On 31 January 1990 fifteen settlers and six soldiers attacked Sabri's house during his absence. They entered the house after breaking all the windows and left after destroying most of the contents of the house.

4 On 8 February 1990 Sabri was arrested by the local military authorities and taken to the Ramallah Military Prison. He was released after three days. No explanation was ever given for the arrest or the subsequent release.

5 On 13 February 1990 three military vehicles appeared at Sabri's house at eight p.m. Settlers and soldiers fenced the house so completely, it was impossible to move in and out of the place. The fence was removed by Sabri's supporters.

6 On 9 July 1990 Sabri's son Samir was shot and killed. The attackers were never apprehended.

There exists a confused record of a military order to demolish Garib's house. The justification is that the house was built illegally. The order was rescinded after Garib's lawyers produced the building permit no. 5498/3 issued on 10 September 1978, only a month before his problems began.

Sabri Garib is adamant that he will not leave his land or sell any of it. The settlers continue to harass and attack him. The behaviour of the security forces in the area depends on the attitude of the officer in charge. The Israeli courts, which have failed to protect him in the past, are unlikely to do so in the future.

Chapter Eight
AS GOD IS MY WITNESS

The story of my friends of the Bedouin tribe of Al Rashaidah started with a visit to the encampment of these brave men. And although that was several months ago, and I am now back in London leading an ordinary, unencumbered life, the echo of that journey and what followed it remain with me, a living component of my psyche, a reminder of the horrors of life which shouldn't occur but do.

All the fifteen-kilometre trip to the unmarked spot south of Bethlehem and ten kilometres west of the Dead Sea needed was horses and I would have been like an innocent cowboy on his way to a place the existence of which is no more than a rumour. My informants had differed as to where the place was, how to get there, what I would see if I found it and whether I would be made welcome. But rumours are beguiling, particularly when they promise the unexpected.

I did find the place and its people, and I was welcomed and satisfied, if not in the personal sense then at least professionally, enough to justify writing this chapter. I travelled to the Al Rashaidah encampment with N.F. in a small car covered with several months' worth of corroding fine dust, windows that had been jammed open for much longer, a speedometer that didn't work and a seat belt locked into place, demanding that one go through the gymnastics of sliding under it to get in or out. N.F., a tall, dark, bespectacled agricultural engineer is part of a Palestinian self-aid group that assists people to stay on the land by teaching them new ways of realizing a better livelihood from it, an activity that flies in the face of Israeli attempts to grab more Arab land on the pretext that it isn't being used.

N.F.'s seemingly simple activity is so sensitive that I am forced to use his acronym, and not tell how I established contact with him nor mention the make of his car or any other clues that might identify him. I will settle for describing him as an articulate and well-informed companion full of infectious hope. His thorough briefing on what to expect made the trip bearable as we travelled over long stretches of bumpy, unpaved road that did the already battered car even more damage.

We came to a stop atop a grey hill, and when the dust settled I could see the desert mountains around us and notice the gradual change from one colour to another as well as the total absence of green vegetation or signs of human life. N.F.'s finger pointed out a tent two hundred yards away, and I could just make out that it was raised on stilts with a rough goat-hair top tied to spikes in the ground. 'There they are; they move the tent depending on the time of year and time of day,' said my knowledgeable companion.

Several figures appeared and rose as we came near. I was introduced to Ali Oudeh Al Rashaidah (Abu Khalid), the chief of the tribe, then the rest of them. We continued to exchange profuse greetings as we sat down cross-legged on mattresses, and N.F. told them that I was an Arab writer interested in 'their case' and that I had been recommended by mutual friends. He made it clear that it was best if I explained my purpose and left me to fend for myself after saying that he was going to inspect the sheep. He had told me that he was trying to educate this tribe in modern, more productive ways of raising sheep and rotating crops.

As I looked round the tent I took in how masculine and good-looking they all were. All had moustaches and three had beards. Their weather-beaten faces and attractive darkness under their white *kufiyas* enhanced their fine features, particularly their black eyes and chiselled chins. We sat in a circle in the shade made by the tent's top, and I moved around it with my eyes, exchanging greetings with each of them individually.

'*Ya halla, Istaz Saïd, ahlan wasahlan* [Welcome, Professor Saïd]. Move you over next to the esteemed Abu Khalid and rest comfortably.'

Pillows were passed from hand to hand and two thick ones were piled up for me to rest my elbows on while I leaned sideways in a gesture of relaxation. Abu Khalid himself repeated the greeting they had given me earlier and I answered him. Each reprise was accompanied with a friendlier smile. The man sitting on the mattress directly across from me was a wiry, animated member of the family by the name of Abu Muhammad.

'Make yourself comfortable, *Istaz* Saïd,' said Abu Muhammad, 'we're only comfortable when our guests are comfortable.'

'The company of good men has always given me comfort, brother Abu Muhammad.'

'May Allah bestow his greetings on you. Would you not be one of the honourable Aburish of Bethany?'

'I am indeed, if my mother was truthful [an accepted polite Bedouin expression].'

'*Ahlan wasahlan, ahlan wasahlan*, the Aburish are known to us, are they not, Abu Khalid?'

Abu Khalid nodded agreement. 'Yes indeed. I remember an Aburish who was with the United Nations, and there was the head of the Aburish, Abu Khalil, may Allah bless his soul, a legend among generous men he was.'

'Only generous men recognize a generous man, may Allah keep you, brother Abu Khalid.'

This exchange of tokens of mutual esteem continued as bitter Arabic coffee was served in handleless cups that were one third filled from an ornate brass Arab coffee pot. I drained my cup twice and then shook it between my thumb and index finger to denote that I didn't want any more.

There still was no way to broach the subject of my visit, or at least I didn't know a way. The Rashaidahs' inherent Arab politeness precluded directness, and I resigned myself to waiting for an opportune moment. We talked in generalities, about everything and nothing, and it all was subordinated to the niceties of the moment. Soon there was another round of Arabic coffee, followed by a round of mint tea, and slowly some of the comments and questions narrowed and began demanding specific responses.

'Do you know the Obediya [a tribe ten miles away], brother Saïd?'

'Yes, without belittling present company, they are men of honour. I know Sheikh Nufan of the Obediya.'

'Do you know the Sawahra [another tribe]?'

'I do not know any of the young people, but I remember Sheikh Hamad, who used to visit my grandfather, may Allah bless both their souls.'

As this exchange continued, I noticed many of my hosts toying with their watches, and attributed it to unease at the presence of an outsider, but I discovered that I was wrong. A few minutes before twelve, Abu Khalid hollered at one of the boys standing around the tent (they are not allowed to sit down with the elders) and ordered him to fetch a transistor radio. He announced to the rest, who behaved as if they had known his purpose all along, that it was time for the news from Radio Jordan. Silence prevailed while we heard the latest developments in the Gulf. As the newscaster worked himself into a state of excitement, everybody shook their heads. Then, out of nowhere, an Israeli warplane flew overhead and drowned the report. Little Abu Muhammad looked skywards angrily, 'May Allah make all their days noisy. We can't do the simplest thing without their interfering with it – not even listen to the news.'

The noise of the jet trailed into the distance, the newscast came to a close and I moved as fast as I could to capitalize on the opening given me by Abu Muhammad, to stop the conversation from focusing on the Gulf crisis.

'How right you are, Abu Muhammad, I almost forgot we're under their evil rule and they're everywhere. Your mountains are peaceful and your presence is so gentle, I forgot all about them, may *ibliss* [the Koranic Devil] take their souls.'

The cackle of voices rose at once, as if on cue, all saying that the Israelis interfered in everything. I pressed on, 'I hope they let you live the way you want to live.'

'You call this life; this is not life. Life is the freedom to roam all the mountains which belong to us, and that they do not allow us. As Allah is my witness, the Israelis wouldn't mind seeing a man sleep with his wife, they're so evil. They defy Him all the time, may He forgive me. We're a patient people and we keep hoping for a miracle, something to stop their interfering ways, but only Allah knows when it will happen. Allah is angry with the Arabs because they have not followed the righteous path and have wasted their money and quarrelled with each other, and that is why he has not seen fit to punish their enemies – so far. Allah doesn't champion those who don't champion their religion and their brothers, their co-religionists. And we have been infiltrated: I didn't believe it when I first heard it, but the King of Saudi Arabia, may Allah curse his soul, is a Jew in disguise and that is why he does the Arabs so much harm.'

I refrained from laughing until everybody else did, and they accompanied their laughter with accusations that Abu Muhammad always exaggerated. Abu Khalid, who had laughed heartily, began to say something then stopped; the whir of an Israeli helicopter cut through the air and his exalted position and good manners didn't countenance shouting. We waited, looking at each other, and I noticed the injured dignity of Abu Khalid and wondered whether he was remembering a time when only Allah interfered with the word of the Sheikh of Al Rashaidah.

When he finally spoke it was as if he was in pain. 'I think that *Istaz* Saïd knows more about the world than we do. What is going to happen to mankind, *Istaz* Saïd, where's all this madness leading to?'

May Allah help me, I said to myself, what am I going to tell this man without injecting unhappiness into this sad but splendid atmosphere and ruining the purpose of my trip?

'Abu Khalid, my brothers, the world and its fate are in the hands of Allah, the final arbiter of our fate. But Abu Muhammad is right: our people have lost their way, and they have wasted their wealth in pursuit of evil. This can not last forever; history is full of examples of how the Almighty makes people like that pay for their trespasses. He will extract His vengeance from them, of that I am sure.'

'Yes, they have defied Him and continue in their blind ways,' lamented Abu Khalid. 'They have allowed the Jews and Christians near our sacred places [Mecca and Medina in Saudi Arabia]. Shame on them, ten times shame on them. How is that possible?'

Again all voices rose to state that the condemned, the oil-rich sheiks and kings, worship money in place of Allah, and all present asked His forgiveness. I had missed an opportunity to steer the conversation towards their problem, and I was contemplating some way of retrieving the situation when nature came to my aid. It was about noon and several men had left the tent and were praying on the adjacent ground (a Muslim can pray anywhere, for the ground is automatically consecrated). I leaned towards Abu Khalid and whispered that I would like to relieve myself. He pointed to a stone wall about forty yards away and told me to go behind it. He regretted that there wasn't a single bathroom or outhouse in the whole community. I couldn't help but think of the solid-gold fixtures that adorn the bathrooms of King Fahd of Saudi Arabia and the Emir of Kuwait, and the bitter refrains of the Rashaidah assumed a disturbing poignancy.

From behind the wall I was able to look at the whole encampment, and noticed that the biggest single structure was a two-room house on the edge of a rock pile. When I returned to the tent the mattresses underneath it had been moved so that they remained in the shade, and my brief absence had obviously given my hosts a chance to consult with each other.

'Brother Saïd, your presence with us is a happy occasion. We welcome a stranger who loses his way, and we are certainly pleased when we have one of the generous Aburish with us. We have been told that you want to write about us, to tell the world our story. That pleases us, and when you write your book, we would like you to send us a copy so we might display it in a place of honour.'

'You are most kind, Abu Khalid, and that is no surprise coming from the head of Al Rashaidah. I will certainly send a copy of the book, which will carry my picture, and I am happy to think that my picture will be among you. As to your story, I will tell it the way you convey it to me, using your own words. This is why I am here, to hear what you have to say and not to depend on the words of outsiders who do not share your experiences and your feelings. I will record what you tell me.'

They laughed at the mention of my picture being among them, and made comments about what a fine figure of a man I was. Abu Khalid said that Abu Muhammad was the man best qualified to tell me their tale of woe and everybody agreed. Abu Muhammad paused dramatically while he clicked his prayer beads faster than he had done before.

'It is a sad story, *Istaz* Saïd, and it is a simple story of simple God-fearing people. Possession of the land is the origin of all feuds.'

He pointed to a limestone hill in the distance. 'Do you see that *jebel* [mountain]? We have feuded with your friends and ours the Obediya over its ownership for hundreds of years, and we have killed each other over it. But the Obediya belong to the land and their claim to the *jebel* is something we understand because they use the land the same way we do, to raise crops and feed their sheep. Now it's the Jews who want the very same *jebel*, and they are not from here, they have no claim, and they want to use the land differently. I don't know where the Jews come from, perhaps you do, and I don't truly care. All I know is that unlike us they take away the land when it isn't needed for their livelihood.'

Everybody invoked the name of Allah and said that Abu Muhammad's words were nothing but the truth. I waited for their exclamation of support to die down and asked Abu Muhammad how much of the land the Jews had expropriated.

Abu Muhammad gestured in the air dramatically. 'All of it, all of the land, may Allah bless you. They have taken most of the land and they want all of it. Let me tell you that in 1966 [a year before the Israelis occupied the West Bank] Al Rashaidah owned fifty-five thousand *donums* [thirteen thousand acres], and it was all ours to do with it what we wanted. At first, soon after they arrived, they confiscated five thousand *donums*, claiming it had no owner. We went to see their governor and told him that we were the owners; he wouldn't accept our word and asked for papers of ownership. We never had such papers. [The tribes in Palestine operated on the basis of *de facto* ownership, which was accepted by Turkey, Britain and Jordan, the previous occupiers.] We told the governor we had used the land for over two hundred years, but he wouldn't listen and he confirmed the confiscation order. But to appease us he told us that the rest of the land was ours, though we had no ownership papers. We believed him; we weren't happy with the decision, but we believed him. This was in 1968.

'Two years later, in 1970, they, the government, told us seven thousand more *donums* didn't belong to us. They violated their word to us. So we went to see the governor to remind him of his promise, but it was a new governor and this new man wasn't as open as the last one. He didn't talk to us – he made threats and told us that we had too much land.

'We became discouraged, and Abu Khalid and I decided that we couldn't deal with the Israelis on our own. We went to Jerusalem and met with Arab leaders and asked for help to keep our land, but they said they couldn't do anything to help us because the Israelis didn't listen to them.

'So the seven thousand *donums* were taken away; a total of twelve thousand *donums* were taken from us the first three years. This created a problem because we had thirty-four thousand head of sheep, and we needed grazing land for them. We were forced to go back to the governor and tell him of our need for grazing land and to tell him that seven wells were located in the confiscated land, and they were vital to maintain the level of our flock. It was like talking to a wall; he didn't care. He insisted that we still had enough land and water.

'After we lost so much land and so many wells things became difficult, and some of our people began to leave, to go to towns and to Jordan. We simply didn't have enough land to keep nine thousand people.'

Abu Khalid, who had been nodding agreement, decided that the last point merited emphasis and elaboration. 'Brother Saïd, we're all one family, we're all Al Rashaidah. Every person you see around this tent is Al Rashaidah and so were the people who left. We had been here for hundreds of years and for hundreds of years we had stayed together, one big family. For some of us to leave is a source of pain for the rest; it is losing members of one's family. The people who left are our own flesh and blood.'

The old bearded man sitting at an angle to me took the edge of his *kufiya* and applied it to his eyes. Silence enveloped us. There was nothing but the echo of the words of Abu Khalid and Abu Muhammad and the obvious pain of the old man, and I put my pad and pen down and bent my head in a moment of unrehearsed reverence. I suspected that they were dwelling on the memory of absent relations, but my own thoughts focused on the stunning similarity between what I was hearing and what the white man had done to the native Americans. After a while I felt comfortable enough to continue.

'Abu Khalid, who left and who made the decision that they were the ones to leave?'

'As in all cases affecting the tribe, the elders met, myself, Abu Muhammad, Abu Hassan and Abu Oudeh. We talked and talked until the moon set. We knew that four wells and the rest of the land wasn't enough for nine thousand people and their sheep, camels and beasts of burden. Abu Oudeh suggested that he should take his branch of the family and move to Jordan. We begged him not to do it, but he knew it had to be done – someone had to leave.

'After Abu Oudeh's decision we went to see the Israeli colonel in Bethlehem to ask for safe passage for Abu Oudeh so he might cross to Jordan. At first he wouldn't see us and kept us waiting for hours. Then when we told his assistants why we were there, the colonel saw us right away and gleefully told us that we were doing the right thing. He insisted that Abu Oudeh's group leave right away, in two days. We agreed; we had no choice.

'Two days later, two thousand of our people began their trek towards Jordan, following a route which took them around the southern end of the Dead Sea. It is a long journey that should take ten days, but their planes without wings [helicopters] kept chasing the sheep and other animals to frighten them and make them go faster. They made the trip in a week, but they lost over four hundred head of sheep, thirty camels and five people, may Allah bless their souls. They are in Jordan now, the group who moved away, but Abu Oudeh died soon after they arrived there; he died from *al gahr* [anger].'

It was now nearly two in the afternoon. A young man whispered in Abu Khalid's ear and the Sheikh rose and announced that lunch was ready. There was a hubbub as to whether we should eat under the tent or in the one-room stone house nearby and a decision was made in favour of the latter. As I walked to the house with Abu Khalid, I apologized for being a bother, but he scolded me for thinking that way and jokingly accused me of being a 'barehead' (a reference to the city people who do not wear an Arab head-dress, and are supposedly effete). He added, 'Brother Saïd, even if there was nothing left of Al Rashaidah, except widows, you'd still be welcome here and you'd still have lunch with us.'

It was a simple square room and the plaster had come off the walls in several places. On one wall there was a framed *sura* of the Koran, a picture of the Dome of the Rock in Jerusalem (Islam's third holiest shrine) and a PLO poster. A study of an Arabian horse adorned the opposite wall, and on the third wall there was a picture of a girl guide and more framed Koranic verses. Mattresses were laid squarely against the walls, and N.F. joined us. We sat around the room cross-legged as a bevy of men and boys spread a plastic sheet over the space in the middle.

The food was brought in on three big aluminium trays: mounds of rice topped with chunks of lamb, and bowls of *laban kishk* (liquefied yoghurt sauce) to pour over the rice and meat. I refused the offer of a spoon, rolled up my shirtsleeves and set to work. And although I couldn't match my hosts' dexterity in mixing all the ingredients together in one ball and popping it in my mouth, I managed well and the food was delicious.

Protocol precluded continuing the history of the tribe that Abu Muhammad and Abu Khalid had been relating to me. Abu Khalid moved from one circle to another, breaking up chunks of meat and placing them in front of people, especially guests like N.F. and me. 'In the name of Allah,' he said, 'I don't want to hear that a guest of Al Rashaidah has gone home hungry. This is fresh meat from our own sheep [*halalnah*], and it isn't city meat, which is kept in storage for days and smells. We butcher every day.'

When the meal was over we lined up outside the room to wash our hands. A smiling boy gave us a bar of soap and poured water from a jug and when we had finished another boy gave us a towel. N.F. told me that we would have to leave in an hour. He had been supervising the spraying of sheep with pesticide to guard them against tics and other vermin. I returned with N.F. to re-form the group that had met earlier under the tent.

N.F. spoke to them in their Bedouin dialect but with respectful familiarity. 'Listen to me, all of you. I can't keep coming back to see you for the sake of small jobs, though your company is as charming as ever. You must listen to what I say or I will never come back. You must spray all your sheep at once, in one day. If you don't and only spray a few hundred then it is a waste of effort because the clean ones have to graze with the infected ones and they'll get infected all over again. The Jews say we don't know what we're doing and we must prove them wrong, and the only way to prove them wrong is to do things right. Unless we adopt new ways to protect our sheep then we are indeed dirty and backward and this supports the Israeli efforts to take our land and our stock from us.

'My organization is willing to help, trying to help, but you must cooperate and listen to us. Without your cooperation, our efforts will fail.'

They commended N.F.'s work as more Arabic coffee made the rounds. They all praised him as a valued brother, one of them, but as usual it was left to Abu Muhammad to deal with the weighty problem.

'N---, we thank you. May Allah bless you [*Barrak Allah feik*]. But what are we to do about the big problem? We talked about it before. We need feed and we need it badly. Whatever land we have left isn't big enough for grazing. The merchants who sell us feed charge us up to eighty per cent interest and now Jewish merchants are coming to see us to increase our indebtedness and when we can't pay them back they offer to buy our flock. As God is my witness, a Jewish merchant came the other day, and he knew how badly in need we are and he offered to buy my flock of a hundred and forty head of sheep at one and a half times the going price. But he also told me that if I sold to him then I must give him an undertaking not to raise any more sheep and that I should go and live somewhere else. It is a problem; we don't have cash to pay for feed. We need loans to help us get by, and we are men of honour and we would pay the loans back. We can't bear eighty per cent interest. Brother N---, there is no time, we are being pressured into doing the unthinkable, to sell what we own to the Jews, who want us to leave this land. Brother N---, please, what are you going to do to help us?'

N.F. spoke of the various institutions and charitable organizations he had contacted and detailed the results of his efforts. He was hopeful that some positive answers were on the way. The debate on the pressures on them to forsake their source of livelihood and leave the land continued until four p.m., frank, animated and full of praise of the Almighty.

When it was time to leave I announced that I would return to listen to the rest of their story. As I said my goodbyes, Abu

Khalid held on to my hand and embraced me, and I embraced him with the fulness of affection of someone leaving a loved one. Abu Muhammad followed suit and whispered, 'Help us, if you can.'

N.F.'s little car was unbearably hot, and my clothes stuck to my body and enough dust came through the windows for parts of my sweat-soaked shirt to cake. Two miles along the road to Bethlehem, I noticed something I had missed on the way out. There was a mosque in the middle of a fenced piece of land in the middle of nowhere. The walls of the mosque were covered with pro-PLO nationalist slogans and drawings of the Palestinian flag. N.F. told me that the mosque was all that was left of the original encampment of Al Rashaidah. Everything else had been razed in 1981, but the Israelis had stopped short of demolishing the mosque.

'Where exactly was the rest of their place? Do we have time to have a look?'

N.F. turned the car round and we drove over a hill for a few hundred yards. It was all in front of us for the naked eye to see: the rubble of a whole village that had been dynamited.

'My God,' I said, 'it looks as if this place was much more substantial than what they have now. All I saw today were six tiny houses and ten tents.'

'Oh yes, they weren't exactly prosperous, but they managed well when they had the land. They had better houses and more water. Of course this land is no longer theirs, it was expropriated, and it is much better than what they have now – unfortunately, it's strategic. It belongs to Kirbat Mayna now, a new Israeli settlement.'

'The poor people! When are you going to take me back to them?'

'Sometime next week.'

The following week trouble flared up in Jerusalem and there were restrictions on travel to Bethlehem and beyond it, to the Al Rashaidah area. The following week things got worse and the whole district where Al Rashaidah are was placed under curfew. Time was running out for my second visit, and I told N.F. and other friends acquainted with the situation to contact me immediately there was a chance of making the trip. I promised to go there on short notice. It was four weeks after my visit to Al Rashaidah that a friend contacted me to tell me that Abu Khalid and Abu Muhammad were in Bethlehem. I told him to keep them there and took a taxi to meet them in Nativity Square.

They were waiting for me, wrapped in *abbas* (camel-hair cloaks) and wearing friendly smiles. We embraced and sat down to have coffee, which we all agreed didn't compare with the bitter delicious variety they served.

'*Barrak Allah feik*, did you rush over here just to see us?'

'Yes, I would go a longer distance to visit honoured friends, and I would have telephoned you, but there are no phones your way.'

'Thanks be to you,' said Abu Muhammad, 'not many people think meeting with Al Rashaidah is worth so much effort.'

'Well, other people follow foolish ways. I am very pleased to see you. I am only sorry that I am leaving in two days and will not have another chance to visit you at home. But perhaps another time, I hope.'

We exchanged pleasantries for over ten minutes after which I decided that there was no time to lose before the night curfew began. 'Abu Muhammad, I need to know the rest of your story, so please can we continue where we left off?'

He had rehearsed what to say, or so it seemed. 'To continue where I was . . . land seizure never stopped, the last time they took away some of our land was a mere two years ago. More and more of our people have had to leave, with each confiscation. We are down to seven thousand *donums* out of the original fifty-five thousand, and we're only one thousand people instead of around ten thousand. The rest of our people have gone to Jordan, Jericho and other places.

'They've moved us, our encampment, three times. It isn't good where we are now, it's in the face of the wind, but that's the only place they'd permit us to settle. The second place to which they moved us is only a mile away from where we are now, but they took that to build one of their settlements, Kirbat Mayna. This settlement has electricity, running water and telephones, but they refuse to supply us with any of this – they tell us we don't need them.

'We're trying to hold on to the sheep; we still have fourteen thousand head, instead of what we used to have. We don't have camels any more. We don't have enough water. We won't be able to hold out for long.

'We can't graze our sheep in the fallow mountains around us because they have declared them protected preserves. The mountains are full of wolves now, and they wander into our land and eat our sheep, but we're afraid to touch them lest the Israelis use this as an excuse to push us out of what we have left.'

Abu Khalid stopped him. 'You should tell Brother Saïd about

when they killed our sheep and camels. We don't even know what caused it, perhaps some of our sheep had strayed into the forbidden area, but they came in in jeeps and had a shoot-out. They killed three hundred and twenty head of sheep and twenty-one camels.

'We stood there and watched helplessly. There was nothing to do, nothing.'

'Did you report this to the authorities?'

He laughed. 'We report everything, but in that case it was soldiers and they claimed the whole thing was justified because we conspired with the PLO. They concluded by telling us that we should sell our land and move away, that it was the best solution.

'They don't punish their own people, Brother Saïd. Things are bad; we don't even have a school to which to send our children and the nearest one is eight kilometres away and the kids can't walk sixteen kilometres a day. The level of our education is getting worse; now we have only two high-school graduates.

'They keep imposing fines on us, and we just can't pay. We can't afford it, and they know that. We have appealed for help from everybody and some, like Brother N---, do, but it isn't enough. In the name of justice, decency and humanity, tell the world to help us, please, my brother, someone must help us.

'Now they have built a new settlement, Maale Amis, on our old land, and the number of people there is increasing so they'll need more land and you know what that means. It isn't fair, no it isn't fair.'

It was another hurried and sad goodbye. Back in Jerusalem I confirmed that only a Quaker group and a Lutheran group were trying to help Al Rashaidah by providing them with seed and paying for pesticides. When I repeated the Al Rashaidah story to people, they just shook their heads and told me that the Al Ta'amra, Shohoud and Arajah tribes were suffering the same fate and facing a bleak future. The confrontation between the Bedouins and the Israelis is an uneven one, to say the least. Someone somewhere must speak out on behalf of these noble men.

Chapter Nine
PROFILES IN COURAGE – MAKRAM SA'AD

It is difficult to describe Makram Sa'ad. To say that he is a thirty-year-old Bethlehem pharmacist with a moustache, a receding hairline and an air of folksiness in the way he walks and talks describes the outward appearance of this unassuming man. However, still waters run deep is a more accurate description of this leading member of a small group who have come to symbolize Palestinian resistance to Israel's policy of abusive taxation without representation. Makram Sa'ad and three fellow Bethlehem pharmacists have refused to pay tax for over two years. They claim that Israeli tax collection is illegal under international law and that all the money goes towards maintaining the Israeli military presence in the West Bank.

It was nine-thirty on the morning of 16 October 1990 and Makram and I were in his pharmacy, Al Razen, waiting to hear from his lawyer whether his sentencing at the Ramallah Military Court, twenty-five miles away, would take place as scheduled. This was the fourth time a date for the sentencing had been given, and although the authorities had refused to reconfirm the date and the chances of a cancellation were high, Makram was still quite concerned lest the existing special conditions be used against him. Because of recent disturbances, cars from Bethlehem were not allowed to enter Jerusalem and, if summonsed, he would have to drive through Jerusalem to get to Ramallah. He wouldn't want to be sentenced *in absentia* because it could work against him; he would at the very least be fined for not obeying a court order to appear or miss out on an offer of a bargain between his lawyer and the court, regardless of the authorities' failure to respond to his enquiries about the date.

'But Makram, why don't you go and wait in Ramallah just in case?'

'If I did that every time they schedule a hearing or a sentencing date and cancel it, I would go out of business, and that's what they want.'

To pass the time Makram told me how offended he was by what the constant delays were doing to outsiders interested enough in his case to want to attend the sentencing. They included a Swedish human rights group, the liberal Israeli human rights activists B'tselem, representatives of Al Haq, the associates of the Committee of International Jurists and the Greek, Belgian and Italian consuls in Jerusalem. Talking about his obvious celebrity status embarrassed him and he changed the subject and gave me a book entitled *Taxation in The West Bank, 1967–1989*, an Al Haq publication. We chatted amiably, but the telephone call from lawyer Osameh Audeh never came and we rightly assumed that the sentencing was postponed. This destructive waiting game was something to which Makram had become accustomed, and the only reaction he gave to the prospect of its continuing was to shake his head.

I first met Makram Sa'ad on 24 August 1990 through the good offices of a mutual friend. He was waiting for me in his pharmacy at eight a.m. and apologized for the early hour, but said it was a good time to talk without disruption. Al Razen pharmacy was a small, impeccably clean place in Mahd (Nativity) Street, the approach road to Bethlehem from Jerusalem. A sense of order in the shop was very apparent and the products were well displayed. Hair gels, powdered milk, antibiotics and throat lozenges, obviously the fast-moving items, were much in evidence. Makram's younger brother, who was not a graduate pharmacist, was there assisting him, and people came in to buy over-the-counter products, have prescriptions filled or drink a cup of coffee. It was an extremely pleasant atmosphere, made more so by Makram's hospitable manner and the obvious esteem he enjoyed among his visitors.

As it was difficult to conduct a conversation without interruption, the pharmacist drove me to a small experimental farm belonging to a friend of his, where we were alone. On the way he stopped several times to offer people lifts and in each case he delivered them to their exact destination. At the farm we settled in a bedroom for the workers and the interview finally began.

I asked Makram to tell me briefly the history of the tax resisters, particularly the group with which he was identified.

'The idea began a long time ago, well before the *intifada*. The United National Leadership didn't want people to pay taxes. But it was a difficult decision which they didn't try to enforce for fear of reprisals against non-payers by the Israeli authorities. They weren't sure our people were ready for reprisals and in many ways they were right.

'Whenever somebody refused to pay taxes, massive pressure by the authorities was directed at them. Among other things, the police would never renew their identity cards, and if you don't have an identity card then you're violating security laws and you can be detained. Or they wouldn't renew drivers' licences and that too can lead to imprisonment. I don't have a licence now because they wouldn't give me a new one. I drive without it; I take my chances.

'The principle behind non-payment of taxes is simple. The UNL's position was that people shouldn't pay taxes because international law considers the imposition of new taxes on the people of an occupied territory illegal [VAT is a totally new tax imposed by the Israelis], and it is highly questionable whether an occupying power can raise the level of taxation. But these two points are too complicated for our people to understand. Instead, UNL wisely based their appeal to people to stop paying taxes on what is happening to the tax money. We pay income tax, excise tax, property tax, municipal and other taxes, and we get nothing back. The Israelis spend no money on public works or health services and extremely little on education and other services. Showing that we weren't getting any of the money back was a better way of explaining the problem, and this was coupled with figures showing that the Israelis use our tax money to support their hated military presence; they use it to finance their continued occupation.

'Beit Sahur [a town to the south of Bethlehem] crystallized the issue. Beit Sahur was the place where the big confrontation over taxation, non-payment that is, took place. You must remember that the Israelis fear non-payment of taxes more than anything else, and Beit Sahur was the test ground.'

'You come from Beit Sahur, don't you, Makram?'

'Yes.'

'Tell me what happened in Beit Sahur, please.'

He apologized for not being in a place where he could offer coffee or tea. 'Well, Beit Sahur was the place where people began refusing to pay taxes; it was the place where this activity took on the semblance of a mass movement. It started with a few people in the community and spread like wildfire and before long no one in the place would pay taxes. So Beit Sahur became a whole town of over ten thousand people in open rebellion against Israeli rule, or what sustains it. What made it worse for the Israelis was the ethnic composition of the town. It is a mixed community of Catholics, Greek Orthodox and Muslims. It sent out a message that all religious and ethnic groups were opposed to Israeli taxation policies.

'At first, the Israelis used one of the old methods they had used against non-payers in the past. They took away their household belongings: fridges, gas ranges and furniture, supposedly the equivalent of the tax overdue. But this policy really backfired. After it was imposed, nobody would pay a penny, not even the people who hadn't joined the movement before. What were the Israelis to do? The government's storage facilities near Sarafand [near Ramallah] were full of household goods. People learned the art of conversation in Beit Sahur, after the Israelis took away all their radios and television sets.

'Each time the Israelis intensified their pressure, the Beit Sahuris responded with a gesture of defiance. The Israelis stopped people from going to school, the army occupied the local schools for three months, so the people responded by turning in their identity cards – thousands of them did that. An amazing community spirit surfaced.

'The army became desperate. They were determined to break the solidarity of the people, and all the traditional measures failed to do it. So, they imposed a state of siege. It lasted forty-two days. One couldn't get in or out of Beit Sahur, and the only time one could move around inside the town was during the day, and even then everybody was subjected to harassment and abuse. This was the most they could do, but we still held the line, nobody gave in.'

'Were you a leader of this movement?'

'There were no leaders; everybody participated. If anyone, the religious leaders were the leaders. The Muslim, Catholic and Orthodox leaders would link arms and march in defiance, and on occasion they prayed together in the main square of the town. We were all Palestinians and there were no leaders; we suffered alike and protested alike.

'Look at it this way: Sheki Aires, head of the so-called Civil Administration of the West Bank – they're really military – he announced that his administration had a surplus of one hundred million Israeli shekels, and everybody knew this was our tax money. Allah knows, the Israelis are stupid. He made this announcement when we were questioning them about what they were doing with our tax money. When the Beit Sahur siege took place, the Israelis had occupied the West Bank for twenty-two years, and they still had no budget for the occupied area, nothing allocated to schools and hospitals and the like.

'And they want us to pay tax. Never. We in Beit Sahur still don't pay. They lifted the siege for one reason only: the international community eventually raised a fuss about their actions, that's why.'

'Were there any individual acts of abuse during the siege, any acts of violence against civilians?'

'All types. Too many beatings to count . . . but fewer than usual because our people were determined not to provoke them. Let me think . . . A bunch of soldiers dropped a stone slab on the head of Edmond Ghannim. The investigation revealed that the soldiers had a bet whether they could hit him or not. Attalh Misleh had a fatal heart attack after soldiers broke into his house and abused his family. Poor Ayad Abu Saadeh, he got a seventeen-year jail sentence. He had a few standing charges against him, but participating in the Beit Sahur boycott sealed his fate.'

'Did the Israelis allow food in?'

'That was the only thing they allowed in – barely enough.'

'Now that they have failed to break the spirit of the people of Beit Sahur, what are they trying to do as an encore?'

'All sorts of things. Even foreign diplomats are not allowed to visit Beit Sahur most of the time. They're afraid; the Israelis are afraid because Beit Sahur got a lot of publicity.'

'Tell me more specifically about what they're doing now.'

'A lot, a lot. They're trying to drive us out, to get us to leave. Hizb Muleidit [a small extreme-right-wing Israeli party] are trying to push us out. Moshe Mrai of that party offers to facilitate the immigration of the Beit Sahur people to the USA, Australia and Canada. He tells them it would solve their tax problem. Then there is the official policy. An Arab is required to pay two shekels in taxes for every cubic metre of water he uses, but an Israeli pays only ninety agora, less than half [a shekel is one hundred agoras]. They have enacted a decree limiting the boundaries of the town, making it impossible for us to expand, to stifle us. We've had a drought and they cut off our water supplies first, in spite of the fact that the water originates in Wadi Al Ghoneim, in Arab territory. They impose curfews frequently, so Beit Sahuris can't go to their places of work in other towns.'

'Are they succeeding? Is this policy meeting with greater success than the siege?'

'Succeeding – no. They can't succeed. But some people are leaving. They've made life hell and some people are leaving. There is no work and some farm land is getting confiscated. We're a marked community. Don't believe that they will leave us alone, not a chance. All they've done is change tactics. They can't do anything that would focus international attention on the place all over again – the outcry was too much even for them. Now they're working like a grinder, slowly.'

We took a short break before continuing. 'I think we've said enough about Beit Sahur. What about you? Where do you fit in?'

He smiled modestly. 'I'd rather your story be about us as a group than about me. There isn't much to my story. I am married to a local girl and I have two children, a boy and a girl.'

'I know you aren't looking for personal glory. But do tell me more about yourself and all that happened to you.'

'I am a local boy, from a big family. My family was poor; we never had much. But I did well in school here and got a scholarship to the University of Malta, where I studied pharmacology. I worked my way through college.'

I interrupted. 'I see this part is difficult for you. Let me rephrase my question. When did your personal troubles with the tax people begin and how?'

'In July '88. I paid all my taxes for '87 and then the Israelis went stupid. They assessed us for all of '88 and wanted all the tax paid in advance. We were deciding whether to pay taxes or not, and the Israelis show up and demand a year's worth of taxes in advance. So they forced us to make a decision.

'They showed up in July '88 and said taxes – now. When I told them the taxes they were asking for weren't due until the end of the year, they referred me to the military. I answered the summons of the military officer, Captain Oudi, and he kept me waiting from eight a.m. until eight p.m., then he talked to me. He was so arrogant and he was trying to humiliate me. By the time he saw me in the evening my final decision had already been made: no payment of taxes. He didn't talk to me; he threatened me. He told me that failure to pay all of the assessment for 1988 tax right away made me liable for arrest. Let me ask you, where in the world do people pay VAT in advance, and that's what the jerk was demanding – stupid, no?

'On 15 September 1988 the military paid a visit to the pharmacy and took me to Oudi for a two-hour interrogation. All Oudi did was to repeat his threats. I said I couldn't and wouldn't pay the tax.

'The day after, they closed all of Mahd Street, leading to my pharmacy. It was a small military operation. And what for? They came into the pharmacy and took all the cosmetic products and took me back with them for a repeat interrogation which got nowhere. So they interrogated me every day for a whole week, and all they did was repeat their unreasonable demands.

'When they got nowhere, they decided to confiscate my car, but they were temporarily stopped by the fact that it was registered in my wife's name, in Nadira's name. They, under a certain Captain Yousi this time, eventually decided to take the car from Nadira. When they appeared to collect it, she refused to tell them where it was or give them the keys because they had no written order of confiscation. As a matter of fact that day she managed to give the keys to a friend who drove the car away. As you can imagine, they finally succeeded and they did take away Nadira's car, a Peugeot 104, an '82 model.

'Is a car like that worth a lot here?'

'Not really – five thousand dollars. But they never stop; they wanted to get back at Nadira because she gave them a hard time. They issued a summons for her to appear in front of the military, along with her father. They interrogated them endlessly and stupidly about my business. They knew nothing; they aren't involved in my business. Nadira is a housewife.'

Makram looked at his watch and told me that he had to go back to his pharmacy, a reasonable request in view of the four hours we had spent together. On the way back he told me that he was the pharmacist on duty since it was a strike day and the other pharmacies were closed. He also told me that in a place like Bethlehem, a pharmacist's duties went beyond the ordinary; he very often prescribed things on the spot to avoid extra expense for those who could be helped without going to see a doctor. We made a date to meet again a week later.

My second meeting with Makram took place in his pharmacy on 23 September. We agreed that there was no way for him to get away for long and that we had to suffer the constant interruptions of customers, but we wanted to continue the interview. In addition I had an interest in seeing him perform his duties.

Most of the people who came into the pharmacy were regular customers known to Makram. Very many of them were looking for remedies for stress-related diseases, self-testing kits for measuring the level of diabetes, analgesics, rash ointments and pills to relieve cramps. Makram confirmed to me that stress-related diseases were prevalent in the community. He advised customers in a language they understood, and I noticed that he occasionally charged different prices for the same medication and for the leading brand of powdered milk. When I asked him he admitted that he charges poorer people less than others.

'Is this across the board, is this a policy that covers everything you dispense here?'

'Yes, yes. Some people just can't afford to pay the full price. Sometimes we don't realize a profit and other times our margins are very low for a pharmacy, down to ten per cent. One must do one's duty. People are in very bad financial shape – what can one do?'

'Let's go back to where we were the last time. What eventually happened to Nadira?'

'Nothing really. They just kept pestering her – that's what they do to people they don't like. Dogs.'

'How about you? Where did things go from there, after they took Nadira's car?'

'For nine months they visited me almost daily. One time they took me with them – put me in jail for four days, ninety-six hours. They demanded an on-the-spot payment of fifteen thousand shekels [US$7500] on account. When I refused, they put me in a cell. An officer came to see me in the cell. He asked for five hundred shekels to close the whole file. Naturally, I refused. I am sure he was pretending to want a bribe, the amount was so small. If I were caught bribing an officer then it would be a hefty jail sentence. Isn't it shameful to behave this way? They released me after issuing a threat that they would revoke my licence as a pharmacist.'

'When they arrest you they search you. Did they ever take away money you were carrying or anything else?'

'Yes, the driver's licence, but not money, because I don't carry any, or no more than a few shekels at a time.' Makram laughed at this.

'But this whole affair sounds odd. If the tax they wanted was the result of a legal demand to pay taxes, then surely they could have done something more than this unmethodical harassment?'

'We have no idea whether the money they demanded in taxes represented a legal demand. Perhaps they just didn't like me, or like my ways. Who knows? What followed was more sinister.'

I waited for five minutes while Makram served two customers.

'You were saying something really bad followed. What was it?'

'Oh yes. On 26 November 1988 they decided I owed them back taxes for the years 1984 to 1987. They said that what I had paid wasn't correct, and that the new figures were based on a re-examination of the accounts and my testimony during the various interrogations.

'I had receipts and letters showing the three years were fully paid, vacated as they say, and I tried to prove that the amounts I had paid were correct, but they wouldn't budge. I told them I wouldn't pay – finally – and they didn't like it.

'On 29 November 1988 a military group in a jeep picked me up. I was taken to the military jail in Ramallah and they handed me a summary judgement [the court is in the same building as the prison] of five thousand shekels for not cooperating with the military authorities. I requested to see a lawyer, but they turned down my request, so I refused to pay. They sentenced me to a ten-day term instead.

'On the last day they got me out for another hearing, but this time I was allowed a lawyer. I was released on bail of five thousand shekels put up by the lawyer. Do you want to hear more?'

'Yes, everything. Was anybody helping you during this period, a political group or the like? Did you solicit such help?'

'No, no. This is an individual case, not a political one. But because three other Bethlehem pharmacists were suffering the same thing, we became a *de facto* group, the pharmacists' group who wouldn't pay taxes. The charges against us were the same and so was the pattern of harassment, only the figures of the money demanded was different. So we retained the same lawyer and combined our defence efforts.'

'Tell me about the others. They were all local, weren't they?'

'Yes, we're all from here. Elias Rashmawi and his brother Hanna Rashmawi and Elana Al Hatlawi.'

'Elana, a woman? She didn't go through what you went through, did she?'

'Yes, I don't know how many times she was imprisoned, but she was put in jail. It was because she was a female and because we banded together that our case became famous.'

There was another wait, of ten minutes this time.

'Let's see, by now things had changed. This was no longer a case of prepayment, but a simple case of refusal to pay, non-payment?'

'Yes, yes. We were challenging their right to levy tax. The '88 [taxes] were owing by now but we still wouldn't pay them.'

'Right, what followed?'

'On 13 February 1989 the military came in two jeeps and a small truck and they took away the contents of my pharmacy. Everything. All I had left was empty shelves; look at these pictures. This was the real test; they obviously wanted me to close down. I borrowed fifty-four thousand dollars from my brother-in-law and reopened in no time at all. My lawyer took the matter of confiscation of the contents of the pharmacy to the High Court. The court issued a restraining order against the removal of more goods until a final decision on the whole case was made. The same order forbade the military from selling the goods.

'The military didn't like the two aspects of the order. By the way, the others suffered the same fate and got the same order. So back to harassment tactics. We were ordered to report to military headquarters every day until June '89. They would keep us there from eight a.m. until two p.m. Every day. People needed medicine. What criminals! But even this didn't work.

'So what do they do – they resort to confiscation again. On 11 July 1989 they again took everything from my pharmacy and the pharmacies of the others.'

'Wait a minute, please. Had anything happened to change the standing order of the High Court?'

'No, they did it in spite of the order. They took away everything. You can imagine what the lawyer said when we finally got a hearing date in court. He sarcastically told them that their military was out of control. We won. We won and got damages – but it doesn't work that simply. We were trying to assess the damages and couldn't agree. Whatever goods we got back from the military hadn't been stored properly and were damaged, defective . . . what a High Court!

'On 16 October 1989 the military took me to the tax office for interrogation. There they beat me up. Two guys beat me up.'

'How badly?'

'They didn't break anything. They were the types who were trained – this was planned.'

'Sorry to insist, but how bad was it?'

'They kept punching me in places that don't bruise. I didn't feel pain, I really didn't. My mind was elsewhere. They kept saying don't move and don't breathe, and kept punching me. But I didn't care anymore. I just didn't care. At one point I was far away and all I could hear was the sentence, "If you move you'll suffer more".'

'They didn't torture Elana, did they?'

'If you mean beat her up, then no. But they did everything else. They thought a girl was the weak link in the group, but they were wrong. They didn't know Elana.'

'Let's stay on her for a minute. What about sexual abuse – any of that?'

'I don't think so, but I would rather not discuss that anyway.'

'OK. Was that the last time they arrested you?'

He leaned back and laughed heartily. 'I promise you they didn't know what they were doing, not a bit. They arrested me one more time and they put me in the women's prison by mistake. I think it was a mistake. I found myself with a bunch of female drug addicts. They kept me for two days.'

The day was coming to an end; it was three-thirty in the afternoon and our intermittent interview had lasted over five hours while people had come and gone. Some visitors had sat down and talked to Makram about community happenings, and others had come in to report the latest Israeli atrocity. As I was flipping through my notebook inspecting my notes, a tall, well-dressed woman carrying two books walked in and kissed Makram on the cheek.

'What a pleasant surprise. Elana, this is Saïd Aburish. He's writing about our case.'

We shook hands and she sat down on a chair opposite me and her startling good looks and engaging smile contradicted the image of her I had created in my mind. She looked like a pretty tea-party lady.

'How is it going?' I asked, fully aware of the question's broad implications.

'As well as expected. When you don't expect anything from them, you're ahead.'

'Makram told me everything. Any regrets that it has gone on for so long and has been painful and complicated?'

'Regrets over doing my duty. Never.'

'So you're still ready to face the consequences?'

'Of course.' And there was the enchanting smile. She continued, 'We'll win, you know. Perhaps not in court, but we're going to win. Now the dentists are refusing to pay their taxes, and several doctors. Dr Jamal got a three-and-a-half-year jail sentence. They sentenced him fast, before the whole thing got publicity. And two dental technicians have also been jailed.'

I pointed to the books she was carrying. 'What are you reading?'

'I'm studying French at the university. Why not? If anything happens then I can continue my studies in prison.'

Elana rushed off to her French class. She showed more agitation about being late for her French than she did over her tax case.

The four Bethlehem resisters were all Christian and better educated than the average Palestinian. It is true that Palestinian Christians possess a greater sense of community than the rest of the population, but others are emulating them, and the resistance to Israeli rule has graduated from simple acts of stone throwing to more sophisticated levels of civil disobedience. This new approach is contagious and carries with it a more serious threat to Israel's ability to hold on to the occupied territories in the face of the selflessness of the resisters.

On 16 October my last question to Makram Sa'ad was whether he was sure that he wanted me to publish his story. His answer was, 'What are they going to do to me? There comes a moment when they can't frighten people anymore. I have reached that point. There is nothing they could do to me, nothing. I am not the type who carries a gun. There are many ways of fighting, and I am fighting for my country my own way. Please publish the story.'

Part Three
People on the Other Side

Chapter Ten
PROFILES IN COURAGE – LEA TZEMEL

Everybody in the West Bank knows her name. In an atmosphere of conflict where the suffering ordinary people attach pejoratives to the names of the famous to express their frustration and lack of faith, the mention of Lea Tzemel's name is accompanied by words of admiration and respect. She is a Jewish Israeli lawyer who specializes in defending Arabs accused of resistance crimes.

At first I didn't want to meet her. It wasn't only that her story or parts of it had been told by many an admiring journalist, but also because I had assigned myself the difficult task of looking beyond the easily available and obvious in favour of unearthing those fundamental issues in the West Bank that are beyond the reach of others. My pompous attitude was eventually eroded by the realization that no true picture of what is happening there is complete without Lea Tzemel. I also nursed a secret belief that my conversations with her would be more revealing than those granted to others.

I walked into her office without appointment, deliberately, at ten a.m. I had been told that it was her busiest hour, and I wanted to witness the atmosphere that made the place a Mecca for the masses in need of solace and legal help who trekked there from all over the West Bank and Gaza. It took a mere five minutes to discover that my informant had understated the situation; her office was a place apart, a small, self-contained world of hope.

Lea Tzemel's Law Office, as the sign on the door announced, was a two-room affair on the fourth floor of a modern stone building on the edge of Salaheddine Street and the Sheikh Jarrah district of Jerusalem. The building had no lift. After the exhausting climb, I walked into a small room full of women wearing *thoubs*. They sat on two worn settees around a small Formica-topped table covered with old magazines. Instead of a reception desk, there was a counter that ran the full length of the room, facing the door. It was staffed by two attractive young ladies (Najat Rabi and Fatin Sandoukah, I was told later) who spoke Arabic and Hebrew interchangeably but without affectation. The three office telephones were either in use or ringing, and I used the receptionists' preoccupation with answering calls and talking to visitors to watch the waiting women and examine the posters on the walls.

The seven women waiting, all around the age of forty, came from different parts of the West Bank and Gaza. The embroidery on their dresses and their dialects revealed that. They spent their time exchanging information about their cases and wishing each other well. In the circumstances, the exclusive female presence was another confirmation that the men of the older generation, the women's husbands and relatives, have been discredited and relegated to secondary roles and that the *intifada* is the work of children who benefit from the backing of a substantial women's auxiliary.

The posters, fourteen in all, gave an idea of the kind of cases Lea Tzemel handled. There was the famous poster of a woman sitting on the ruins of her demolished house with her hands raised pleadingly towards heaven, another in English, French and Italian demanded freedom for the Palestinians, a third was full of pictures of people deported to Jordan by Israel, a fourth appealed to the Israeli military authorities to reopen the Arab universities of the West Bank and the rest dealt with cases of torture, prison conditions and the pleas of international groups for a just peace, and there were several on behalf of Israeli human rights organizations.

Eventually one of the receptionists was free long enough to look at me in a way that enquired about my purpose. I introduced myself and told her that I wanted to see Mrs Tzemel for an interview. I was asked to wait five minutes because she had someone with her and two telephone calls waiting.

The door to the second room was open, and I could hear the distinctive, scratchy voice of a woman speaking in Arabic, Hebrew, English and exclaiming in French. It was apparent that she was talking on the phone and interviewing at the same time, and both conversations revealed the sort of woman who is determined to make the most of her day. Meanwhile, the receptionists were talking to waiting ladies, passing folders to and receiving them from the inside office, answering complicated telephone enquiries themselves and shouting for Lea and her assistant Samir to pick up one phone or the other.

Among the questions I heard the receptionists answer without referring to Lea was one about the possible release of all detainees under the age of seventeen. Another sought confirmation of a court date, several asked whether Lea had the time to handle another case and there was the oft-repeated, all-inclusive 'Any news?'.

The receptionists' ability to cope, the pace at which they had to work was utterly remarkable, particularly so when one considered that their dedication was accompanied by an extraordinary politeness and patience in situations that militated against both. After twenty minutes of watching and listening, one of the receptionists led me into the second, even smaller office. There were more posters, two cheap petty bureaucrats' desks with Lea Tzemel and Samir Abu Shakra behind them and three chairs for visitors.

I had seen Lea Tzemel before, the day the sentencing of my cousins Amer and Nasser was last postponed. This time I stood in front of her desk, introduced myself and asked if it would be possible to spend two days with her, watching her perform her duties. Lea Tzemel shook my hand without standing up and told me that she didn't have much time to talk to me. Eventually, after I insisted that nothing less than being with her for that length of time would do, we agreed on a date two weeks thence. I thanked her and left after a short talk with Samir.

My brief encounter with Lea Tzemel left me with two impressions: her incredibly blue eyes that promised a sharper vision than possessed by normal mortals and the unmistakable energy she emitted. Her eyes were those of a restless eagle; they moved to take in everything and drew people to them like a magnet. Her energy transcended the evident ability to conduct several multilingual conversations simultaneously and lent her a quickness of decision and the talent for reducing the massively complicated to brief, all-inclusive sentences impossible to misinterpret. When I was in her office, she had turned to the person she had been interviewing, held him in her gaze and said, 'Call me in exactly one month from today – before noon. I won't talk to you if you call before and I won't talk to you if you're late calling. Write it down instead of nodding agreement.'

I went back to Lea Tzemel's office at eight-thirty a.m. on 1 October 1990. She was already there, alone, and was using one of the telephones in reception. Speaking in a mixture of Hebrew and Arabic, she was telling someone off for not informing her of a change in a hearing date. She gestured for me to wait.

She banged the phone down, ran from behind the counter to grab her bag and walked out, saying, 'Let's go. We can't be late.' I trotted a few steps behind as all five foot four inches of her sped down the stairs, kicking out of the way her baggy blue polka-dot trousers, which were topped by a simple white blouse. 'Come on, let's go.' By the time I got in her small Renault, she had already started the engine, and I barely had time to buckle my seat belt before the car was on its way to the District Court in Jerusalem.

'Good morning.'

She smiled. 'Good morning. I am glad you were on time. The District Court is just around the corner, but we've got to be there on time. Otherwise God knows what will happen.'

'I thought we were spending the day at the Ramallah Military Court.'

'We are, we are. But I have to take care of this small matter first.'

'What goes on in the Jerusalem District Court?'

'A kid. He's from the environs of Jerusalem and Jerusalem was annexed by the Israelis, so the District Court has jurisdiction. Military courts are for the occupied territories.'

It was not far. Lea parked the car in a hurry and marched into the District Court building with me in pursuit, after we had been customarily searched and asked to produce our identity documents. Lea's client was in the central waiting area. Kanaan Muhammad Suleiman Mashri, a redhead of sixteen, wore the standard blue jeans and stood alone, afraid and at a complete loss as to why he was in court. Lea hurriedly told me that he was free on bail after being detained for violating a curfew order in Jabal Al Mukhabir two months before. She faced him.

'Are you alone?'

'Yes.'

'Your family didn't come?'

'No.'

'What if they sentence you to jail? Who is going to tell your family?'

'I don't know.'

'What do you mean, you don't know? Why aren't they here?'

'I don't know.'

She threw up her hands in a gesture of despair, then, while telling us to wait, ran into a corner room and came out wearing a black robe. We walked into the courtroom in the middle of the proceedings. Kanaan sat next to Lea in front and I sat in the back.

Another teenager, manacled to a police officer, was brought in and unshackled to stand in the dock. There were four women, one man, six security officers, two defendants and the comely female judge of about fifty. Everything was in Hebrew.

The two cases ahead of Kanaan's didn't last long, for the lawyers struck a bargain with the judge. When Kanaan's case came up, Lea stood up right hand on hip while with her left hand she waved her pencil. She and the judge exchanged words for five minutes after which our group of three left.

Outside in the hallway Lea explained to Kanaan that she had obtained a delay of hearing because he was a minor and needed the presence of an adult member of his family. She asked whether his family had a telephone, and he said that they didn't but the neighbours did. She asked him to send a message via the neighbours asking one of his parents to call her urgently that afternoon, and he said that he had no money. She got her purse out of her bag and gave him a five-shekel piece and shouted, 'They must call me this afternoon. Call them now – the phone is over there. Use the rest of the money to get home just in case they don't get the message. Do you understand? Get going then.'

Once again I had a hard time keeping up with her. We were on our way to Ramallah at nine forty-five. She handled the car with the agility of a Lebanese taxi driver, and the speed at which she drove made it difficult for me to take notes.

'Lea, does what took place earlier happen very often?'

'Yes, yes. And I never know the reason behind it.'

'What do you mean?'

'Well, the kid still doesn't understand what he did, how serious it is. Perhaps he just thought that he'd be told to go home. Who knows? Maybe his family doesn't have the money for the trip to court – he probably walked over. Or perhaps it's just a case of expecting the Jewish lawyer to perform miracles. Who knows?'

'Will he be sentenced to a jail term?'

'Probably. He did violate the curfew. But I'll try to make it as light as possible. He just doesn't understand that walking around in his small village when there is a curfew is a crime.'

The thought that Kanaan's family might not have the money to make a two-mile trip to court made me pause for a moment.

'Now, tell me about yourself please,' I asked.

'What do you want to know?'

'Everything. But first, do people like this boy pay you?'

'When they can.'

'And when they can't?'

'They don't.'

'Can you handle cases this way? Can you afford it?'

'What choice do I have?'

'What about help from outside sources?'

'It would be self-defeating. They all have an axe to grind.'

'What about the PLO? I understand they pay legal fees.'

'Taking money from them is against the law. Do you think that I would jeopardize what I am doing for a little money?'

'So you depend totally on what people pay when they can pay?'

'Yes. It isn't easy.'

'Do some of your defendants sometimes pretend they can't pay when they could?'

'Often.'

'It must be hell to be rewarded that way.'

'Yes, it is. But what's the choice? To stop and make the really needy suffer? I can't do that.'

'What about other Israeli lawyers? Are any of them doing what you're doing?'

'Well, Felicia [Felicia Langer, the left-wing lawyer who wrote *With My Own Eyes*] started it all. But she's retired now. She's back in Germany. But yes, there are a few Jewish Israeli lawyers who work with Arab kids. But most of the time they go for big cases with publicity value. They don't handle a joker like Kanaan.'

We both laughed.

'It looks to me as if yours is an extremely demanding job. How much of your time does it take?'

'Most of my hours, my life, let alone time.'

'What about your family? How do they feel about you spending your life like this?'

'Michel approves. He agrees with what I am doing. My son is twenty; he's going into the army in a week. My daughter is nine. I try to spend as much time with her as possible.'

'I take it Michel is your husband. What does he do?'

'He writes for two French newspapers.'

'Liberal ones, I take it.'

'Yes, left of centre, though his family was French conservative. His father was the Chief Rabbi of Strasbourg.'

'But in spite of this home atmosphere, your son didn't refuse to serve in the army?'

'No, why should he? He is a citizen and so am I. Opposing unjust occupation laws and demanding equality for the Arabs isn't the same as violating the laws of the state.'

'Could you elaborate on this point, please.'

'I am not going to argue why Arabs should be equal. It is self-evident. But the laws of occupation are unjust – certainly the administrative detention nonsense and related matters are. They were supposed to be temporary measures, and years after here we are – not that I accepted the original enactment. I am questioning the validity of the laws. That has little to do with disobeying the established laws of the land, which are unrelated.'

'So you'd never think of doing anything illegal to help anybody, or advising them to do something illegal?'

'No.'

'Never?'

'No. There is no need for that. If enough people oppose unjust laws, then the government will change them. That's a much better way.'

'What if the unjust laws of the land are never changed or get worse?'

'I'd rather not think about that.'

When we reached Ramallah I tried to put my note pad in the back pocket of my trousers, but Lea took it away from me and put it in her bag to avoid its confiscation by the security guards. We walked through the various checkpoints with me pretending to be her assistant.

I sat in the back of the minor crimes court watching Lea Tzemel at work. The black lawyer's gown made for someone twice her size couldn't contain her. She talked to fellow-lawyers, held short conferences with the advocate-general, demanded and was granted a pre-hearing meeting with her clients and in between made copious notes and put them in the many thick folders she carried in her bag. At eleven-thirty the judge entered.

Lea's first client was accused of the simple act of throwing stones at an Israeli army patrol without causing injury. He had been in detention for three months. When the indictment was read he pleaded guilty. Lea rose and began by presenting her credentials, and the judge nodded for her to proceed. His gesture was a combination of 'go ahead' and 'we've met before, Mrs Tzemel'. With that, pencil in hand as earlier that morning, Lea began her defence.

According to the volunteer translator, who happened to be sitting next to me, the case for the defence was very simple: three months of detention were enough punishment, the whole law governing administrative detention was highly questionable and giving the lad a harsh sentence would be counter-productive and turn him into a committed stone-thrower.

Lea spoke for twenty minutes, reinforcing every point she made. The administrative detention law was inherited from emergency laws enacted by the British in the 1940s, when they ruled Palestine. Since international law requires an occupying power to refrain from altering 'the laws existing therein', and Israel cannot change the content of these laws but only the manner in which they are applied, then Israeli orders detaining people for long periods of time were illegal, since they change the content of the law. Even for someone wholly dependent on a kind translator, the attack Lea Tzemel waged on this point was most impressive; certainly the judge and the other members of the court seemed to be mesmerized by her superior talent. But the following exchange between her and the judge smacked of the banal. The judge dismissed her point, saying that it was beyond his court's jurisdiction and continued to emphasize that the stone-throwing incident was unprovoked. Lea accepted the absence of provocation but hammered home the fact that the sentence the teenager had already served was more than enough. Finally, the judge ordered that the administrative detention be extended for another month, and the court was adjourned.

My question to her about why the judge decided to delay the sentencing produced the expected answer: because it would be difficult to justify a four-month prison sentence and he saw fit to impose it through administrative detention, which doesn't have to be justified. In answer to my natural follow-up question, Lea confirmed that this was indeed usual.

We walked around the courtyard talking while we waited for Lea's next case. She told me that one thousand four hundred military orders had been introduced in amendment of the laws existing before Israeli occupation. Israeli military orders altered the law that suited them best. For example, administrative detention was originally British, but the amended laws dealing with land ownership were originally Turkish and other orders amended Jordanian laws. The diversity of the laws of the previous rulers had proved very useful. Suddenly Lea laughed and told me that there was a military order amending an old law, the result of which was to stop Arab farmers from planting aubergines. She had been totally puzzled by the new order until she discovered that Arab-grown aubergines were competing with Israeli ones, something the military wanted to stop. She laughed bitterly and shook her head throughout her story. I found it pleasing that the smallest things still bothered her, that she had not learned to accommodate the unreasonable in life.

At one-fifteen Lea's second case was called. This time the defendant was a seventeen-year-old who, along with four others, was charged with threatening the life of another teenager suspected of collaborating with the Israelis. All five defendants had denied the charge, so it was a case of the plaintiff's case against theirs. In this case Lea's defence was even more basic: the detention of her client was unjustified; there was no substantiation for the plaintiff's claim.

By contrast, the advocate-general equated the alleged threat against the plaintiff's life with a threat against the security of the state. But there was no proof of a threat against the plaintiff's life, retorted Lea. Ah, said the advocate-general, detention for making a threat against the security of the state can be based on unsubstantiated suspicion, and this was the same. Lea's anger echoed beyond the courtroom, and she asked whether applying this standard wouldn't mean that the state is capable of placing the whole population of the West Bank under detention.

I noticed the judge becoming uncomfortable. He didn't want his court to become the venue for this debate. This time the deliberations took a long time, but the outcome was the same: further detention for the accused until a more detailed study of the case had been made.

We were about to drive back to Jerusalem when someone approached Lea's car and whispered something through the window. He pulled back and said, 'It's only two miles away.'

'What is it, Lea.'

'A drug dealer.'

'What about him?'

'He's been killed. We'll see in a minute.'

It was a small house and nearly twenty people were sitting on small chairs in front, with the victim's family in the middle receiving condolences. Lea pulled up a chair next to the unshaven brother of the victim, and I sat near her.

'I am in a hurry. Tell me what happened,' she said.

The man told her how four men shot his brother with a submachine-gun and then escaped. The killers were known to the victim and his family, but the brother alleged that the motive for the murder eluded him. Lea folded her notebook angrily and we left.

'What is this all about?' I asked in the car.

'He was a drug dealer. Taleb Abu Arreyssi was a known drug dealer. Trouble developed and they killed him. The brother was lying.'

'I have no frame of reference for this. Please explain it to me slowly.'

'The security people use Arab drug dealers as informers. They help them with their trade, or look the other way, in return for the dealer supplying them with information about fellow-Arabs. Then trouble develops: the guy refuses to act as a spy or reneges on promises he's made, or sometimes they want to stop dealing and informing. The security people can't afford to have someone go back on the tacit cooperation agreement because it would mean that the rest of them would do it. So they eliminate him.'

'This is truly unbelievable. There is no way to limit the use of drugs to Arabs. Surely the government must know that drugs will inevitably reach Israeli youth.'

'Go tell them. Everything this government does is so short-sighted as to be ludicrous.'

'And you say there are a lot of drug dealers?'

'Yes, hundreds. The drugs come from Lebanon; the army helps with them getting here. We already have a drug problem on both sides.'

'God help us – what next?'

'God is not doing a good job of helping in this part of the world.'

I waited a while, watching her face tighten with thoughts about drugs and what they do to people.

'How many clients do you have, Lea?'

'I don't know; it changes all the time. A little more than two hundred.'

'It must be difficult all this, the seeming helplessness of it all.'

'Yes, it's all very difficult.'

'How do they feel about you on the other side? What do the Israelis think of what you're doing?'

'I am still the lawyer to terrorists to a lot of them, but it isn't as bad as it used to be.'

'Really? How was it at the beginning?'

'Much, much worse. There were years of social isolation. It was hell. Things improved after '82, after Israel invaded Lebanon. More and more Israelis objected to what the government was doing, so the focus of hate shifted from me to other people and I was no longer in the limelight as a weird happening.'

'That's good. Did the others who became dissatisfied with government policy do anything to help you?'

'We communicated and discussed cooperating and I thought of working with some groups like Matzpan [a socialist group], but it didn't work. A group has to have aims and it has to identify them, and most of the time such aims are political. I didn't want that. I wanted and want to challenge the legality of the occupation and its policies and through that stop what the Zionists are doing to the Arabs.'

'It sounds as if you're anti-Zionist?'

'Without reservation. The Zionists dream of building a state which includes all of the West Bank except parts of Jordan. It's absurd. All historical dreams are changed and amended as they go along, so why can't they be reasonable and do the same thing?'

'Is the Zionist dream religious in nature? Is that why it's uncompromising?'

'It is religious, but what you say is utter nonsense. Even religions change; most Christians have stopped blaming the Jews for the killing of Christ. Why can't they change? Because they don't want to change, they want to conquer and be heroes.'

'Historical redress?'

'Yes.'

'When did you begin to see it all this way?'

'After college. I finished Law School at the Hebrew University in '67. Until then I was most apolitical. Then came the '67 war and the conquest of the West Bank and Gaza. I started asking questions, but no one in Israel wanted to give me answers. They objected to why I was asking the questions, not their content. Questioning what was happening automatically reduced me to an outsider. I wasn't part of the conspiracy. I don't want to be part of any conspiracy which denies human beings their rights.'

The car came to a stop in front of Lea's office. It was after three and she still hadn't had lunch. I regretted my inability to continue our conversation and to be hospitable and left her to go to another appointment. We made a date for the following day and said a slow, heavy goodbye.

At ten the next morning we were at the High Court in the building known as Maskobia (meaning Muscovite – a carry-over from the days when it belonged to the Russian Orthodox Church). As we were about to enter, I stopped to look at the pock-marks of battle and remembered that the building had been fought over viciously during the 1948 war, when I was a teenager living in Bethany. Standing next to me, Lea was reading the Hebrew graffiti near the entrance.

She translated it for me: 'Court martial for the Arabs, not the justice of the Supreme Court.' She was annoyed by my inclination to dismiss the whole thing as the work of cranks. 'They are taking over the country, your cranks,' she said as we walked inside.

Samir Abu Shakra, Lea's able assistant, was already there waiting for us, wearing his usual smile of defiance. I was glad to see him and asked whether he would sit next to me and translate for me, as the unknown gentleman had done the day before. He agreed and the three of us went to the small canteen for a coffee.

'What kind of case have we got today?' I asked.

'House demolition,' Lea answered.

'Tell me about it, one of you.'

'It is an order demolishing someone's home because it was used by kids throwing stones at Israeli patrols.'

'And you're contesting the legality of it all?'

'No, there's too much precedent for that. It's a three-room house. One room is a living room and bedroom, the second is an above-ground well and the third is used for animals. The demolition order specified that the residence of the family be destroyed. To me, that means the living room-bedroom. I am trying to save the other two rooms.'

'What are the chances of success?'

'We'll see. It's time to go.'

This courtroom was quite impressive. The chairs of the three members of the court were on a high platform, and they were deep-cushioned and comfortable-looking. The advocate-general, to the left of the judges and the right of the spectators, merited a chair and a desk of quality. The lawyers operated from the front benches. At the back of the room were bookshelves full of volumes on British, American and Canadian law. The judges emerged in black robes.

Samir told me that the middle-aged judge was Gabriel Bach, who was handsome and neatly dressed in a French way. Shoshona Netanyahu, sister of the extreme-right-wing Israeli Deputy Foreign Minister, was the member of the right, and Yacoub Martz, also an impressive-looking man, was the member of the left.

Lea's case was first on the list. The advocate-general related the history of the case and maintained that all three rooms of the house constituted a residence. He described the two rooms Lea was trying to save from demolition as subsidiary to the main room. Lea contested these claims vigorously, questioning how the word 'residence' could possibly be applied to a well or a place for animals. As she continued her defence, the judge and the two members of the court questioned her in detail about the use of the other rooms and whether the whole place constituted one unit. Gabriel Bach and Yacoub Martz were satisfied but not Shoshona Netanyahu. A vicious female dispute ensued, and I told Samir Abu Shakra to stop his translation activity because I was much more interested in the physical postures of the two women.

Lea Tzemel was earthy, animated and angry, while Shoshona Netanyahu was coldly condescending. Lea spoke with a raspy voice and gestured continuously, while her opponent modulated a thin voice with care and found it beneath her dignity to resort to gestures for emphasis. The member of the right assumed an ever haughtier demeanour the longer things went on, and I got the impression she found the whole business of arguing with a populist lawyer demeaning.

This case, too, was postponed. Further investigation was needed. On our way out of the court-house I stopped twice to examine posters depicting the good life in Israel. They purported to show a country rejoicing in nothing but sun and fun. Samir left us and Lea and I decided to sit in a small prefabricated café outside. Lea banged the little table with her fist and told me that Shoshona Netanyahu had insisted that a residence is a whole structure and not part of it. '*Balgan, Balgan*,' she shouted. When she saw me questioning what the word meant, she repeated, 'Chaos, chaos.'

Soon she was on the telephone talking to her office with a bagel in her free hand. She settled down after making three calls.

'Lea, is this the time to ask you my concluding questions or should I wait and come to see you tomorrow?'

'Now, please. Tomorrow is going to be hell. They've got him again.'

'Got who?'

'Kamal Sheikh Amin. He was under administrative detention for seven years – seven years without trial. They've just taken him in.'

'Why?'

She was agitated and her gestures matched her words. 'Who the hell knows why? Every time things sour, when there's tension, they take him in. He's gone anyway, not much of him left.'

I chose not to pursue this line of questioning because I knew the

Israeli military authorities did detain people without having to give a reason.

'Lea, may I backtrack?'

'Sure.'

'Where did your family come from?'

'Poland in 1933.'

'Were they religious?'

'Somewhat, certainly conservative. Not political, but very conservative.'

'Do they agree with you?'

'Not necessarily, but they support me.'

'Now, do you have any words of advice to all the parties involved in the Arab–Israeli conflict?'

'Yes. To the Israelis: be human. To America: be American, don't interfere. To the Arabs: be human, develop, become individuals. They should do this not only in the occupied territories but everywhere.'

'What should Israel do more specifically?'

'Israel belongs to the Middle East, not to America. They should be kind and try to belong to the Middle East and try to build bridges to the people of the Middle East. They live here and not in Brooklyn.'

'What do you think of what they're doing now in the occupied territories?'

'Everything they do is aimed at pushing the people of the territories out, at evicting them. They should stop that and work towards a modern unified Middle East where Israel would become the Jewish division.'

'Is that where it's heading on a long-term basis? Is that what will happen?'

'Not soon. The immediate future is hell. The Israelis are greedy and the Arabs haven't changed enough. But on a long-term basis, they have to live with each other; they must live with each other or perish.'

'So you're hopeful – on a long-term basis.'

'Yes.'

'I haven't seen anything to justify that. Tell me more of why you're hopeful.'

'Look, I have lived long enough to see an *intifada*. It's almost enough for a lifetime – a whole people in rebellion for freedom. From 1967 until 1987 I lost hope in the human condition, I lost hope in the Arabs as human beings because they took all the Israelis dished out without kicking back. Then a bunch of children told me that I was wrong and it was delicious. I had been wrong and my very first thoughts were right. You can't stamp out man's quest for freedom. Do you know what that means or have you been away sheltered in London for too long?'

I didn't answer her question. I said a brief goodbye and walked away, sheepishly. As I looked back she was making another telephone call, probably to check on another case. I had an urge to run back and tell her that my faith too, even if only temporarily, had been restored, that my doubts about the human condition had melted in the heat of her passion for freedom. But I didn't. I raised my hand and waved dramatically – hopefully not a last farewell.

Chapter Eleven
A CONFUSING TIME

There is no better way to learn what is happening in the West Bank than to examine everyday occurrences and conversations, for these reveal much about Israeli attitudes towards the Arabs. Even when soldiers are obeying orders, how they do things is telling, particularly since much is left to the discretion of the individual.

The following bizarre incident took place on the morning of 26 August 1990. I leave it to the reader to determine the exact time. The place is the eastern slope of Bethany, a little north of the Greek Orthodox monastery, to the right of the boys' school, a tiny bit to the left of where my cousin Randa lives. In Bethany, this is an accurate description of place.

An Israeli soldier armed with an M16 rifle is standing guard at an improvised road block. My fifteen-year-old cousin is walking by on his way to the centre of the village. The soldier orders him to stop, and my cousin, thinking this is the usual ID check, reaches into his pocket and produces it. The soldier examines the card and returns it. He continues, '*Maha shaa*?' (What time is it?)

When my cousin says that he doesn't understand Hebrew, the soldier repeats the question in Arabic. '*Sho al saa*?'

Cousin: I don't know.

Soldier: But you're wearing a watch, can't you tell the time, you stupid Arab?

Cousin: My watch doesn't work.

Soldier: Why do you wear it then, dumbo?

Cousin: I like to wear it.

Soldier: It's ten o'clock, isn't it?

Cousin: Not necessarily.

Soldier: Show me your watch.

My cousin doesn't move. The soldier grabs his wrist and looks to see the time. It says eleven. As my cousin stands motionless with fear, the soldier pulls off the cheap watch with its metal bracelet, throws it on the ground and smashes it with the butt of his rifle. The soldier's mates, standing a mere ten yards away, laugh and egg him on. My cousin moves away slowly, head bowed in helpless anger, but the soldier takes a few steps towards him, kicks his backside and orders him to go home.

The background to this utterly absurd incident is simple: 26 August is the date the Israelis set the clock back one hour, but the PLO refused to follow suit and ordered West Bankers to maintain 'old time'. My cousin was following PLO time, which annoyed the Israeli soldier, who viewed this as an act of defiance.

When I heard the story a few hours later, I hurriedly tried to determine the number of ugly incidents that took place that day as a result of Israeli–PLO failure to agree on a single time. I couldn't. Thousands, some people told me, while others claimed the number ran into the tens of thousands. I managed to verify six separate incidents in Jerusalem and decided the episodes justified an investigation. To get more information, I met with my young cousin, in spite of family claims that he was upset and moping.

Me: Did you expect something like this to happen to you when you didn't reset your watch?

Cousin: Yes, they do it every year.

Me: Why didn't you at least take off your watch to avoid trouble?

Cousin: Why should I? It's my watch.

Me: Is it policy? Are all of you kids agreed that you should wear your watches and maintain PLO time in spite of the obvious danger?

Cousin: Yes.

Me: Who issued the instructions for you to do this?

Cousin: Nobody issued instructions, but the PLO tells us when to set the clock. The rest is up to us. We choose to follow PLO time.

Me: Have Israeli soldiers ever done anything more than smash watches and kick ass?

Cousin: Yes.

Me: What?

Cousin: They take watches away – they just pocket them. Also there were several incidents last year when some of my friends got afraid, panicked and tried to run away. When you try to run away and you're caught, they detain you. Usually for two weeks but it depends whether you resist or not.

Me: Did anything happen to your friends during the periods of detention?

Cousin: They beat them and kept asking them what time it was.

Me: And what did they say?

Cousin: They couldn't tell the time anyway because their watches had either been smashed or confiscated.

Me: Wasn't there a clock somewhere?

Cousin: Yes, in the police station there was one, but my friends refused to read it because it showed Israeli time.

Me: What are you going to do about a new watch?

Cousin: Not much. My father is out of work.

Me: What would you do if I bought you one?

Cousin: Wear it and show PLO time.

The following day I missed a meeting I had scheduled at the American Colony Hotel with American freelance writer Arlene Phillips. We had agreed to meet at six p.m. She, deferentially, had assumed I was following PLO time while I, thinking she lived on the Israeli side, thought Israeli time was in force. The misunderstanding produced more laughter than hard feeling.

The issue of whose time West Bankers follow for the period of two weeks when this becomes an issue is an example of how capable of stupidity the human mind is. More than anything else, it is illusory activity like this that separates Arab and Israeli; many of the contentious issues one discovers at street level are fabricated. This is not to say that genuine differences in cultural conceptions do not exist in abundance. These differences have a tendency to show themselves through individual action because governmental and group behaviour guard against their exposure.

Two days after the incident I was in the company of an agricultural engineer on my way back to Bethlehem from my visit to the Rashaidah Bedouin tribe. We were stopped by an Israeli patrol manning a checkpoint. A sergeant stuck his head through the window of the car on my side. Sergeant (in unaccented Arabic but with disdain): Identity card?

Me: This is my passport.

Sergeant: American, ha?

Me: Yes.

Sergeant: Were you born here?

Me: Yes, in Bethany.

Sergeant: And where do you live?
Me: In London.
Sergeant (shaking his head): You were born here, carry an American passport and live in London?
Me: Yes.
Sergeant: You're an impostor.
Me: That's a bit hard, isn't it?
The sergeant ignored my protest, threw the passport on my lap and walked around the car to talk to my companion.
Sergeant: ID card?
Driver: Here.
Sergeant: You live in Bethlehem?
Driver: Yes.
Sergeant (noticing the driver's hand was bandaged): What happened to your hand?
Driver: A jackass bit it.
Sergeant: Why?
Driver: What do you expect from a jackass?
The sergeant became furious and I was afraid he might hurt my friend, but he didn't. Instead, he turned to one of his colleagues and said, 'Check with headquarters whether jackasses bite people.'
The soldier went to the radio and talked animatedly for two to three minutes. He came back and nodded to the sergeant. The sergeant ordered us to move, telling us, 'I thought you were lying.'

The two contrasting incidents of the soldier who destroyed my cousin's watch because it showed PLO time and the sergeant who innocently overlooked an insult demonstrate the personal nature of the daily confrontations between Israelis and Palestinians. The outcome of both depended on the attitude of the individuals involved, and not on any laws or regulations governing the specific situation.

Weeks later I was in an impeccably clean Israeli taxi that was taking me to a meeting in west Jerusalem. I sat in the back and tried to catch up with world happenings by reading the *International Herald Tribune*, which I spread in front of me so my face hid behind it. In the wake of the Temple Mount–Harram Al Sherrif massacre, the atmosphere in Jerusalem was more tense than usual.

The driver addressed me in Arabic. 'Do you know who lives up there?'

I lowered the paper and answered him in English. 'I am sorry, but I am afraid I don't speak Arabic.'

He changed to English. 'Are you sure you can't speak Arabic?'

'Yes.'

'But you look like an Arab.'

I still tried to hide my identity to avoid the pervasive air of hate choking Jerusalem. 'That's true, but I was born in the United States. My parents are Arab.'

'Do you feel like an Arab?'

'I can't answer that question because I don't know what it's supposed to mean.'

'Do you hate us?'

'No, certainly not. There are good people everywhere, and I don't hate anybody.'

'That's a good diplomatic answer, but tell me, how do you feel about things?'

'I feel that we should have peace.'

'We all feel that, but there are some jerks on both sides who don't want peace.'

'I know.'

'Do you know who lived in that street I showed you?'

'Back there?'

'Yes, on Jablonski Street.'

'I have no idea.'

'Are you sure? You look like a man who knows a great deal.'

'I promise you, I have no idea who lives on that street.'

'Shamir the Midget [Prime Minister Yitshak Shamir of Israel].'

'Oh.'

'How do you like him?'

'It's not for me to say. It's the Israeli people who elect him to office.'

'Look, I'll make you a deal. Do you agree?'

'I think you better tell me what sort of deal you have in mind.'

'You people want to kill him, don't you? I'll do it for you for money.'

'No . . . thanks. I am not in the business, thank you very much.'

'Are you sure?'

'Absolutely.'

'Really, really sure?'

'As sure as I am of anything, and I don't want to talk about it, even if you're joking.'

'I am not joking, but OK.'

I returned to the *Herald Tribune*, thankful that our criminal conversation had come to an end and determined not to start another. Suddenly I heard Arabic music coming from the front, the famous Egyptian singer Um Kulsoum doing her classic rendition of 'You Are My Life'. I kept to my newspaper – but not for long.

'Do you like this music?'

'Sorry?'

'I said do you like this music?'

I couldn't help it; I smiled. 'Yes, most of it.'

'Why do you pretend you're American?

'I am an American citizen, and it's easier most of the time. It's a way of avoiding trouble.'

'But believe me, the Arabs are better people than the Americans, and they have culture.' He reverted to Arabic. 'It's the loveliest music in the world, you know.'

'Yes, in some ways.'

'In all ways, it's better than singing "Tutti Frutti". I was born in Haifa in an Arab neighbourhood, and this is how I feel. I don't understand their music or anything they do, the new people.'

'I see.'

'Only people with no soul would not love this music and the words.'

'I see.'

'Do you know who those people are who don't love it?'

'No.'

'German Jews. They have no soul. Someone took away their soul and now you and I suffer.'

We reached our destination. I was torn between continuing the conversation and being thankful that my journey was over. The taxi driver refused to take a tip; he shouted 'Allah be with you' and drove away.

There was something very sad about the Israeli taxi driver. His initial dramatic way of telling me that he and I had something in common eventually gave way to a much gentler approach, the use of music to help me overcome my fear of communicating with him openly. The statement he made deserved a better hearing, and I have regretted my inability to be more forthcoming.

The Israeli journalist I was meeting in the famous Fink's Café on King George Street was considered one of Israel's leading experts on the West Bank and things Arab. A mutual friend was of the opinion that an exchange of views would be beneficial to both of us.

Fink's is a cross between an Italian café and a Central European meeting house for men of letters. The place has an atmosphere of homey decadence aided by the presence of many pictures of

Jerusalem at the turn of the century, along with checked table cloths and matchboxes that proclaim it one of the world's most famous bars. The owner is dark, bald and takes his proprietorship seriously.

I spotted the journalist and moved towards him. He stood up.

'You must be Saïd!'

'Yes, hello. It's very nice of you to come on such short notice.'

'Well thank you for contacting me. I couldn't think of anywhere else. I hope this place is to your liking.'

For over an hour we talked about books on the Middle East, how inadequate most of them were and how difficult it was to publish books about the Arab–Israeli problem. We agreed that the world was tired of the Arabs and the Israelis and their common and individual problems. To us, most people wished the dilemma of the Middle East would disappear but showed little stomach for doing anything that would make this wish come true.

We moved to more immediate considerations of the widening divide between Arabs of the West Bank and the Israelis, even in mixed communities in Jerusalem, and lamented this unfortunate development. It all sounded like a wake for what might have been. Inevitably, the conversation narrowed and we began to talk about ourselves and what we were doing.

'You're from Bethany, aren't you?'

'Yes, I was born and raised there but left the place in '48.'

'How many of you are there in your immediate family?'

'Seven, five boys and two girls.'

'I bet you're scattered all over the place. Where do you all live?'

'The US, UK, Egypt, Holland, Portugal and Saudi Arabia.'

'But you're still Palestinian?'

'Yes, all of us.'

'I bet you have a hundred nephews and nieces.'

'Not quite. Sixteen, but that's enough.'

'Only sixteen?'

'Yes, what's wrong with sixteen?'

'Nothing, it's a small number for Arabs.'

'I don't know about that, but it's plenty. Who can afford a lot of kids nowadays!'

'That's amazing – I mean coming from Bethany, I thought you would have a lot of kids.'

'Things have changed. People don't have as many kids any more.'

'How many of you married cousins from Bethany?'

'None.'

'Not a single one of you married a cousin from Bethany?'

'Not from Bethany or any other place where our cousins are.'

'That is truly remarkable.'

'Not only that, I can't even think of a cousin who married another cousin.'

'Why not?'

'I don't know what you mean by why not.'

'Well, I thought Arabs had a lot of kids and always married first cousins.'

'Not us. Anyway, it is a less frequent occurrence everywhere now.'

'But your wives and husbands are all Arabs?'

'No . . . four are non-Arabs.'

'This is really interesting.'

'I don't know how interesting it is.'

'What do your sisters and brothers and brothers-in-law do?'

'I see you're curious. Let's see. One brother owns an electronic supply company, another is a middle executive with a trading company and two are in the travel business. One of my brothers-in-law is the manager of Sheraton Hotels in Portugal and the other is a surgeon. One sister works – Mona – she owns a fashion boutique in Lisbon.'

'Amazing, and it all started in Bethany.'

'Yes, but Bethany itself has changed . . . you'd be surprised, things have moved forward four hundred years during the past forty.'

'And you feel Bethany is your home?'

'A spiritual one, yes.'

After two hours more of conversation, we parted company. It was apparent to me that this expert's knowledge was completely out of date; it stopped at 1948 if not earlier. If a so-called expert has no appreciation of how much the Arabs have changed in fifty years, then there is little hope. After all, he was one of the people responsible for educating the Israelis in Arab ways, but – unlike the attractive and friendly taxi driver – his parents had come to Israel from Germany, and we were cultures apart.

If the journalist's attitude exemplifies the antiquated official thinking towards Arabs, then the feelings of Z.B., an Israeli architect, are, unfortunately, more representative of the middle-class Israelis, who suffer from simple, inactive but seriously harmful prejudices. Z.B. is a kind and generous man, but he manifests a narrow preoccupation with self that stands in the way of greater understanding between the Israelis and the Arabs.

Z.B. is hardly a person who hears about the Arabs at second hand or blindly follows the line of the Israeli government. On the contrary, he speaks good Arabic, a considerable amount of his work is with Arabs, and he is well acquainted with their grievances and aspirations. In fact, it is because of his potential as a bridge-builder and his belief that he is a friend of the Arabs, that his case becomes fascinating.

'Things are really bad. For the first time since 1967 I can no longer go to places in the West Bank which I used to visit regularly. My Arab friends don't want to see me because their Arab neighbours would think they're traitors and it is unsafe for me anyway. The division between the two sides is getting wider and wider.

'You must have a more sensible Palestinian leadership which should deal with basic things and not with politics. They must work on developing the infrastructure and building things for the future. Politics is not the real problem – the real problem is improving people's lives. We can help them, if they'd let us, but they're preoccupied with nonsense.'

'My friend, I understand that. But look at it this way: they want to run their own affairs and after that if they want your help then maybe something could be worked out, but first they're entitled to decide their own future.'

'Arabs can't run their own affairs. They need outside help with everything. The West Bank isn't self-sufficient, and we must develop it. We have to do something about improving things.'

'I don't know how to get this through to you, but the people of the West Bank and Gaza want to be left alone to manage their own affairs.'

'We can't leave them alone. All they would do is cause trouble for us. They are not economically developed. They have to attain economic self-sufficiency and then other things might be considered, and to reach that point they need us badly.'

'But you've occupied the West Bank for twenty-three years, and you haven't done much. As a matter of fact you haven't done anything, so how could you say it should all be left to you?'

'That may be true, but we can start now. We can work with them to make them attain self-sufficiency. Without self-sufficiency people can't aspire to anything.'

'Do you realize that this is a self-refuting argument? Israel itself has never been self-sufficient. If it weren't for US aid, the whole place would collapse and I can show you that on a small piece of paper.'

'That's different.'

'Why?'

'Because we pay the United States back in other ways – we help them maintain their position in the Middle East.'

'I see. Let me stay with your vision for the West Bank. How long would any plan to make the West Bank self-sufficient take and what would come after that?'

'How long it would take depends on the Arabs, on how good they are and how interested they are. And after that, if they attain self-sufficiency, perhaps we will make them Israeli citizens.'

'So you're not thinking of giving them independence?'

'No, no, they don't need independence.'

'All the thousands of kids who riot, go to prison, suffer torture and risk their lives for independence aren't enough proof that they want to be on their own?'

'Too much has been made of this, you know. The leadership eggs the kids on, and they can be stopped. Anyway, not much happens to those kids when they go to prison. They eat better than they do at home and they learn Hebrew.'

The cruelty of the statement made me stop for a while, but it was obvious that it was not a slip of the tongue and that Z.B. truly believed what he said. I suppressed my anger and continued.

'Are you telling me that the *intifada* can disappear overnight and that you have no sympathy whatsoever with the suffering of the children?'

'Suffering – putting a few kids in prison isn't suffering. I will tell you what suffering is. My family came from Latvia, and all of them were in concentration camps during the war. Only my aunt and my father survived, and you expect me to compare that with a little arm-twisting of a bunch of kids.'

'But what you're saying will do nothing except produce more wars in the future. The Arabs won't stand for not being allowed to decide their own future. Sooner or later a Saddam Hussein will come and tell them war is their only way out.'

'If the Arabs are foolish enough to want another war then it will be different this time. We're tired of them starting wars. If they start another one, then we will rain atomic bombs on the whole of the Middle East.'

'Is what you say representative of Israeli thinking?'

'No. A lot of people here don't want anything to do with the Arabs. I want to make them citizens, after they make sense out of their economic situation. I want to help the Arabs, and very few people in Israel are concerned with that; they want to get rid of them. One thing is sure: no one here wants the Arabs to have their own state.'

'It all sounds like some form of colonialism to me, deciding the future of a people without their consent.'

'And what's wrong with colonialism?'

The meetings with the journalist and the architect left me in deep despair. My need for words of comfort and understanding pushed me towards familiar territory. My friend Yehuda Litani is a remarkable man of principle in a world that cries for more. A former Israeli television correspondent and Middle East Editor of the *Jerusalem Post*, he resigned his last position when the Israeli government appointed a right-wing editor to influence the newspaper's policies.

For me, no trip to Jerusalem is complete without several meetings with Yehuda during which we exchange news and views and I am brought up to date with what is happening. We entertain ourselves with pleasant dreams of how wonderful it would be if sense prevailed and the present policies of hate were abandoned. It is a mark of Yehuda's integrity and humanity that he has never referred to the disputed land as anything except 'Israel–Palestine' or 'Palestine–Israel'.

After the changes in Eastern Europe, Yehuda was one of many Israelis who visited countries from which their ancestors came to Israel, in his case Poland. Yehuda's words are a living monument to how pain and human experience can expand the mind rather than narrow it and how they can contribute to greater human understanding.

'It was incredible, just incredible. What impressed me most was the sense of identity the Poles had. In many ways, it was as if communism never was; it was a true reversion to Polish culture as shown by how people felt and behaved. For over forty years Russia tried to impose an outside system on them which didn't reflect their character, but it didn't work and their Polishness triumphed. There are lessons to be learned there for everybody, not only for Israel and what it is trying to do here but for the United States and others who wander around trying to infect others with their ways.

'After a group of us saw Walesa – God he's remarkable – and we saw a few other people, I decided to go on a sentimental journey.

I went to the graveyard where my ancestors were buried. Everything was all right until I was physically there, then I couldn't take it.

'Each little story I had heard as a child, all the good and bad things my family had experienced, lived, came alive. I was shaking all over; I couldn't take it. I cried, I really cried. What a confrontation with the past, with myself, that was.

'I guess that's what you feel when you come back here, Saïd. It's probably easier for me; after all, I am an Israeli and I have a country, and I really like this place – with all its faults. I belong, but you're still in the middle and because of that the pull towards this place must be stronger for you than the pull of Poland for me. The whole thing made me understand more.

'Then, after a week in Warsaw, something funny happened. The food isn't terrific there, as you know; Polish food is so-so. I couldn't eat after a week, I just couldn't eat, my subconscious was telling me that I didn't want Polish food. So there I was walking in the middle of Warsaw and I started laughing at myself – nothing happened, but I was laughing at myself. I desperately wanted a plate of hummus, I just felt like hummus and it explained why I didn't want to eat Polish food. It was a strange urge for pita bread and hummus. It was a startling revelation which told me how Middle Eastern I was.

'The other day I was on my way to investigate a story in a village near Nablus. And there I was with a map looking for the village but lost. I saw an old man along the road and I asked him for directions. The old man just smiled at me, grabbed a handful of earth and smelled it. He told me that one has to belong to that earth to know where things are, then he told me where to go. He made me wonder.'

Yehuda Litani's instinctive and intellectual senses endow him with an enviable appreciation of the things that matter. His reflections on the Polish situation tell us much about Israel's attempt to impose itself on the Palestinians; the graves of his ancestors and his pain-filled visit enhanced his awareness of how the Arabs feel about their heritage; and his story about wanting hummus was nothing but an assertion that he too belonged to the Middle East. He still refuses to think of anything except a 'Palestine–Israel' or 'Israel–Palestine' and though a seasoned journalist who has seen enough to make him cynical, he remains hopeful and fully committed to peace. 'If they want peace, they'll find it. With good will everything is possible, everything.'

A day after my last meeting with Yehuda Litani, I returned to

Bethany to find my aunt sitting in the kitchen with a large pitcher of lemonade in front of her. When I made a comment about how much lemonade she had made, she told me that she had made it for an Israeli military group of three people who had come to talk to her about cousin Muhammad, an *intifada* boy who is the subject of continuous investigations.

'But it doesn't look as if they had any of it.'

'No, they wouldn't, not a drop. Perhaps they thought I had poisoned it or something.'

'I doubt it, it's probably regulations. They're not allowed to accept things from people while on duty.'

'No, no. In the past they used to have a cup of coffee or tea, but they don't any more. They don't want to have anything to do with us any more. To hell with them; this is the last time I offer them anything. All they do is come here to chase our kids. I really don't want anything to do with them any more.'

Unlike my aunt, I refused and refuse to close the door on communications with what Arabs call 'people on the other side'. But I made a decision to delay further investigation of Israeli attitudes until the latter part of my trip. I did not want my discouraging findings in this area to pre-empt my search for signs of hope.

Chapter Twelve
CONVERSATIONS WITH PEOPLE ON THE OTHER SIDE

Two weeks before my return to London I decided to renew my exploration of the attitude of Israeli individuals and groups towards what is happening in the West Bank. I had seen enough to suspect that relations between Arabs and the Israelis were deteriorating much faster than the world outside realized, and I needed more Israeli voices to confirm or refute this suspicion.

Several attempts to meet with 'representative' Israelis failed; they refused to be interviewed by a Palestinian. The reasons given fell into two types: many said that a Palestinian writer wouldn't and couldn't be impartial while others stated that the existing tense atmosphere was not conducive to holding 'a constructive meeting'. It is therefore important to remember that what follows suffers from this constraint, although I still believe that the ones who talked to me had much of importance to say.

What follows are relatively lengthy, focused interviews with people who knew my purpose and were prepared to answer questions. Though hardly a cross-section of the population, they were chosen from different walks of life and reflect different outlooks. As elsewhere in this book, the decision to withhold the names of the interviewees was mine. Even in Israel the atmosphere is too fluid and frayed and the risk of misinterpretation and consequent damage to the welfare of the interviewee is always present.

I had been looking forward to my meeting with one of Israel's leading writers with the nervousness of a groupie about to meet her idol. The man had written with remarkable insight about the relationship of the conqueror (the Israelis) to the defeated (the Arabs) and eloquently exposed the evils of the relationship and what it portends for both sides. As a result I had written him a complimentary letter and we had had a friendly correspondence but had never met.

As with communications between people on different sides of this great divide, our telephone conversation, which had started easily, soon developed its own uncertainty. He, aware of the unfriendly conditions that exist on the ground, was reluctant to suggest a meeting place and this made me nervous and equally reluctant. Eventually we agreed to have tea at the famous King David Hotel.

We had no difficulty in identifying each other. He walked into the place with the certain step of a man at peace with himself and where he was; he possessed an enviable sense of presence. Our greetings, in a combination of Arabic and English, were friendly. We sat in a corner of the huge lobby and ordered tea.

For over twenty minutes we talked shop: writing, publishing, the problem of having works translated and how spiritually satisfying it was to devote oneself full time to writing. Everything the man said confirmed my previous image of him; I was in the presence of an exceptional talent and a very sensitive and kind man. Inevitably the conversation drifted to how things stood between the Arabs and the Israelis.

'Are you working on a book?' he asked.

'Yes, I am researching one. I haven't yet decided what form it will take. But I am also here looking for hope. Things look so bleak from the outside, I thought I might find a glimpse of hope here, something on the ground that the rest of the world is neglecting.'

'You're here looking for hope? Well, you won't find it. Things are bad and getting worse; I never thought it would reach this point.'

'I must admit that I haven't seen any, but I thought you might point me towards something. You don't think there's anything which offers hope?'

'I am afraid not. Whatever hope existed evaporated with the Gulf crisis. Now nobody is working together any more – the positions have hardened.'

'That's sad. Why?'

'The Palestinians support Saddam. On the other hand, the Israelis, even the most liberal, who wanted their government to conduct a constructive dialogue with the Palestinians, have given up. Even small groups which used to meet to discuss things have suspended their contacts because of this, because of the Gulf crisis.'

'Because of Palestinian support for Saddam?'

'Yes.'

'Let's pretend I don't have any opinion about that. Why are the Israelis so angered by Palestinian identification with Saddam?'

'Because Saddam wants to destroy Israel, and when the Palestinians support him it reveals that's what they want also. Taken a step further, this means that Palestinians' claims that they want peace are not true.'

'Interesting. Nobody sees the Palestinian identification with Saddam as a reflection of their frustration and desperation?'

'No, not really. You've got to see it from this side. How could we possibly support Palestinian desire for self-determination when they join forces with someone who wants to destroy our country? It makes it impossible for those who have supported independence for the Palestinians and accepted their statements about peace with Israel. It supports the contention of Israeli hardliners who say that the only reason the Palestinians want to be independent is to prepare for another go at us.'

'Are you telling me that there is nobody in Israel at this moment in time who advocates giving the Palestinians the right of self-determination?'

'Of course there are. But we have been silenced for now. The best way to help those who support Palestinian rights is for the Palestinians to recant and renounce Saddam. If that happens then it will take some time before believers in Palestinian rights can say anything. In the meanwhile those who take a hard line against the Palestinians have been strengthened – for them the present situation was God-sent.'

'Tell me, how do Israelis feel about the other side, the anti-Saddam Arabs, the traditionalist regimes of Saudi Arabia and the oil sheikhs?'

'They think they're a bunch of corrupt, backward clowns. We have nothing in common with people like them.'

'I see, but what would have happened if the Palestinians had supported this group, the oil-rich?'

'Nothing.'

'You don't care if the Palestinians support the corrupt ones, but you don't want them to back a modern tyrant?'

'I guess that's true. Our concern is our safety and the people you mention are not a threat to the state of Israel.'

'So indirectly, or even directly, your objection is to Palestinian politics? It sounds as if you are dictating to them how they should behave.'

'Not really, though it looks that way. We just don't want them joining those who want us eliminated.'

'But it does smack of wanting them to adopt a specific attitude or you won't accept any of their claims?'

'On a short-term basis, yes.'

'It doesn't sound like a good formula for peace, one which says either you follow my ways or nothing for you.'

'In reality, the ideal solution for the Israelis is if the Palestinians give up Arab politics altogether. Let me turn what I said around and ask you a question: if we give the Palestinians some form of independence would they still be involved in Arab politics and the rest of the Arab world or would they use their energy to build a Palestinian state?'

'I would think both. But surely you know that there is no way to isolate the Palestinians from the rest of the Arabs. After all, they are Arabs culturally and religiously. A total cut-off from the rest of the Arabs isn't possible.'

'I thought you would say that. In that case the future is bleak indeed.'

'Let me backtrack for a minute. Why are you in such a state about Saddam? The mere mention of his name generates unrealistic fear here, even in someone like you.'

'I have said what he wants to do and he is militarily powerful and, who knows, he might be able to do something.'

'I know he is marching towards attaining military parity with Israel, though he isn't there yet. Is this what frightens people here?'

'Yes.'

'How do you feel personally? Have you been operating on the basis that over two hundred million Arabs will never attain military parity with Israel?'

He leaned back in his chair and thought for a moment. 'To be honest, yes.'

'My friend, you have already told me two things which are not acceptable. One is the fact that you want the Palestinians to isolate themselves from the rest of the Arabs and the second is that you can't accept the Arabs as equals.'

'Perhaps.'

We talked for another hour. We agreed that the world had blindly, and for over forty years, addressed itself to only half of the Arab–Israeli problem: the part concerning territory and who has the right to it, whether the fence was a mile one way or the other. The second half of the Arab–Israeli problem, that of supremacy in the Middle East, had never received any attention. To us, it was the second half that mattered most because it dealt with the bigger problem of whether the two sides are able to live with each other. We parted as friends, genuinely wishing each other *salam* and *shalom* and promising to stay in touch. Whatever differences of opinion we had, and they were as substantial as they were obvious, what mattered most was that we had been able to exchange views. Perhaps when next we meet, our differences will be smaller.

She was a tall, attractive girl of twenty working in the office of an Israeli acquaintance of mine for the summer, after which she intended to return to the Hebrew University to continue her ancient history course. It took me more than a week to convince her that my interest in her was academic, that I wanted to hear the opinions of someone her age on the problems of the Arabs and the Israelis.

After she agreed to be interviewed, my offer of a drink was turned down in favour of tea. She seldom drank, was working her way through college, belonged to no political party and her parents were average middle-class people who didn't hold strong views on anything. They were socially liberal, allowing her a free hand.

'Do you know a lot of Arabs?'

'Not a lot – three or four only – but I see a great many of them because they're around.'

'How did you meet the ones you know?'

'One at university and the others at work.'

'Are you friendly with them?'

'We get along, we don't have much to do with each other, but when we do it's all right.'

'What does that mean exactly?'

'It means we're not good friends, but we don't have problems.'

'It sounds as if you expect problems when you meet Arabs, do you?'

She smiles. 'Well, yes.'

'What kind?'

'The general kind. After all, we don't get along, the Arabs and the Israelis.'

'So they're not personal problems but ones that have to do with the overall problem?'

'Yes, I guess that's what it is.'

'How do you avoid having arguments or problems with the Arabs you know?'

'We don't discuss them, we don't talk about things which create argument.'

'So your contact is perfunctory, superficial?'

'Yes, with the guy at the university I just say hello and we talk about archaeology. The guys in our office don't discuss anything with us except work, that's all.'

'So there is no personal discussion about the way you live or things of that sort?'

'No, never.'

'Because it would cause trouble?'

'Yes. Also we have our own idea of how they live and I am sure they have theirs.'

'The Arabs at your office, do you think that they do their work well?'

'Not bad, but it isn't for me to decide these things.'

'Does anything happen with them that wouldn't happen with Israelis doing the same work?'

'Sure, sometimes they don't come to work because there's trouble. When there is a curfew in the towns where they live they can't come to work and there have been occasions when they have been afraid to come to work.'

'How does the boss feel about them staying away from work?'

'He doesn't mind. He's a very nice man. He actually worries about them.'

'So he's kind to them?'

'Yes, very kind. He has an Arab servant in his house and he's kind to him also. He goes to visit Arab friends he has all the time.'

'How about you, do you ever go to the Arab side to see things?'

'Me, no, never.'

'You have no curiosity about what happens there?'

'It's dangerous to go to Arab areas, so why should I go?'

'To find out how they live and how they feel about the Israelis?'

'We know how the Arabs live.'

'How?'

'I think you'd be insulted. But the Arabs are lazy and they are not very clean.'

'Who told you that?'

'I don't know, it's common knowledge.'

'Do Israeli students your age at the university think the same way?'

'Most of them, yes. But there are some who belong to leftist groups, a minority, but they're always saying that we should give the Arabs their political rights.'

'Do you agree with giving them their rights?'

'I don't know.'

'What is your own personal opinion? How do you feel about the Arabs?'

'I don't mind them.'

'Do you think that they should have their own country?'

'I don't mind really, but I don't want them to cause us problems. Sure they should have somewhere to live.' •

'How about the West Bank? Would you agree to give the Arabs the West Bank?'

'I don't know. We have millions of Jews coming from Eastern Europe and we need room for them. I don't want to be rude, but the Arabs have so much land everywhere, so why don't they go there instead and leave us in this small country?'

'Suppose I tell you that they don't want to go anywhere else and they want a country in the West Bank. How would you feel about that?'

'Well, in that case there's a big problem.'

What made the interview so difficult was the genuine innocence of my interviewee. She told me that most university students were neither liberal-left nor anti-Arab-right but people like her who wanted to live in a purely Jewish state not vulnerable to outside threats. I avoided questioning her about the historical rights and wrongs of the situation because that would have been useless. The limit of her concern with the Arabs was that they should not cause trouble for her and her family or the Jewish state to which they belonged.

Five people were invited and accepted the invitation, but only three showed up at the house of my Israeli journalist friend. Our mutual host insisted that the remaining two's failure to appear had nothing to do with me and the proposed interview but that the *aliya* were notoriously unreliable. (Historically the term *aliya* referred to all Jewish immigration to Israel but now it is used more specifically to mean the Soviet Jews who have been pouring in in great numbers in recent years.) I wanted to investigate how their presence might influence the politics of Israel and the future of the

West Bank. After all, the most conservative estimate suggests that the *aliya* will in two years total twenty per cent of the electorate of Israel.

The most striking thing about the two women and one man who showed up to meet me was their old-fashioned appearance. They looked like Second World War pictures of Eastern European refugees. Everything they wore was drab, giving them a boring and depressing aura. They were between forty-five and fifty-five and the lack of colour seemed to penetrate their personalities; even their smiles were full of tired sadness.

We had to communicate through my friend, for they spoke nothing but Russian and a smattering of newly acquired Hebrew. Their Hebrew was the result of Israeli government-sponsored lessons and when I asked them about that they went through a language learner's recital of words they thought were funny and giggled freely.

My next question concerned their professions. The man was an architect, one of the women was a chemist and the second woman was a schoolteacher. They set my question aside and volunteered statements about how long it had taken them to obtain exit visas to leave the Soviet Union. They were quite sceptical about the changes taking place in their former country and convinced that communism in one ugly form or another will reappear in the near future. To them this meant that many Jews wishing to come to Israel will once again be denied the opportunity to do so.

One couldn't help but express genuine sympathy with their tales of woe; what they had suffered made understandable their fears of the Soviet system and how it works. Like victims of oppression everywhere, including the Palestinians, they wanted to dwell on the history of their suffering rather than on their present situation. They showed a distinct lack of interest in talking about life in Israel and its natural extension, the influence this will have on the Arab–Israeli problem.

'Is any of you holding a job?'

They were all unemployed, each receiving the equivalent of six thousand dollars in annual unemployment benefits, an amount greater than the salaries they received in the Soviet Union. Furthermore, this amount of money afforded them a better lifestyle than their former income provided.

I turned to the architect and asked him why, in view of the huge building programme being undertaken by the Israeli government, he still had no job. His answer, through my friend, was accompanied by gestures and giggles, and my friend, somewhat embarrassed, told me that the man had been offered two jobs that he had turned down because the employers insisted on paying him legally whereas he insisted on being paid under the table. I, too, laughed and offered a 'Welcome to the Middle East'.

It was time to address more substantive issues, and I asked them to tell me what feelings they had on the Arab–Israeli problem. By the sound of things, they were far from up to date. They had no idea that the PLO had accepted Israel's right to exist within secure boundaries and were amazed by my disclosure to the contrary. They couldn't understand why the Arabs would view their presence in Israel with trepidation; the prospect of them replacing Palestinian Arabs hadn't occurred to them. They dwelled on how much they had suffered and presented an argument for their entitlement to 'a home'. Interestingly, they revealed very little anti-Arab prejudice except an indirect one: because the Soviet press had been pro-Arab, they were automatically anti-Arab, since to them whatever the Soviet press had espoused was either dishonest or flawed. Still, they didn't wish the Arabs any harm.

'Would any of you live in a settlement located on land expropriated from the Arabs?'

This question provoked animated discussion among them, and my friend confirmed my suspicion that they wanted to agree on the implications of the question before answering. I have no doubt about the veracity of the answer. They all said that the jobs for which they were qualified required that they live in cities – even the school teacher. To them, the prospect of living in an agricultural settlement was not an issue, and therefore they had formulated no opinion on it. They smiled at me as if to say that there was nothing to worry about, the problem was solved.

I turned the question around and asked them how they felt about the general issue of Israelis settling on Arab land and made clear that this was indeed a big problem. Their answer was another confirmation that their thinking was outmoded, a throwback to the original Arab–Israeli argument, 1948 vintage. This time they couldn't understand why the Arabs attached so much importance to a small piece of land when there was so much land in Jordan, Syria and Iraq. Neither the difference between the Palestinians and other Arabs nor the attachment of people to the land of Palestine made any sense to them. It would have been useless to try to confront them with the idea of the Palestinians' desire to have their own country, so I changed direction.

'Would you have gone to another country besides Israel had the opportunity existed?'

The overall answer, to which each interviewee contributed a part, amounted to a condemnation of the attitude of a neglectful world. It contained considerable bitterness about the fact that the doors of other countries were closed to them and praise for the various Jewish groups that had helped them immigrate to Israel. They refused to make a clear statement of whether they would have gone somewhere else, but they insisted that Israel was 'home' and therefore their worries were over.

'So you feel like Israelis, despite the fact that you do not speak Hebrew?'

They all said yes. The reason behind the unqualified answer was the same: in Israel they were not discriminated against. It was a difficult interview made more so by the interviewees' inclination to give close-ended answers, but I chose to return to the reason for the meeting. 'Ask them if they could tell me all they know and feel towards the Palestinians,' I said to my friend.

Only one of them, the schoolteacher, had seen, met, an Arab at close range, but she still had no way of communicating with the other person involved in the encounter. None of them had visited the Arab areas or had any interest in undertaking such a visit. They didn't even have any idea about the various attempts to convene an international conference to resolve the Arab–Israeli problem. They kept repeating that their only concern was to lead simple, ordinary, middle-class lives in a place where they were safe, but they made it plain that they would not tolerate anything or anyone who threatened that innocent pursuit or the government that offered them the opportunity to aspire to it, Israel.

The results of my second batch of interviews with people on the Israeli side proved more discouraging than those of the first. Even my writer friend displayed a lack of awareness of Arab ambitions and sensibilities and all saw the Arabs as people who lived by bread alone. If one accepts the simple premise that any Arab–Israeli peace must rest on the assumption that both sides are equal, then I have seen very little on the Israeli side to suggest acceptability of this basic human notion. Whatever idea the Israelis have of peaceful co-existence with the Arabs contains the seeds of its own destruction because it assumes that the Arab is not their equal. More bluntly, it assumes that the Arab is an inferior person. That will never stop me from stating that the world would be the less without the likes of Yehuda Litani, and that I found the uncomplicated friendliness of the taxi driver touching beyond words. Sadly, people like them represent a minority whose position is being assailed by the weight of a majority that is opposed to acceptance of the Palestinians and the rest of the Arabs and promises to prolong the tragedy of the past fifty years into the foreseeable future.

Part Four
Palestinians – the Worst and the Best

Chapter Thirteen
A PARANOID CULTURE

My childhood friend Saleh Hussein Al Khatib, whom I remember as someone with a sunny outlook on life, has turned cynical and bitter over the years. He is my age, fifty-five, but his schooling came to an end at the age of fifteen. He lives in Bethany, earns a living driving a tourist bus and has the average West Banker's insatiable thirst for politics. This he tries to satisfy by reading most of the local newspapers and magazines, following Israeli and Jordanian radio and television news reports and through endless discussions of Palestinian and Arab politics with his relatives and friends.

Saleh's social and educational background – he is a villager with two years of high school – is typical of most West Bankers and so are his modest financial position, the fact that he has a son supporting himself through university and his preoccupation with politics. Even his physical appearance is characteristic: he is five foot six with a paunch, a receding hairline and light, Italian-made clothes.

The West Bank is a society where politics are of immediate and constant concern but where the level of discussion is annoyingly shallow, reflecting an absence of solid education or any awareness of world politics and how they affect the Middle East. Nevertheless, a few days of listening to other people convinced me that Saleh's anger and bitterness against everybody and everything are his most characteristic trait. This attitude is truly representative of the local people and deserves investigation because it reflects the thinking of a large segment of the population, namely the middle-aged parents of the *intifada* generation, a group distinguished by its inability to do anything except complain.

Having established that Saleh's choking anger – 'all Arab leaders should be shot' – mirrors a universal Palestinian malaise, I decided to incorporate a new, sharp question in all the interviews I was conducting with people from the political, educational, business, medical and social-work fields in the West Bank. Without exposing my purpose, I asked them whether the history of Palestine has turned its people into a paranoid nation.

Everybody said yes, and everybody added that the paranoia of the Palestinians is justified. The best summary answer was given by Haidar Al Husseini, Chairman of the Family Planning Centre and a member of one of the leading Palestinian families. He said, 'Of course we're paranoid. Yes, indeed we're a paranoid nation. I think it's only natural after a century of abuse. Yes, it's to be expected.'

But the views of urbane social worker Al Husseini, Oxford-educated politician Sari Nusseibeh, physician Samir Abu Khalaf, university professor Jad Izhaq and others, though necessary to confirm the existence of the Palestinian disease, were not what I was after. The awareness of this group of the presence of a national paranoia did not mean that they were among its victims, because of their superior financial, educational and social backgrounds, and I wanted to deal with the real patient, the average man in the street, the Saleh Al Khatibs of this world. I wanted to discover how this morbid condition manifests itself, and what influence, if any, it has on the current problems of the West Bank and its future.

Because the average West Banker is suspicious enough to give false answers, it is almost impossible to conduct formal structured interviews with people here. So I resorted to carrying out my interviews in the informal, unstructured manner of everyday conversations with partners who were told that their names would be withheld to protect them.

All the people with whom I spoke agreed strongly that things in the West Bank and the Arab world are drastically wrong and attribute their personal anguish, which they express with the bitterness of the totally alienated, to this sad state of affairs. It is axiomatic that this group do not have the intellectual skills to deal with what they perceive except in an emotional, exaggerated and unconstructive way. I wanted them to be representative of the larger mass of the people. In other words, my interviewees are examples of typical people who blame the problems of the West Bank and the wider Arab problems on forces they can't influence or control. These forces are the people, organizations and governments that, according to them, have played havoc with their Palestinian lives throughout this century and continue to plague them.

In the language of my interviewees these outside forces are always 'they' and 'them'. When talking about such forces, the average West Banker is loath to identify them by name even when that is simpler, because the constant use of personal pronouns adds to the sinister nature of the supposedly evil powers in question. For example, in talking about Arab leaders, both Palestinians and others, West Bankers often say, 'They're not interested in doing anything to help us,' or 'The only thing which interests them is to line their pockets.' When lamenting the behaviour of PLO leaders in particular, the complaint changes to 'They don't listen to us'. Occasionally I had difficulty determining who 'they' were, only to discover that this is a deliberate vagueness by people who are happy to use this very inclusive term to describe all those whom they accuse of being responsible for their problems.

It took me a while to discover the extent to which the use of 'they' represented an abdication from responsibility for Palestinian and Arab failure: a clear statement that the speaker, and people like him or her, are totally blameless. This act of self-absolution is reinforced by the use of 'they' for local political leaders, as in 'they come from the same families who have mismanaged our affairs since the turn of the century' or the poisonous 'they want us to continue to sacrifice while they make a lot of money trading in our lives'.

'They' are always the bad people who do harmful things to the interests of the West Bankers, but this useful word becomes broader or narrower in scope, depending on who is supposed to be doing what to whom. For example, in 'They will never allow an Arab or Muslim leader to be powerful', 'they' is the West, opposed to the aspirations of all Arabs and Muslims that affect the Muslim and Arab worlds and the people of the West Bank. On the other hand, 'They don't like Palestinians because we're better educated' refers to the Arabs of the oil-rich states. The term's meaning shrinks in 'They don't know how much we're suffering', which refers to the PLO in general, and 'All they want to do is hold press conferences', used to describe PLO leaders in the West Bank. 'They will never grant the Palestinians a country of their own' speaks for itself.

To me, the people of the West Bank making the statements are not only representative of a particular age group, an older group of people who watch the *intifada* and its children from a distance and who are separated from this event and its movers by a generation gap in outlook of much more than a hundred years.

They are the people of the West Bank who lost wars and suffer the consequences of defeat including the loss of hope, the fearful group that still represents a large segment of the West Bank's population, Haidar Al Husseini's paranoid nation.

Only through a closer look at the causes of the prevailing paranoia and whether they are real or imagined can we tell whether the patient is worthy of sympathy. Because there is universal acceptance here that Israel and the West are the enemies of the Palestinians in particular and of the Arabs in general, analysing this aspect of the case is not likely to yield rewarding results. This is why, in this narrative, the West and Israel assume a subsidiary role that is only mentioned in so far as it contributes to the more telling inter-Arab situation. It is in dissecting the relationship between West Bankers and fellow-Arabs, including their own leadership here and the PLO in Tunisia, that we are likely to find a more revealing answer as to whether this national neurosis is justified.

'They are ignorant,' said a man who owned a small coffee-house in Salaheddine Street in Jerusalem. 'They are very ignorant people,' he repeated while drawing on his cigarette and wiping his hand on his dirty sweater.

After establishing that here 'they' referred to Arab leaders, I asked my thin, mustachioed friend to justify his harsh accusation. He continued, 'When Dayan [the late Israeli Chief of Staff and Defence Minister Moshe Dayan] visited King Hassan of Morocco, the king took him on a tour of all his palaces. In his memoirs Dayan stated that there wasn't a single book in all the palaces. Wouldn't you say that was an indication of ignorance – a king who never reads?'

'That's only one man, what about the rest of the Arab leaders?'

He exposed his yellow teeth with a big smile. 'Well, they're no better. King Fahd [of Saudi Arabia] has a hundred billion dollars. He's a gambler and a womanizer. Anybody who has that much money when there's poverty in Saudi Arabia is ignorant. The Emir of Kuwait got married every Thursday and had two hundred wedding dresses ready for the bride to select one she liked. That's ignorance. Hussein [King Hussein of Jordan] has many girlfriends and his wife is American and America hates us. Having an American wife under these circumstances is ignorance. President Mubarak of Egypt takes orders from the CIA and they say the CIA writes his speeches for him. Listening to outsiders is ignorance, particularly when they hate us. Assad [Hafez Al, the President of Syria] hasn't been out of his palace for years because he's afraid of his own people and doesn't know their wishes. It is an extremely ignorant way to behave. And let us not forget [Yasser] Arafat. He is actually a good man, but he is ignorant about the corruption of the people around him, and all he does with his time is kiss African leaders.'

'What about Saddam Hussein?'

'He's a butcher [*safah*], but he's on our side. Come to think of it, we don't have anything except him and Arafat. Arafat's mistakes are different.'

'How are Arafat's mistakes different?'

'He still works for us,' he answered, making it clear he didn't want to say more.

'It seems to me that you are equating ignórance with who is doing the most for you. Is this correct?'

'Yes, that's true.'

I repeated the list of accusations made by the coffee-house owner to an employee of the local cigarette company, a forty-five-year-old middle executive, and he readily endorsed them, calmly, while adjusting his tie to underline the importance of what he was about to say.

This time my follow-up question came naturally. 'If these leaders are ignorant and this is accepted by all Arabs, then why don't the people of Saudi Arabia, Egypt, Jordan, Syria and Morocco do something about them? Why don't they change their leaders?'

The answer was preceded by a snigger of derision; this man wanted me to defer to his pomposity. 'Because the people follow whoever is in office. They're ignorant.'

'Are you saying it isn't only the leaders who are ignorant but the people as well?'

'Yes, they're no good.'

'Why?'

'As I said, they're ignorant, backward.'

'And this affects you, I mean the people of the West Bank, and your welfare, does it?'

'Yes, they could do more to help us but they don't.'

'Was it always this way? Did the Arabs always have ignorant leaders and people?'

He smoothed his hair back with his hand. 'No, it's worse than before, much worse than before. Look at what the Arabs have done with the oil money. The leaders build palaces for themselves and mosques to keep the people busy – they don't build schools and hospitals – palaces. King Fahd has a palace in Spain worth a billion dollars, a whole billion dollars. Hassan of Morocco has ten of them, ten palaces, and his country is poor. And our rich people are no better. You should know, ninety per cent of the people in casinos in London are Arabs. They gamble away many millions every night. What about ---- -- -------- of the PLO? He has a London house worth ten million pounds sterling. No? Shame on them, the leaders in our history were different – very different, more sensible.'

'But Saudi Arabia and Kuwait and other oil-rich countries built schools and hospitals, didn't they?'

'Yes, perhaps, but not enough. Also, what about money for the poor Arabs here and in Jordan, Syria, and Yemen – what about money to build schools and hospitals in these places? The cost of the palace in Spain would make a huge difference.'

'So you're now talking about what the Arabs do with their money as an indication of ignorance?'

He adjusted his glasses, again with a sense of self-importance.

'Yes, ignorance and corruption, yes, yes. They squander it. God, think of what the West Bank could do with a billion dollars. Imagine, it would change the whole educational system. And look at what money has done to them, their behaviour. It is all against Islam and against our traditions. In the past, in history, caliphs shared the wealth with their people, they cared about the welfare of their people, but they don't now.'

'Can you give me examples, more specific ones, of areas where the Arabs aren't as good as they used to be?'

'Yes, there was equality under Islam and there isn't now. The leaders used to listen to the people, particularly learned ones and religious leaders and now they don't. We had our ways and were masters in our land and now we are followers of the West and its ways. If you examine our problem, the Palestinian problem, you'll see that even in recent history we have taken steps backwards. In 1948 the Arabs wanted all Palestine; they didn't concede anything to the Jews and they were willing to fight and sacrifice for what they wanted. When we lost '48 [the 1948 Arab–Israeli war] we settled for less, we settled for wanting the refugees to go back to the part of Palestine the Jews occupied. Nothing happened until the 1967 war; after we lost that we asked for less than after '48. Now we've accepted Israel. But the Israelis know us. They won't give us back a thing. Why should they when they know all we do is take steps backward? Sooner or later we will give up our claim to the West Bank and Gaza. How is that for an example?'

'It's good. Besides the Palestinian problem, is there anything political which demonstrates that the Arabs are taking backwards steps?'

'Yes . . . right now, look at Saddam. He appealed to the Arabs and Muslims to declare a jihad against the West but no one listens. Believe me, forty or fifty years ago millions would have heeded his call and the West would have been in trouble. Today nobody moved; everybody is afraid. If Nasser [the late Gamal Abdel Nasser of Egypt] had declared a jihad, my God . . . people would have risen, but now we're asleep. Look at it this way: the West used to be afraid of jihad in olden times and now all they do is laugh at us.

'Let me tell you something else which shows how bad things are. Saudi Arabia, Egypt and Syria and other Arabs are lined up against Saddam, they're with the West. They want to fight a fellow-Arab and Muslim openly. In the past we were brothers: an Arab never fought an Arab. Not now, not any more.'

'Are you doing anything to help Saddam?'

'Yes, I have just told you how I feel.' And once again he smoothed his hair back like a pretty Italian taxi driver.

The owner of the local grocery store who had listened to the executive's answers could no longer contain himself, and I accepted his offer to join the conversation. He wasn't neat or precious, this one – he had the calloused hands of a worker and wore his Western clothes loosely, but not as an affectation. He leaned forward.

'There is a big story behind the divisions in the Arab world. As you know, in the twenties, thirties and forties the West occupied many of the Arab countries; we were colonies. But the people didn't like it; we wanted to be independent. The West went through the motions of giving us our independence. Independence, my ass [*teezi*]. The West were very clever; they pretended they were giving us independence and they made believe that they were leaving us alone but they put their people in office, they put in people who would obey them to run our governments. Now the West have what they want without us complaining about colonialism: they have the House of Saud and the Emir of Kuwait to do their work for them. What does the West want besides oil? Nothing, they don't want anything else – surely not dates and sand. So it's the oil they want and the oil they control through kings, emirs and sheikhs.'

'But our mutual friend here suggested that the Arab people are also guilty. How does the average Arab participate in this surrender to the West?'

Both men laughed and the grocer continued. 'The leaders, who are loyal to the West, have corrupted the people so the people won't protest against their action. Don't you see that?'

I shook my head to say no and waited.

'When we were young, people cared about each other. They helped their neighbours, gave alms to the poor and tended the sick – and they didn't drink and gamble – and they obeyed the Koran. There was dignity in the way we behaved towards each other. Now it's dollars; people don't care about anything except money. It's the oil dollars which have corrupted us because they have ruined our society.'

'I understand what you're saying but I don't see how it relates to leaders corrupting the people. How?'

'It started with oil: it is a conspiracy between the West and the people they left in power, the people who run the oil countries. The West give the leaders a lot of money for the oil and tell them to use part of it to corrupt the people, to mislead them away from wanting to control the oil. They want the people to think what they are getting is good when in fact they should be getting ten times as much money because the leaders are selling the oil to the West for a cheap price. Yes, they make the people think they're benefiting when they deserve more. Also the leaders and their lackies show the people how to misuse money, to corrupt our values and traditions. Oil, the way its money has been used, has done more harm than good to the Arabs. Even Palestinians who went to work in Saudi Arabia and Kuwait began to behave like the people there – they succumbed, became corrupt. If we weren't corrupt we could buy Israel with the money we waste.'

'But it hasn't all been wasted. We now have more doctors, engineers, lawyers and other educated people than ever before. Isn't that progress of some sort?'

'The doctors, engineers and lawyers are out for themselves, they don't help society. We have a doctor who demands money before treatment – that's all he cares about. Engineers build palaces, not canals or housing, and all lawyers do is defend the rich and refuse help to the poor.'

'Is the doctor who charges in advance a local?'

'Yes, he's my second cousin, the son of a dog.'

'So you're saying there isn't a community spirit any more?'

'Yes. There's only the dollar.'

The grocer eventually told me that he is unable to help anyone himself because he has a large family and after all one's family comes first.

A few days after the meeting with the executive and the grocer, I held another with a builder who doubles as a muezzin (a prayer caller from the minaret of a mosque) in the village of At Tour.

I tried to steer the conversation towards some obvious social ills.

'There's a population explosion here. By the looks of things most people have large families which they can't afford, and they admit that. What is going to happen if the population keeps growing at an unaffordable rate?'

'I don't know.'

'Do people practise birth control? Is anybody encouraging the use of contraception?'

'Very few practise birth control and nobody preaches the use of contraception. It's against religion.'

'But don't you think that something needs to be done? Most people simply can't afford large families.'

'I know. Economic conditions are bad and they're going to get worse.'

'What do you suggest people should do?'

He irreverently put his hands in front of him to resemble a pair of scissors and made as if he were snipping something and laughed.

'Seriously, what do you think should be done?'

'It's a religious problem; I have no answer.'

'But you're a believer, you observe the rules of religion. Is there any way of handling this situation from within religion?'

'It's no different from the rest of the Arab countries: they all have a high birth rate, even Egypt, which is very crowded. In a way everybody deals with the problem, but not openly. The groups which advocate birth control call it family planning, or they talk about it in secret. The religious groups and politicians are against birth control when they speak out. Politicians in particular know there is a problem but they pretend it isn't there. It isn't a popular issue, so they either go against it or ignore it. What is more serious than what they say is the example they set. Look at the House of Saud: they've gone from one person to six thousand in three generations.'

'I am not clear on one thing: are you personally for or against birth control?'

'My opinion doesn't matter; I am a simple man. What I am saying is that you can't do anything except with guidance from above. The politicians and the people in power are the ones who set the example for the average person.'

'So these are the important things, guidance and setting an example, are they?'

'Yes, this is totally lacking in the Arab countries; there's no one to emulate. We've always suffered because of lack of example and it is a big social problem.'

'Can you give me other examples in addition to the area of birth control?'

'Yes. For example, we tell our children not to lie, then *Al Ahram* [a semi-official Egyptian daily newspaper] prints a story once a month telling us that an Egyptian doctor has invented a cure for cancer. It's a big lie. How many times do you invent a cure for cancer? *Al Ahram* is not alone; all our newspapers lie to the people. We tell our children not to steal, then they discover that our political leaders steal billions of dollars. Arab leaders constantly speak of their brotherly feelings towards the Palestinians and then they refuse them permits to work in their countries. Qaddafi [Colonel Mua'mmar Qaddafi of Libya] accuses Mubarak of Egypt of being a traitor, then he makes up with him and goes to Cairo to embrace him. Some of our Palestinian leaders talk about the rights of the refugees while they have never been near a refugee camp to see how they live because they think it's all beneath their dignity. Everybody talks about Arab unity and all it means is that they want the other Arabs to follow them. The press, leaders and governments have no principles. Even religion has been corrupted and manipulated; all religious people do is support the people in power in their country. The top people in our countries are rotten. Simple people like myself can't do anything. I don't even talk about these things normally.'

'What is the solution then? You say people live by example and guidance and there isn't any or it's bad. What can be done?'

'There is no solution. Perhaps a return to true, politically free religion and violence. The Arab world must be destroyed and we must begin anew; there isn't much chance to reform things from within what exists. We need a new Al Hajaj [Abu Museilmah Al Hajaj, an Arab military leader who beheaded thousands of Iraqis for being liars and cheats].'

'Do you think Saddam Hussein is a modern-day Hajaj?'

'Yes, he's not afraid to kill people and that's what's needed. He executes corrupt people who take bribes and he sentences those who shirk their military duty to prison terms and he even deals with religious people who lie. Saddam is tough; you've got to hand it to him.'

'But there is no freedom in Iraq. Doesn't that matter?'

'No it doesn't. I didn't say anything about freedom – what freedom? There's no freedom anywhere in the Arab world, but

Saddam has given the common man dignity. We want dignity. Dignity is more important than freedom.'

'Dignity without freedom?'

'Yes, why not? Islam never gave people freedom, but it gave them equality and dignity.'

'So you think a man who executes people for the most minor of disagreements with his opinion can give the people dignity?'

'They [the Arab leaders] all execute people. The House of Saud chops their heads off, in Syria they disappear forever, in Egypt they're tortured to death, Qaddafi blows them up and the PLO kills them and then declares they're martyrs. All these guys behave the same way, really. At least Saddam is for the average man, not for a select few. Do you know why they [the West] are against Saddam? It isn't because he kills people, it's because he wants more money for the oil to give to the average man, and to use against Israel.'

'So freedom is not an issue in any Arab country?'

'No.'

'Shouldn't it be?'

'I am not sure. Read your history. We don't have a tradition of freedom and democracy, that's why not. On the other hand, equality is something else, equality is in the Koran and that's what we want.'

'But how do you get equality without freedom?'

'Equality is imposed by the ruler, if he's a just ruler then he treats people equally.'

'So equality doesn't come through collective action, through awareness on the part of the people?'

'No, no, we're too backward for what you say. We must be practical and go for equality by a just ruler.'

He went on as I wearily turned off the recording machine, remembering that this man who so admired Saddam for punishing those who don't perform their military duties refused to answer when I asked him if he had done his national service.

Two days later, I was with an employee at a travel agency, a pleasant fifty-year-old man, bald and with a winning smile. He chain-smoked throughout the interview.

'In the fifties and sixties there were political movements that preached freedom in the Arab world. There were political parties, trades unions, socialist organizations and the press in Lebanon and Egypt. What happened to them?'

'You're right, these movements existed, but they weren't very serious. Most of the ideas came from outside, not from our tradition.

Anyhow, the oil money destroyed all that. The oil was discovered in the most backward Arab countries and they imposed their way on the rest of us. Every time a Palestinian, Lebanese or Egyptian went to work in an oil-rich country, they had to give up whatever freedom they had because they lived, dressed and spoke like their hosts. The people of these countries care about one thing and one thing only, money. The people don't care about important things any more, just money.'

'So it's the people, is it?'

'Yes, of course, we must recognize that, the people.' He giggled, waited a minute then continued. 'There's something wrong with us, you know. How many honest ones are there among the two hundred million Arabs? Three million Israelis keep beating us, that should tell you a great deal. How many people are willing to make a sacrifice for an Arab cause? How many true, loyal Palestinians do we have? Maybe twenty thousand. Look at the Lebanese: if you listen to them then there's no reason for the problems in their country. It's all very bad.'

'Do you belong to a political party or group that devotes itself to changing things?'

'God forbid, no, no. They're all liars, there isn't a single honest party or group in the whole Arab world.'

'All of them? Does that include the political groups here?'

'Yes, I don't mind saying it: the ones here are liars, perhaps the biggest. And the rest, all of them.'

'Give me examples of lies by politicians and political groups, if you would.'

'Look at how many times we have been told the Arabs are ready to defeat Israel; even Nasser did that. They lie to us all the time.'

'Is lying the domain of politics and politicians or is it common to all the people?'

'The Arabs are liars, in and out of politics.'

'Why do you say that?'

'I have answered about politicians. About the rest, it's because they are.'

'But why are they?'

'It's part of our culture to exaggerate things. I really don't know. We have two hundred words for lion and no words for social workers like we have from Western charity organizations. It's all nonsense.'

'What about your wife, son, doctor, neighbour, boss etc. – do you believe them?'

'I believe all of them.'

'You believe they tell the truth, that they aren't liars?'

'Yes.'

'So the Arabs aren't liars.'

'Yes, they are, when they have something to gain.'

'Do you do the same when you have something to gain?'

His smile was broad. 'Yes, I guess.'

'Like when?'

'When I sell some tickets for people to go abroad. I don't tell them about the cheap ones.'

'Let's leave that alone. Tell me more about the political leadership here.'

'They're certainly liars. They tell us they're working for us and they're not. Look at their names: they belong to the same families that have led the Palestinians since the turn of the century. They don't want to help us, they want to be leaders – they don't even like the average person. So they lie to us to tell us it's our rights they are concerned with and that isn't true.'

'And the Arab leaders outside?'

'They are the same.'

'Why do they all do it?'

'To make the people happy.'

'But that happens everywhere.'

'It's different in other places. In our case it has produced bad results. We're taking steps backwards as a result of their lies.'

'But a lie has an end, it is eventually discovered. Why don't the people do something about it when they find out?'

'They won't let us.'

'Who's "they"?'

'The people in power, the politicians.'

'Not the people?'

'The people go along.'

'So there's no hope?'

'Yes, there is, if we destroy everything and start from scratch.'

'How do you start from scratch?'

'What I meant is that we should go back to the old values.'

'Are you talking of going back to Islam?'

'Why not? It's better than what we have.'

'Are you doing anything to help with this process of starting anew?'

'There isn't much a person in my position can do. No, they won't listen to me and I don't want to get involved.'

My last interviewee was a fifty-two-year-old schoolteacher who takes himself very seriously. Thin and gentlemanly, he kept his hands on his knees throughout our talk.

'What in your estimation is the reason behind our social ills?'

'Money. When you have it it corrupts and it also corrupts when you don't have it and it is available, because you want it.'

'Please elaborate on what you're saying.'

'Gladly. The people who have lots of money no longer have a social conscience. Look at the oil-rich Arabs. The ones who don't have it are in need. This means they're corruptible; a person in need is always corruptible.'

'Does money lead to an overall loss of values?'

'Of course. Our tradition is clear about how money should be used. In our tradition the only thing which distinguishes one person from another is reverence [*al taqua*]. But we don't follow our tradition, we follow outside, Western ways.'

'So it's Western influence?'

'Undoubtedly, the West wants us to behave like them. They don't accept our ways. What do you think?'

I smiled. 'It's your opinion that matters. How does the West go about achieving their purpose?'

'The people in power do it for them. Look at the curriculum in schools: there's very little about our tradition and more about the West; the rulers decree this to please their Western masters. Look at the way women dress. What's wrong with our native frock? They've given us music, chewing gum and jeans. I think we can live very well without them.'

'What is the answer?'

'To go back to our old ways.'

'What is stopping us?'

'They won't let us.'

'Who is "they"?'

'Our political leaders. They want Western ways. After all, the West keeps them in power because they buy their perfume and fancy cars and arms which they can't use or will not harm Israel.'

'And you believe buying these things harms us?'

'Yes, they do. We don't need all these material things. What we need is values and we don't have values any more.'

'Tell me, how would going back to the old ways change things for the better?'

'First you avoid the confusion of what you want in life. Our old ways called for justice for all [*adle*]. That's enough, that's more important than parliaments, elections and all the stuff we worry about. We don't have justice now and when you don't have justice, you don't have anything. Justice stops the stealing and lying, and abuse of power. We must go back to the ways of justice.'

'Do the Israelis provide the people with justice?'

'No, no, there is no justice in Israel, none. But they're clever, they provide justice for their own people. We must do like them and provide justice for our own people and not worry about the rest.'

'Do you preach this to other people?'

'No . . . I am only a schoolteacher. Who's going to listen to me? I can't do anything.'

And so my interviews aimed at determining the nature of the Palestinians' paranoia came to an end. The preoccupation with the purely political and the ensuing bitterness are certainly there. The interviewees, aged between thirty-six and fifty-six, have the same negative answer to what they consider the problems besetting the Arab world: a reversion to Islam and the old ways without a coherent understanding of what that entails. This wish to revert to the past is all the more amazing because not one of this group belonged to a Muslim fundamentalist movement, so it is more in the nature of a protest than an ideological commitment.

To my interviewees what exists now is corruption, ignorance, abuse of power and wealth, social and political disintegration and conspiracies by the ruling class and Western supporters against the people. There was no admission that anything good has happened to the Arabs lately, no acceptance that some of the oil money has filtered through to the people. Their concern was with what oil wealth has done to the Arab character. All existing governments, political movements and organizations got short shrift; not a single one was worthy of respect.

When they discussed the Palestinian problem in isolation, things got worse. To them, there is an absence of an Arab will to fight for Palestinian rights, coupled with a Palestinian leadership whose only interest is in perpetuating its dominant position. Arab leaders follow the dictates of an anti-Palestinian West, and the Arab people, including Palestinians who had a chance to amass it, are only interested in increasing their wealth. In all it is a hopeless situation with no one to respect or look up to – except someone who would use violence to achieve his aims, a Saddam Hussein.

Not one interviewee had any attachment to the idea of freedom; they all thought freedom through democratic systems wasn't possible. There is considerable interest in equality and justice. Saddam

Hussein appeals because he gives the illusion of believing in equality. Very little was said about his support of the Palestinians, and this took second place to the bigger problem of the haves and have-nots.

Above all, it is the character of the interviewees that lends support to their critical, damning statements of everything Arab. None of them has ever done anything but complain. Not one has served in the army, done charity work or tried to take a clear moral or political position on anything. In reality the group blamed others for qualities they themselves possess. The 'they' my interviewees talked about are people who in one way or another contribute towards Arab weakness, which harms the attainment of the rights of the Palestinian people, and they themselves are guilty of this crime.

The use of 'they' in the West Bank, and to a lesser degree in other parts of the Arab world, by a whole generation of people between the ages of thirty and sixty (including some highly educated people) is a symptom of a culture unable to cope with its own problems because the most basic requirement, the will of the people to change their condition, is absent. There is no 'they': the critic and the person criticized are one and the same. Mercifully, this elaborate Arab double-think, the attempt to shirk responsibility, does not exist in the younger generation. The older generation are already on their way out and being replaced by the younger generation of the *intifada*, who are altogether different.

Chapter Fourteen
CHILDREN OF THE *INTIFADA*

We have seen them, and we think we know them. But there is much more to them than the romantic image of fearless young men throwing stones at armed soldiers while covering their faces with their native head-dress. The children of the *intifada* are in many ways the most genuine revolutionary movement to erupt in the Middle East this century and their angry visible protests are but a small manifestation of a much larger rage that threatens traditional Arab society and ultimately governments and institutions.

For weeks I observed them at close range without asking a question, and even that is hugely revealing. They dress, talk and behave differently, and are not an extension of their elders but an amalgam of elements old and new that owes much to diverse influences rather than a specific one. They are separate; everything about them is distinct.

The standard dress is Western, with blue jeans the most universal component. What is worn above these is eclectic, but the shoes are usually trainers. These youngsters emit the endearing look of free souls; they look as if they are enjoying doing their own thing. There is a striking tidiness about them, and one gets the impression that each of them considers himself or herself the representative of a whole class who view untidiness as detracting from the overall image.

Their language is light and they are brief and to the point: a clear attempt at avoiding the inherent repetitiveness of Arabic. They use simple words and short sentences and avoid cumbersome preambles. Among themselves the language is lighter, hip, and is full of deliberate modern playfulness, but with their elders they accommodate ordinary usage and there is a change in tempo. For example, when an *intifada* youth asks someone of his own age whether he is leaving a place he says '*mashi?*' (leaving?). But when talking to an older person, he reverts to '*b'dak timshi?*' (do you intend to leave?) It is as if the decision-making process is different between their group and others.

The everyday behaviour of this generation of rebels is no less telling. Within their group there is an obvious sense of camaraderie and fun – they are natural teasers – but with their elders they are respectful and deliberately distant. When they are together a strange un-Arabness is near the surface in the way they walk – a firm step – and greet each other – less effusive and more relaxed. They gesture less and seldom raise their voices. With older people they are responsive but not obedient in an old-fashioned, unquestioning way. The act itself rather than their relationship to the older person is likely to determine their response.

My first structured meeting with a group of *intifada* children took a lot of time to organize because I wanted them – more accurately, their parents – to be as demographically representative as possible. I ended up with the sons of a schoolteacher, a stonemason, a bus driver, a hotel owner and a newspaper reporter. They came to see me dressed typically, slightly apprehensive but not afraid, and we met in the modest living room of my aunt's house. They refused my offer of tea or coffee and wanted to get down to business right away. They all agreed they belonged to the *intifada*.

'What is the aim of the *intifada*?' I asked. Without my knowledge, the reporter's son had been appointed to handle the heavy questions. He moved his bulky frame forward and clasped his hands between his knees.

'It is an independence movement. We want to be free from Israeli rule and control, and we want to have our own government which would run our affairs.'

'Do you think you can achieve this through the methods you're using at present?'

'Maybe . . . it is difficult to tell.'

'Well, do you think you can achieve your aims alone without outside help?'

'This is also impossible to tell, but in either case we're under an obligation to try. We will not accept what is going on, so we must do the most we can. But we are not alone. Who told you we're alone? The organization [the PLO] is behind us and so are the rest of the Arab countries, and some Muslim countries and many friendly people everywhere.'

'Are you telling me that the *intifada* is part of the PLO?' Their voices rose all at once and I looked at the hotelier's trilingual son and asked him to answer.

'The *intifada* is not part of the PLO. Both the *intifada* and the PLO are voices of the Palestinian people, but the PLO is good at diplomacy so they handle that while we deal with here, with the Israelis.'

I continued to address myself to him. 'But the PLO has declared a State of Palestine with Yasser Arafat as its head. If you go along with the PLO then you must be part of that state. Are you?'

His gestures impressed me as being softer than the usual Arab ones, perhaps because of exposure to foreign visitors to his father's establishment. 'Well, if a state is necessary then it is necessary. I guess they had to declare a state in order to be recognized by other countries. Why not? We'll go along with it.'

'Why are you reluctant to say that you're part of the PLO? What is the problem?'

'There is no problem, none whatsoever. The PLO speaks for us, we accept that, but we don't want to be a small part of the PLO without having any say in our own affairs.'

At this point, I turned to the group as a whole. 'Are you saying that you don't have a voice in deciding what the PLO is and does? Is this a problem?' They all said yes, quietly and with some reluctance.

'If you had a voice in determining what the PLO is and what it does, how would it be different?'

A new voice demanded to be heard, that of the delicately built son of the stonemason, and he took the floor. 'We are not saying that it would be different, but we're saying it was created before our time and too bad that they didn't take us into consideration.'

'So you are objecting to the way it operates because it doesn't reflect your wishes, are you?'

'We're not objecting to anything. We like the PLO and accept it as our representative.'

'Let me put it differently. If I asked you personally what you would do with the PLO as it exists now, how you would change it, what would you say?'

He looked around apprehensively but got several encouraging nods to proceed. 'I would get rid of some of the old people.'

'Why?'

'They're out of touch.'

'How?'

'They don't know what's happening here, on the ground, where we are.'

'Like what? What is happening that they don't know?'

'Like how we feel.'

'How do you feel?'

'Occasionally, I feel they're out of step, but I don't like to talk about little differences.'

'Who would you get rid of then? Arafat?'

He raised his hand as if to stop me. 'No, no. He's good. He's good and he is our leader.'

'Tell me who then.'

'It isn't really specific old people, it's people who follow the old ways, the old thinking and ways of leadership.'

'Tell me more.'

'I think that you should talk to my friends. They have a point of view on these things.'

He sat back to relax, and I went back to the first person who answered me. 'Do you agree that you should get rid of the old ways and the people who represent them?'

'Yes, I think we all agree on that.'

'Since you refuse to mention names, then what old ways do you want to discard?'

'The ones which give some of our leaders inferiority complexes in dealing with the West and the oil-rich Arabs.'

Taken aback by the complexity and sophistication of the answer, I asked, 'How does this inferiority complex show? Tell me about it.'

'They think nothing can be done for the Palestinian people without the approval of the West and the oil-rich Arabs.'

'Let me ask all of you: do you think you can win without the help of the oil people?'

Their voices rose as one. They assured me they thought they could win without the help of the oil-rich Arabs. They said that the oil people were backward and that cooperating with them as the PLO does vitiates the organization's effectiveness and weakens its moral position because the oil-rich Arabs are corrupt and corruption is contagious. They wanted the Palestinians to try to win without their support.

When I repeated the same question regarding the West, the answer was the same but the reasons for it differed. According to this group of young people, the only thing the West understands is power and trying to deal with the West means using power, perhaps violence.

As a result, one can't negotiate or deal with the West; one must confront it.

By this time I had tired of listening to their ambivalent attitude towards the PLO and their unfriendly feelings towards the oil-rich Arabs and the West and wanted to know more about what they were for, apart from wanting the right of self-determination.

'What do you want in addition to independence for the Palestinians?'

One said, 'Freedom and unity with other Arab countries.' Another spoke of 'freedom and following our own ways' and the others repeated 'political freedom and freedom from the old ways'.

I concluded my first talk with this young group by making arrangements for a follow-up meeting. I decided that I needed to clarify the type of relationship they had with their community and their families in order to focus more closely on what they were saying. A meeting was arranged with three of their mothers and my two aunts, who also have *intifada*-age children. To avoid wasting time, I double-checked the teenagers' background and confirmed that they were average students with no personal problems and that they did typify most people of their age.

The mothers were amused that anyone would think they were important enough to be interviewed. 'Ladies, I met with [I mentioned the names of my teenage interviewees], may Allah bless them. They are good lads who would make any parent proud. Tell me – they're all committed to the *intifada* and the Palestinian cause – do you approve?'

They all said that they didn't object, but pointed out that their approval or lack of it made little difference to the kids, who were determined to go their own way.

'So they don't listen to you?'

'Yes and no. They listen to us on small things, but we never tell them anything on the national issues and they wouldn't listen.'

'Are you happy with the way they are or would you want them to be different?'

'Among themselves, they're very nice lads, but I don't think they like us. At least they don't seem to approve of us,' said one mother.

'How?'

'First, they don't trust us. They don't share anything with us; in fact they don't share anything with anyone who is older than twenty.'

'What is the reason for that, their suspicion of people over twenty?'

They all said it was because the kids thought they knew better and told funny stories of how the kids make jokes about the older generation.

'I still don't understand why they have such a strong disapproval of people over twenty?'

One woman took the lead and spoke before the others. 'They don't like what we did to them . . . just look at what we did to them. We left them without a country and with a lot of trouble. And there's no opportunity here. What do they have to look forward to?'

'So they blame you for their problems, *sit* [madam]?'

'Yes, of course. It's only natural. People leave children a country, education and money, but we are not leaving them with anything. Nothing.'

'And the feeling of disapproval of older people, is it against both fathers and mothers?'

They all agreed that it was stronger against the fathers because it is the men who do things and it is the fathers who left the young people with nothing.

'Do the fathers know this?'

Another lady stepped in. 'Yes, they do, more than us. In my family my son has very little to do with his father. He even finds it easier to talk to him through me.'

'And the reason is politics, pure and simple.'

'Politics, schmolitics, I don't know. The reason is, like the rest of them, he doesn't respect his father.'

'But it isn't personal, is it?'

'No, they don't have quarrels with them, if that's what you mean. They just look down on them. They think they're failures.'

'What do you think they want, the young men of the *intifada*?'

'They want a country, they want Palestine. But their fathers wanted a country and look what happened. Nothing happened; things got worse the harder they tried.'

'Is there any difference between the way the young people want a country and the way their fathers wanted a country? What do you think?'

They all said that there was an enormous difference between the ways of the kids and the ways their fathers followed. To the mothers, the fathers were well-intentioned but fickle; they never pursued what they wanted. But their children of the *intifada* were organized and disciplined, perhaps because they were more educated and aware than their fathers were. Having got from the mothers the direction I wanted, I met with the kids again.

'How do you fellows feel about the older generation?'

The spokesman had decided to reassume his position, and waded in heavily. 'They're failures. They fought the Jews for over seventy years and have nothing to show for it, not a thing.'

'Do you blame them for this or do you blame outside influences and outsiders?'

'What outsiders and outside influences? That's too easy. We blame them.'

'What could they have done differently?'

He shook his head very hard. 'What did they do right?'

'Tell me.'

'Nothing.'

'Then tell me what they did wrong.'

'Lack of organization, lack of discipline, lack of sensible leadership and fear.'

'Fear of what?'

'Everything. They feared the Jews and didn't know how to fight them. They feared their leadership and obeyed it blindly even when it was wrong. They feared their sacrifices would be in vain and didn't sacrifice as much as they should have.'

'Let me ask your friend here a question. Do you think that you have more discipline than the older generation?'

The smiling, curly-haired son of the schoolteacher put both hands on his knees. 'Yes, considerably more. They couldn't organize anything, it was all so funny . . . not well done, just confused.'

'So you obviously didn't learn your discipline from them – from where then?'

He gave me a bitter-sweet smile. 'The Israelis, we learned our discipline from the Israelis.'

The shocking revelation made me think of the full cycle things have come, that it was the Germans who infected the Jews, stiffening Israel's backbone with discipline. He continued without prompting. 'The Israelis are organized and disciplined and they act as a whole, not as individuals.'

'And you and your group do that? You act as a whole without regard to the individual?'

'Yes. Yes, we do.'

I turned to one of them who so far had been quiet. 'Do you agree with this fear business – what, to you, was your father afraid of when he was your age?'

'Sacrifice, they were afraid of sacrifice, and they still are. Look at the way they behave in the presence of Israeli soldiers. They're afraid of them, afraid that they would put them in jail. But we aren't, we aren't afraid of jail, but they are.'

'What about the fear of their leadership? Do you think that was bad?'

'Of course it was and it is. We aren't afraid of our leaders. If you're afraid of your leaders then you've already lost your freedom and you've lost what you're fighting for. Look at it this way: suppose Arafat is a dictator who wants everything for himself, then why should we fight the Israelis just to please him. He would make us slaves and it would be the same as now.'

'So you're fighting with Arafat because he is not a dictator? You think he is not a dictator?'

'I don't think Arafat is a dictator. He is not – definitely not.'

'So one of the reasons you're willing to fight for him is because he would establish a democratic Palestine – is that so?'

He stared at me with the look of someone who knew he was being tricked, and he and the rest of them had gone over these things too often to be caught by someone like me. 'I don't fight for Arafat or any other individual. I fight for me, my freedom and my country, I fight for Palestine.'

'What if Arafat tells you to do something of which you disapprove? What would you do?'

'We would tell him that we disapprove.'

'What if he carries on with things of which you disapprove and he persists in doing that – what then?'

'We would replace him.'

'Are you sure?'

'Yes, that's why he would never do it.'

'You're sure of that as well?'

'Yes, he knows we're not afraid.'

It was time to broaden the scope of my questions.

'Do you think education is behind your thinking? That you think differently because you're more educated and advanced than the older generation?'

They all said yes. 'So you think education is important?'

The stonemason's son felt the question was directed at him rather than the others. 'Education is very important. The Jews beat us because they were better educated; it's that simple.'

'So you're devoted to your schools, are you?'

'Yes, but there's more to education than that. Education is more than schools and books. We learn from the Israelis, from TV and from each other, and we don't follow the uneducated ways of the older generation.'

'Are you saying there's no home education?'

'No, not really. They don't have anything to teach us.'

'But aren't family ties still strong here?'

'Yes.'

'What would happen if your family was insistent that you don't do something?'

'I wouldn't listen, but they wouldn't do it anyway.'

'Allow me to rephrase that . . . would you go against your family for what you consider the common good?'

'Yes.'

'Under what specific circumstances?'

'At one point they told me to be active in the *intifada*. I told them to mind their own business.'

'Anything else?'

'Yes, they always tell me to look out for myself, and I tell them I am a member of a group. My friends and I are the same. Do you understand that?'

'Yes, I do. Can anybody else think of examples against the wishes of their families?'

The bus driver's son raised his hand. 'Some parents don't like the way we dress, but it's the way we dress and that's our business. They even told us not to form the local soccer team because the Israelis would think it's only an excuse to meet and work against them. We formed the team; we know what we're doing and we don't need any guidance.'

'Let me address this question to all of you. Do you think the failure of the older generation is a Palestinian thing or does it apply to all the Arabs? Are the older generations in other countries failures as well?'

It was a question for the leader to answer and he accepted his responsibility. 'It is the same throughout the Arab world; it is an Arab failure. There is no country in the whole Arab world where the older generation left the people with something. Palestinian problems are different, but this problem is everywhere. The young Arabs don't have anything to be proud of or emulate.'

'So you believe the older Arab generation is bad across the board with nothing to recommend it?'

'Yes, they are a generation of treason.'

'That's a strong term, did you just make it up or is it common?'

'We all use it.'

'Why are they traitors?'

'They destroyed our values, our ways, and gave us nothing.'

I stood up to stretch and deliberately made light of what I was about to say. 'Look, you're wearing jeans and sneakers and things Western. Did they do more than that, than adopt Western ways?'

'There's more to it than clothes. They left us nothing to be proud of. They destroyed everything, lost everything. We imitate, but they behave like slaves.'

'Where is the hope then?'

'We are the hope. There is nothing else.'

'Specifically, what would you do?'

'Resist the Israelis in a disciplined way, resist the West in a unified, disciplined way, adopt the effective ways of others, particularly how to organize, kill those who collaborate with the West and Israel and eliminate corruption and fear. You can't have a nation without doing these things.'

'Who beside yourselves would help you attain all these things?'

'Nobody. The governments are bad, the old generation is very bad, the West and Israel are against us, the religious people are in the Dark Ages and the Arab press is all corrupt. The PLO tries, but it's a mess. I don't know.'

'What do you mean by the PLO tries to help?'

'They try. They're not successful most of the time.'

'Is that their fault?'

'It's impossible to tell, but we must assume our responsibility. It could be that others are in the way but they should try harder and stop being afraid of others.'

I thanked my group and decided that I needed to speak to others who have done more than talk about things and throw the occasional stone at Israeli patrols. I wanted to get closer to the *intifada*'s hard core, people who had suffered detention and perhaps torture; after all, even in numbers they represent a high proportion of the *intifada*'s children.

Arranging a meeting with former detainees proved much more difficult than the previous ones as they were more suspicious. A pretext was used to guard the secrecy of the meeting, even from their own parents, and we finally gathered in a small room on neutral territory.

I began our uneasy conversation by reiterating my wish to hear their opinions on everything, particularly their attitude towards the Gulf crisis and what, if anything, detention had done to their thinking.

My first question about what was happening in the Gulf produced heaps of invective against the United States, formless angry shouts worthy of a mob. Of the two major accusations they made, the one denouncing Jewish control of America and American foreign policy held nothing new. The second assumed a sharper edge because of the anger of the moment. According to my interviewees, the United States, and to a lesser extent its Western allies, are irrevocably committed to anti-Arab, anti-Muslim policies that amount to a twentieth-century crusade.

The pack soon produced a leader, a seventeen-year-old redhead in jeans with a stubbly moustache and scared, restless eyes. He had an ability to derive authority from speaking softly. I asked him to give me his assessment of what the Gulf crisis was all about.

'The Americans want to control the oil through their stooges,' he said. 'They don't want the real Arabs, the people, to realize the benefit of oil income. Saddam wants to use the oil money for the masses and to strengthen his army to fight Israel. That's why America and the West oppose Saddam, for these two reasons.'

As he paused, I repeated a statement I had used with other West Bank people who were condemning the oil-rich countries. I said that the Emir of Kuwait used to build mosques, schools and hospitals in his country and other Arab and Muslim nations.

'He gave away very little money, perhaps five per cent, and the rest he kept for himself and his family, the way they do in Saudi Arabia, Qatar and all the oil-rich countries.' He recited grossly inflated figures of the wealth of these countries' leaders (such as the Emir of Kuwait has five hundred billion dollars, King Fahd of Saudi Arabia has two hundred billion).

When I cast doubt on these figures the nine voices rose again in another rehearsed answer. In the view of these teenagers, the United States and the West conceal the figures of the 'corrupt leaders'' deposits in their banks to avoid alienating the poor Arab majority. The group refused to accept that the leaders of the oil-rich countries were capable of good deeds.

I then turned to a quiet sixteen-year-old, who, I had been told, had suffered two brief periods of detention. 'Tell me, do you believe that Saddam and Arafat want oil money to fight Israel?'

'Yes, of course. Nasser was the first man to try to use oil money against outside interests.'

'How would they use the oil money to fight Israel?'

'Saddam already has a big army and he wants to make it bigger and more powerful. Arafat needs money to build a Palestinian army; many people would join an Arafat army, but he doesn't have the money. Nasser wanted the money for the same thing, to expand and support his big army, to buy modern arms. If he had got what he wanted Israel wouldn't have defeated us the last go round.'

When I pointed out that America wasn't alone in opposing Saddam, that the UN, USSR, Britain, France and others were lined up against him, the UN received some rough treatment. 'Why,' asked my friend, 'doesn't the UN implement the various resolutions requiring Israel to withdraw from the West Bank and Gaza and internationalize Jerusalem? Why does America veto all the anti-Israeli resolutions at the United Nations?'

'But what about the other Arabs? Where are you on Egypt, Saudi Arabia, Syria, Morocco and the rest, the ones allied with the West?'

This straightforward question was greeted with howls of laughter and suggestions of naïvety. The Arab leaders of these countries were described as traitors who don't represent their people, and the Arabs of the souk and the mosque were solidly behind Saddam and Arafat and the building of strong Arab armies to reclaim Arab rights in Palestine. Mubarak of Egypt and Fahd of Saudi Arabia and the rest were no more than the agents of American imperialism maintained in office by American power, which doesn't want to see Israel threatened.

I returned to the leader. 'If it were left to the Arab people whether they should support Saddam and Arafat, then what do you think they should do?'

'Every man, woman and child should declare war against America. We should attack them and their oil interests everywhere.'

'Every Arab man, woman and child?'

'Every Arab and every Muslim.'

'A total war?'

'Yes.'

I recrossed my legs uncomfortably, waiting for the qualification that never came. 'Do you approve of hostage taking?'

His young eyes avoided mine and looked at the floor. Silence prevailed while everybody watched him. He put his hands in his jeans pockets and stretched his legs away from the straight-backed chair. His words echoed pro-Saddam and pro-Arafat official reports. 'It's a necessary and defensive move in the case of Iraq. Arafat is opposed to it.' His statement was met with approval from the group.

I decided to change the subject, to bring matters closer to home. I asked whether they had suffered torture during their detention by the Israelis. Two had been tortured, they said, and the spontaneity of the details of their answers rang true.

Their hands had been tied in front of them, they told me, and they were made to crouch through lengthy interrogations. Whenever their legs had given way, they were kicked and beaten with truncheons. They were doused with buckets of cold water to revive them for more of the same. Every member of the group had suffered beatings after being arrested. Some had difficulty in talking about this so I didn't press them for further details.

I continued, 'Are you ready to suffer detentions, perhaps torture, for what you believe all over again?'

The loud yes they all gave me was accompanied by wild gestures.

'Has it worked? Have your sacrifices been justified?'

Inevitably there was another unanimous yes. 'So you will continue with what you're doing now to achieve your aim?'

For the third time the leader took over. 'The aim of stone throwing was to let the world know how things in the West Bank were. Now the world knows but the world hasn't done anything to help us. Perhaps it is time to change tactics.'

'Let me ask all of you if you believe the time has come to move from stone throwing to something else?'

Only one of them said no. The rest said the only language the world understands is that of violence. We fell silent. Someone rose to go home. I shook hands all around and made them promises to tell their story the way they told it to me.

The political, religious and sociological implications of what was said by the *intifada* children and their mothers are clear. They identify with the struggle between the haves and the have-nots. They see themselves as the vanguard of a revolution against the old order, both in the West Bank and throughout the Arab world, but see their elders as a generation of treason. They are willing to suffer and sacrifice because to them that is what distinguishes them from the failures of the past, the failure to accept that winning wars involves suffering and sacrifices. To them, the present Arab leadership is corrupt and must be replaced, and people like Saddam and Arafat, though far from perfect, offer hope. The United States and the West are enemies opposed to Arab progress that threatens their oil interests, and the United Nations is morally corrupt because it follows a double standard that exempts Israel from treatment it metes out to others. Above all, they believe in discipline and self-reliance.

If, as the world is beginning to accept, the old order in the Arab world cannot continue because it contains the seeds of its own destruction, then this children's movement may rise to provide an alternative to the old ways. Developments in Eastern Europe and other places support the thesis that freedom movements are infectious, and there are signs that other youngsters in the Arab world are beginning to take their lead from the *intifada*'s children. Everything happening in the Middle East seems to suggest the existence of a vacuum in the relationship between rulers and the people. The *intifada* is the most developed movement available to fill this vacuum and much of the future of the Middle East could well have its roots in the first stone thrown in the West Bank a mere three years ago.

Chapter Fifteen
THE PLO AND THE PEOPLE

The United Nations and other international organizations, the United States and the West, the Soviet Union and the Arab countries, in fact most of the world, recognize the Palestine Liberation Organization as the sole representative of the Palestinian people. Most of these governments and international bodies temper this recognition with reservations, minor in many cases but considerable in others.

More importantly, the Palestinians, including the people of the West Bank, have traditionally accepted the PLO as their representative and have been inclined to treat it as their government in exile, even since it has been headquartered in far-away Tunisia. This solid but undocumented relationship between the PLO and the Palestinian people has afforded the organization its international legitimacy and stature.

Now, however, the Palestinians in general and the West Bankers in particular are beginning to develop reservations if not outright misgivings about the PLO, and this trend constitutes a long-term threat to the PLO's position of leadership. The growing restraint in the West Bankers' attitude towards the PLO is important and examining it tells us a great deal about the feelings of the people who will ultimately determine the prospects for peace – as they are affected by the people of the West Bank. However, for now, and perhaps for the foreseeable future, the PLO's role is relatively secure, and West Bankers view their differences with the PLO as an internal quarrel that does not affect their common purpose against Israel.

At this point a brief review of the structure and history of the PLO is useful. The PLO is an amalgam, a composite of the various

Palestinian political groups founded in the sixties and seventies to do battle with Israel to recover Palestinian Arab rights. Though differing in political ideology, these groups chose to create an umbrella organization, the PLO, to pursue their overall common goal and placed this unity of purpose above substantial disagreements over the methods to be used.

Fatah was and is the largest PLO group and it espoused a relatively moderate political line. Because of its size and its acceptance by equally moderate Arab countries who provided the PLO with moral and financial support, Fatah assumed the leadership of the PLO and Yasser Arafat became its chairman. To give the organization the semblance of a representative body, Arafat controls it through the Palestine National Council, which resembles a parliament in exile. But it is the ubiquitous and energetic Yasser Arafat himself, a descendant of the famous Husseini family, who is the driving force behind the organization and indeed the symbol of the Palestinian quest for a homeland. He towers above his contemporaries, so it is hard to imagine the organization without him.

Until three years ago, when the *intifada* began, the PLO followed unclear policies that called for the eventual emasculation of the State of Israel in favour of the creation in Palestine of a multi-religious state comprised of Muslims, Christians and Jews. These often confused policies got nowhere; undoing the Jewish state proved beyond the PLO's capabilities. But the nature of the PLO's ambition endeared it to all Palestinians who were desperate to have their own country, or at least a voice in their own affairs, especially those displaced by the 1948 Arab–Israeli war, who lived in refugee camps, and the Arab countries with no Palestinian ground under their feet. So although the PLO's appeal was universal, its pull was strongest among those who wanted to reclaim all of Palestine.

The *intifada*, spontaneous as it was, erupted without guidance in the West Bank and Gaza and forced a change in the PLO's political position and its constituency. Afraid that the movement might produce its own leadership to replace that of the PLO, Arafat brilliantly adopted the *intifada* and in the process accepted its implicit policy of settling for creating a Palestinian state in the territories occupied by Israel after the 1967 war: the West Bank and Gaza. By reducing its demands to match those of the *intifada*, the PLO strengthened its position in the West Bank and Gaza, but weakened it among those who still dreamt of returning to Jaffa and Haifa and the pre-1948 Palestine – that is, the rest of what was Israel before the '67 war.

But the *intifada* and the important change of policy it dictated have so far produced no tangible results for the people responsible for this remarkable change in direction. It is true that recognition and acceptance of the PLO has become more widespread internationally, and the movement has generated considerable sympathy for Palestinian aspirations throughout the world, but for the people of the West Bank and Gaza nothing much has changed and the harsh realities of the Israeli occupation dominate their lives. This failure to change things for the better has led the West Bankers to reassess everything that affects their lives and this includes their relationship with the PLO, the organization that has always represented them and was entrusted with transforming their sacrifices into solid tangible political gains, namely the attainment of independence from Israel.

It should be pointed out that, under normal conditions, sitting in judgement on an Arab country means passing judgement on its leaders, because in the Middle East an organization and its leaders are one and the same. Remarkably, this is not true in this case. Yasser Arafat escapes whatever criticism is directed against the PLO; he is considered above it all, a living symbol of Palestinianism.

The PLO has modified its position and its functions, occasionally admirably, both outside and within the West Bank, and in fact it is beholden to the West Bank people, whose policies it saw fit to adopt. Outside, the PLO retains its functions of mouthpiece for the Palestinian people in international and Arab forums, custodian of the idea of a Palestinian homeland in the eyes of the world, and overall the body entrusted with negotiating the realization of this dream of an independent Palestine. In addition, the PLO maintains an armed force, collects money from the Palestinian diaspora, and receives aid money from the Arab governments. Then there are functions that are decided outside but affect internal workings, such as remitting money to keep the *intifada* and the infrastructure of the West Bank going and the appointment of local West Bank political leaders.

Within the West Bank, the PLO's efforts can be traced in greater detail. The *intifada* is supported through aid money to detained children and their families and payments to lawyers to defend them. The PLO spends money to organize and publicize certain groups and activities including strikes, study groups and political and religious entities. Beyond that, to keep the infrastructure of the West Bank from collapsing, the PLO pays money to support educational and health-care establishments, agricultural-development programmes and civic affairs down to football. Some of the PLO's schemes are elaborate, as when they send specialists to help with the development of the textile business or organize for Italian companies to buy olive oil from West Bank growers.

In the all-important area of selecting and appointing local leaders to deputize for it, the PLO appears to have worked in two ways. They either appoint their own choices in positions of leadership or they adopt local people who have made their mark on their own but who share with them a mutuality of interest. In either case, the PLO's control over the leaders in the West Bank is total because they control their lifeline, money, and because it is impossible for local leaders to function without that and an umbrella organization with which the people identify.

The reasons behind the West Bankers' recent widespread disquiet over their relationship with the PLO are these: the PLO's seeming inability to produce tangible political results to alleviate local conditions, unhappiness with the organization's local leaders and accusations of corruption and mismanagement of much-needed money.

The failure to produce tangible political results produces a greater sense of frustration in the West Bank than among the PLO command abroad because people here have suffered the brunt of Israeli occupation for twenty-three years and living conditions are getting worse by the week. Unlike the PLO in Tunisia, West Bankers don't place much faith in diplomatic gains that might eventually lead to a political solution to their problem. So when the PLO in exile celebrates recognition of its role by a new country, the increasing awareness of people in the West of the plight of the Palestinians or the opening of a political dialogue with the United States, these things do not have the same impact on West Bankers and the average person dismisses them as poor substitutes for their real needs.

What matters here are basics such as jobs and food and the other necessities of everyday life, and there is widespread belief that a political solution would alleviate the problems caused by a lack of these. Subtle diplomatic gains are cynically overlooked because they do not produce results to which the people can relate. Unemployment in the West Bank stands at twenty-five per cent of the workforce and is climbing. The continuing closure of schools and universities blunts parents' plans to give their children a better education than they had and the existing health facilities are under pressure to cope with the problems resulting from the *intifada*, including the little-publicized epidemics of stress-related diseases such as diabetes, hypertension and heart problems. Israeli brutality is an everyday occurrence and many families have had children killed, wounded or detained and lost their lands and homes.

So West Bankers are critical of the PLO because it has failed to translate the sacrifices of the people here into meaningful political gains, the first step towards an improvement in living conditions. The arguments over whether the PLO in exile is doing its best, and whether it is the Israelis who are standing in the way of a solution, are too complicated for people here and most consider them irrelevant anyway. Unfairly, all they are ready to accept is that the PLO leadership has failed and when confronted with facts about Israeli intransigence they dismiss them, saying, 'There must be a way for our people to do better.'

Beyond failing to solve the core political problem, the PLO is condemned for relying on the wrong local leaders – in the words of a West Banker, 'a leadership without feeling' (*zaama bdoun ihsas*). Only two West Bank leaders with PLO connections are above criticism, and indeed merit praise, Faisal Al Husseini and Ziad Abu Zayyad.

In addition to the fact that he is the son of the most popular Palestinian leader this century (Abdel Kader Al Husseini led the Arab forces in 1948 and died in battle), Faisal himself differs markedly from the others. Not only does he have an appealing populist personality, he also presides over several important and effective local organizations such as the Land Office, which monitors Israel's attempts to grab most of the West Bank land, and the Palestinian Human Rights Organization. His organizations undertake much essential work and in doing so are celebrated at the lowest level of society.

The lawyer Ziad Abu Zayyad is a villager who worked his way through law school and attained his position of leadership against massive social odds. This exceptionally talented man devotes much of his time to defending *intifada* children. He also publishes a Hebrew-language bulletin that educates the Israelis in the evil deeds of their government and his command of Hebrew and knowledge of Israeli ways provide the Palestinian leadership with a much-needed understanding of the thinking of 'the other side'.

The rest of the PLO-appointed or approved West Bank leaders fall short of the mark. To the people, they suffer from the same malady: they are bourgeois and out of touch, a condemnation strong enough to discredit them and vitiate their effectiveness.

A closer look is necessary to demonstrate the seriousness of this situation.

Next to Faisal Al Husseini, the best known pro- or crypto-PLO West Bank leader is Sari Nusseibeh, an Oxford-educated former professor of philosophy at Beir Zeit University. Sari Nusseibeh is a good-looking, pleasant, hospitable man who is a good conversationalist and has an enviable ability to enjoy the little things in life.

Nusseibeh's elevation to leadership followed the outbreak of the *intifada*; he was among those who successfully articulated the frustration behind it. The PLO, anxious to adopt the *intifada*, reached out to Nusseibeh and others and confirmed them as local leaders. But Nusseibeh's skill in speaking to the outside world was never matched by an ability to deal with local people, the constituency he supposedly represents. His is a classic case of someone rising to the top because of recognition from outside. However, while the appealing intellectualism of Nusseibeh endeared him to the PLO in exile and the international press, it did nothing to enhance his position with the people here, who are the real issue.

Personal attributes aside, it is the ability to move and lead people that matters under revolutionary conditions and when judged by this yardstick Nusseibeh is totally lacking. So why did the PLO in exile appoint Nusseibeh and others to their positions of power and suffer inevitable damage to the Palestinian cause when they knew that they were unfit for the job?

Sari Nusseibeh's rise to power owes more to his name than it does to his ability to lead the people of the West Bank. He is a member of an old bourgeois family who have lived in Jerusalem for over a thousand years and have held the keys to the Church of the Holy Sepulchre for all this time. His father, the late Anwar Nusseibeh, was a well-known lawyer and politician who served in a number of cabinet posts in Jordan when that country controlled the West Bank. Two of Sari's uncles have also served as members of the Jordanian government and presently many of his relatives occupy important positions throughout the Arab world. Simply stated, the PLO saw Sari Nusseibeh as born to rule, with little regard as to how despised this class is by the grass-roots movement. As a local taxi driver put it, 'The Nusseibehs and others want to run our lives regardless of what ideology we follow or what government represents us.'

To complete the picture, it should be pointed out that Nusseibeh was put ahead of others, even when the losers were more talented and energetic and had solid credentials at street level. In fact, many highly talented people have been alienated by the PLO's penchant for dealing in accordance with an antiquated feudal policy and thinking.

So Sari Nusseibeh is a symptom of a much larger problem that threatens to erode the PLO's popularity in the West Bank, and unless confronted, this problem will cripple the PLO and perhaps destroy it. The adoption of a selfish, narrow-minded policy by the Palestinian leadership is relatively new; until ten years ago the PLO behaved like a revolutionary organization with a broad base of appeal to large segments of the Palestinians.

The PLO's slippage into this destructive position is worth analysing. Years ago, when all the PLO did was field militias to skirmish with Israeli border patrols and deal with the problems of creating a Palestinian national awareness, the PLO, like revolutionary movements elsewhere, needed fighters and intellectuals more than anything else. For the most part, the fighters and intellectuals belonged to the refugee camps and villages, although others came from the open atmosphere of Beirut and the universities of the West. But the moment the PLO turned conservative in order to deal with conservative Arab regimes who belatedly accepted it, it completely lost its revolutionary *élan*. The conservative oil sheikhs wanted to work with fellow-Palestinian conservatives and made it plain that they resented the PLO's revolutionary corps. So the PLO turned to the Palestinian bourgeoisie for new recruits, people to deal with the Arab establishment. Suddenly the old Palestinian names resurfaced, those who had been discredited for their failure to provide a Palestinian homeland in the thirties, forties and fifties. They are not fighters and have no stomach for suffering, but they are the money men who liaise with sheikhs and emirs, act as ambassadors to European capitals and assume positions as consultants and advisers to Yasser Arafat.

To the people of the West Bank, the consequences of this transformation were an unforgivable crime. They bitterly point out that these people were nowhere to be seen during the difficult years of the PLO's struggle for recognition, and make accusations that the establishment will always take care of its own. Old Palestinian names such as Husseini, Nusseibeh, Masri and others took over important PLO positions – if not the whole organization – and the credentials of many of them have nothing to do with the Palestinians; rather, they are the darlings of Arab kings and presidents.

West Bankers emphasize that the Palestinian bourgeoisie has

always abused its people and recite many stories in support of this claim. ('I get better treatment from the Israelis,' said one.) This is undoubtedly true, and I am deeply shocked by this powerful group's utter insensitivity to the needs of the common man and the privilege to which they cling. They insist on being called *beik*, a corruption of the old Turkish title of Bey, and still do anything to avoid submitting to the requirements of daily life. For example, they would never consider standing in line at a bank or obeying a local policeman and demand special treatment in restaurants and other public places. Above all, the average Palestinian scorns their 'privileged involvement' by pointing out that not a single child from the Husseini, Masri, or Nusseibeh families has been detained, because their children find the national sport, or rather duty, of throwing stones at Israeli soldiers beneath their dignity.

Where does all this leave Sari Nusseibeh and his like in the eyes of West Bankers? The simple answer is that while his services may be required as a spokesman to the Western press, he is not wanted as a leader. His presence and that of others who rose to the top on the back of privilege is the source of unarticulated but deeply felt strain between the PLO and the people of the West Bank.

The third and perhaps most damaging issue separating the PLO from its West Bank constituency is the problem of corruption. As our concern is PLO–West Bank relations, we must understand the definition used by West Bankers. To them, 'corruption' has not only its normal, universally accepted meaning but also embraces the source of money and the lifestyle of those overseas PLO leaders who live like oriental potentates while claiming Palestinian leadership. Until the Gulf crisis the main topic of conversation in the West Bank was the corruption within the PLO's ranks in the West Bank and elsewhere.

Specifically, PLO officers overseas are criticized for abusing their position within that organization to make money from Arab leaders, and for their lifestyle. In the words of a West Banker, 'They live like the oil kings and sheikhs.' PLO leaders in the West Bank are accused of personally using money given for communal activity. Even second-tier PLO local leaders are accused of spending small fortunes whenever they travel abroad. Allegedly, they gamble in Monte Carlo and chase all the blondes in the world. One is said to have run up a bill of thirty thousand pounds in a Cairo hotel in three days.

I have investigated a number of these allegations and have come to the conclusion that many of them are correct. If we accept the premise that revolutionary movements are intrinsically lacking in organization and are often corrupt, then exposing them tells us a great deal about their atmosphere and inner workings. In this case such an investigation will illuminate an issue that has considerable bearing on the PLO's relations with the West Bank and the area's future.

It is true that several members of the PLO National Council, the PLO parliament, have acted as go-betweens, ambassadors, to rich Arab countries and it is also true that they have made money in the process. One of Arafat's closest advisers was totally penniless until he was entrusted with liaising with Saudi Arabia on PLO issues. In this role he made a personal fortune because King Fahd liked him and gave him money every time he made a donation to the PLO. (It is said that he stocked up with the latest bawdy jokes every time he went to see the king.) Some, even those who made their money through recognizable business successes, live in a style no less opulent than that of the world's leading industrialists. They do live in houses that cost ten million pounds and spend over a hundred thousand pounds on one party. Some of them do spend an inordinate amount of time gambling. It is also true, as they are fond of pointing out, that this is their money and not PLO money, but this is not the issue. The question repeated by the people of the West Bank is whether this lifestyle is compatible with being leaders of a movement that represents a poor people, many of whom are beginning to suffer real hunger.

The complaint of West Bankers is undoubtedly justified. As a believer in heroic capitalism, I have nothing against people enjoying the fruits of their labour, although naturally I resent excess. However, the issue here is whether the Palestinian people are entitled to expect certain things from their so-called representatives. I do agree that members of the Palestine National Council spending too much time in casinos is harmful to the Palestinian cause and it is equally reprehensible for some of them to spend small fortunes on parties. Yasser Arafat owes it to the Palestinians to get rid of these people.

If West Bankers accuse rich Palestinians overseas of corruption because they have too much money and live in a style unbecoming to political leaders, then they save their strongest criticism for local PLO leaders who pocket funds earmarked to support the *intifada* and its children. So harsh is their censure that most of the language they use is unfit to print.

Because much of the information one gets in the West Bank is exaggerated, fabricated or tailored to fit specific political purposes, I have personally investigated three reported cases of corruption. Two were minor but, although undoubtedly exaggerated, not without foundation – in each case a rumour got bigger and bigger in the telling. In both instances the person had managed to live beyond his recognized means, buying in one case an expensive car and in the other a house that he couldn't honestly afford. But in both cases there is not much more to it than that and the money turned out to be less than reported. While both parties are guilty of offensive, criminal behaviour that an independence movement can ill afford, it is nevertheless the kind of moral slippage associated with their function. The third case was much more serious in both scale and implications.

The person in question is a major PLO operative in Ramallah, a relatively prosperous town north of Jerusalem. A local notable and businessman, he was able to repay an overdraft of half a million dollars from money given to him by the PLO to invigorate the local resistance movement. There is reason to believe that he has been able to siphon off more than the sum already mentioned, or so it seems from his rather confusing bank statements.

I have looked into this man's background and have determined that he is of some value to the PLO. Besides having a local following, he is a good organizer who carries weight with most of the community. If the man's dishonesty is known to the PLO command in Tunisia, this is a classic example of the ends justifying the means, and it is reasonable to assume the PLO feels the same about the two previously mentioned petty thieves and many others. But all this is unlikely to be a reflection of thought-out policy, and the more probable answer is much simpler: Arafat's extraordinarily busy schedule has unfortunately precluded attention to internal matters.

Corruption aside, West Bankers harp on the fact that the PLO has appointed men of doubtful qualities to lead the people of the West Bank. Sari Nusseibeh has talent but he lives and behaves more like a member of the Western literati than a Palestinian leader, and my observations reveal he is more comfortable talking to a young Italian freelance reporter than to a West Bank Arab. Everything about the man, from his sandals to his haircut, makes him look and act like a sixties hippie and that doesn't work in the West Bank because people want their leaders to look the part.

Many West Bankers who are aware of the shortcomings of their local PLO leadership take the view that a change in allegiance at this point would undermine the gains made by the Palestinians and play into the hands of the Israelis, which they can ill afford. They think that a change or an attempt at change in the leadership would undermine the much-admired Arafat and lead to turmoil that would give Israel a chance to continue and prolong its harsh occupation policies unopposed. This would indeed be a high cost to pay without the guarantee that a new leadership would be better. Taken further, this thinking suggests that there is no alternative to the PLO at present. Most arguments for change are dismissed by this group on the pretext of *mish wa'atou*: it is untimely. People who adopt this line of thinking tend to be more educated than the general population.

A second group of Palestinians reason along the same lines, but state that the PLO is necessary and reform from within is the only change possible. They, too, see Arafat as a noble leader who leads a blameless life that includes a rare lack of interest in money, and believe these qualities augur well for a return to the PLO's honest revolutionary ways. Cleverly, they regard as a good omen Arafat's present estrangement from the oil-rich sheikhs and kings as a result of the war in the Gulf. They believe that PLO corruption is a result of money and where it came from and view the PLO's present lack of funds – the Saudis and the rest of the oil-rich states are no longer subsidizing the PLO – as a good way to separate the good guys from the mercenaries.

The third group, some twenty or twenty-five per cent of the West Bank population, believe the PLO has failed and they are looking for an alternative political force to replace it. This group is throwing its lot behind the radical Muslim fundamentalist groups Hamas and Islamic Jihad and PLO radicals such as the Democratic Front for the Liberation of Palestine. Hamas and Islamic Jihad are gathering strength because the ranks of people who are opposed to the PLO are growing, as are the numbers of people who are dejected by the PLO's failure to produce concrete results.

For now, the moderate PLO is able to maintain its local position because the Muslim groups and the radicals have been unable to field acceptable leaders and because some of their policies, while acceptable in an opposition group, are too extreme for a representative body – they frighten even some of their own supporters. The leaderships of Hamas, Islamic Jihad and the hardliners cannot complete with Arafat and his team on an individual basis and their 'Haifa before Jerusalem' slogan, a clear statement that they want all of Palestine back, represents a regressive demand that, hopefully, will keep many people from joining their ranks. For the present, this leaves secure the primary position of the moderates, the PLO. But should the organization's quest for a reasonable response to the demands for independence for the West Bank and Gaza be turned down by the outside world and should it fail to heed the justified demands to put its house in order, then the Islamic groups will inevitably become acceptable and their elevation to a primary position would make the prospects for peace more remote than they are now.

Postscript: On 29 January 1991 the Israeli authorities placed Sari Nusseibeh under administrative detention, claiming that he had been spying for Iraq. This is a patently ridiculous accusation, and a clear demonstration of Israeli short-sightedness. While this unfortunate development does not alter my overall assessment of the man's leadership qualifications, I join others in demanding his early release and wish him and his family well.

Chapter Sixteen
THERE IS A PALESTINIAN STATE

The idea of a Palestinian state has been the subject of endless debate in international forums. Its supporters, the PLO and others, emphasize elements that augur well for its viability while its detractors, Israel and some doubters in the West, concentrate on its impracticality. But in the West Bank something akin to a functioning *de facto* Palestinian entity is already in existence and while Yasser Arafat is not its head, he is certainly its father figure.

Despite the singular aberration of the Israeli settlements, implanted as they are as an alien presence with little reference to their surroundings, the facts show that the West Bank is not only Arab in nature but is run by Arabs as efficiently as any Arab state, and I know them all. Not only have the Israelis failed to change the character of life here, but the Israeli conquest of this land has never been complete. No integration or assimilation and certainly no total subjugation has taken place, and the Israeli presence is limited to military control. Integration and assimilation are opposed by Arabs and Israelis, respectively fearing loss of identity and a change in character of the Jewish state, while to subjugation the *intifada* is the West Bank's answer.

The Israeli government and indeed Israeli politicians out of office, the Israeli press and the Israeli public on all levels equate Israeli ability to 'quell disturbances' with actual control of the West Bank and so does the PLO, which also narrowmindedly concentrates on the trappings of power rather than its substance. In truth, the Israelis have no control beyond their ability to demonstrate that they are militarily in charge and they aren't even interested. The moment an Israeli patrol leaves an Arab town, the place reclaims its totally Arab identity. When it comes to the other aspects of life the Israelis are guilty of criminal negligence, as, to a much lesser degree, is the politically oriented PLO.

The Israeli ability to maintain a military presence in the West Bank can be seen as affording them the chance to establish more settlements and a better line of defence against an organized Arab military threat from outside. But Israel claims there are no plans to build more settlements and the only military threat of that sort in recent years came from Saddam Hussein and involved the use of ground-to-ground missiles, a situation where occupying the West Bank hardly matters. Moreover, the small number of troops deployed are solid testimony that no organized Arab military threat exists.

So what is Israel doing beyond 'suppressing' a bunch of stone-throwing kids and the occasional inevitable escalation of such events? The answer is nothing. Both Arabs and Israelis agree that Israel's only interest is in collecting taxes, in reality a subsidiary issue since these taxes go towards funding their military presence. There are personal taxes, corporate taxes, VAT, property taxes, licence taxes and heavy indirect taxes, but since Israel does nothing but field an unpopular army of occupation this army is entrusted with tax collecting. As the case of Makram Sa'ad has already demonstrated, the resistance to paying taxes is spreading, forcing the military to revert to its primary function of punishing people. Thus it goes round and round.

Everything else that affects life in the West Bank is in the hands of the local Arab population. This includes education, health care, agriculture, public building, small industries, town planning, electricity, road maintenance and the management of buses, taxis, hotels, tour companies and the Holy Places.

The commitment to education among West Bankers, as aggressive as that among oppressed people anywhere, is probably the strongest in the Arab world. In spite of Israeli antipathy towards institutions of middle and higher education (because they are natural breeding grounds for anti-Israeli feelings) and consequent orders to have them shut on the tiniest pretext, the march towards better education continues.

West Bankers run their own elementary and high schools, colleges, technical training centres, nursing schools and universities and many of the institutions are accredited worldwide. There are Islamic schools giving a classical Muslim education (such as Al Makassed), church schools leaning towards traditional Western education run by missionaries assisted by local people (the Jesuit

Frères College), PLO-supported schools with a mixed curriculum (Al Ibrahimia), independent private schools and others affiliated with schools throughout the Arab world. They prepare students to take the entrance examinations of Jordanian, Egyptian, British, American and other universities and have an admirable record of success, their students performing well above average.

The schools are not only well run administratively and educationally, there is a singularly constructive relationship between teacher and pupil. It is here, in the commitment and devotion of teachers and the response of their students, that a West Bank oneness expresses itself. All behave as if they are on a religious mission, and students point out the teacher's sacrifices (they would make more money teaching in an oil-rich country) and teachers proudly identify their successes ('We've sent twenty students to England in the past two years').

The health facilities in the West Bank are lacking by European standards, but they are relatively well run and completely Palestinian. And they go beyond immediate health care to include health studies, counselling services and preventive medicine. The engaging, energetic Dr Selim Al Husseini has admirably put all the data on the West Bank's health problems on a computer, and the equally constructive Miree Ghoneim of the Family Planning Centre adduces endless statistical support for the improvement in the welfare of the West Bank mother and child. Dr Samir Abu Khalaf sums up the overall improvement in the attitude of the population: 'They know better now.'

The Israelis inherited nine public hospitals when they marched into here after the 1967 war, but they have shut down two of them and have done very little to expand the facilities of the others. Palestinian hospitals have taken up the slack while rejecting the ephemeral Israeli attempts to help (legally, the Israeli government is under an obligation to rechannel some of the tax money it collects into health services, but has done nothing whatsoever in this regard). This Palestinian ability to cope came in spite of a dramatic increase in population (2.2 per cent a year is regarded by many as a safe figure, though others disagree).

Palestinian doctors Rustum Al Nammari, Wafiq Nazzal, Samir Abu Khalaf and Selim Al Husseini are full of an infectious sense of responsibility and hospital facilities are being expanded both vertically and horizontally, in terms of the extent of services and their quality and depth. The hospitals survive on donations from outside (from the rich Arab countries, the PLO, and wealthy

Palestinians among others), work with the British Medical Association, cooperate on a local level with Italian, Swedish and other medical aid workers, and send thirty technicians at a time to be trained by the Cooperative Society of Geneva. And they still have time to plan turning Al Makassed into a teaching hospital and to educate the population in dietary improvements.

Roving health units using mobile vans visit small villages where no health care is available and offer across-the-board medical services that include eye and dental care. Palestinian organizations, political, religious and otherwise, vie as to who has more vans, offers broader services and visits more villages. The PLO has first-class medical teams as does the Islamic political movement, Hamas, along with the Catholic, Greek Orthodox and other religious groups and the Communist Party. Even when a political background is present, the efforts are apolitical, and the Communist, Catholic and Muslim units operate on a strict and admirably humane basis. The vans and their support units are manned by a local peace corps of committed young men and women and use whatever is made available to them most effectively. In fact, so successful is this programme that the UN and many Third World countries would do well to study it with a view to adopting its methods.

Agriculture is another area where local talent is being applied with surprising results. I know of six non-profit Arab organizations (except for the Applied Research Institute of Bethlehem and its offshoots, they would rather remain anonymous) whose staffs work diligently to help both large and small farmers in their efforts to improve yields, protect livestock, rotate crops and educate people in other modern methods of agriculture. As a result the per acre yield of crops such as tomatoes, aubergines and fava beans has almost doubled, land previously left fallow because it was considered untillable has been successfully planted with citrus fruits, new fruits such as guava and mangoes have been introduced and even those biblical standards, the olive and the fig, get better care and yield more and of a higher quality.

I have seen young agricultural engineers trek to God-forsaken Bedouin encampments to teach people how to use insecticides and protect sheep and camel flocks against killer diarrhoea and educate people in maximizing the breeding cycle. Producers' cooperatives are operating successfully in the Jordan valley, Ramallah's apple-growing area and other places. In one dramatic example, improvements in the methods of raising chickens since 1967 have led to a one thousand per cent increase in their West Bank population and the production of eggs has risen by over three hundred per cent, thus providing a much-needed source of protein.

These achievements have been possible despite a massive land-expropriation programme by the Israeli government that took away most of the grazing land, and deliberate Israeli competition in fruit and vegetables.

On the local administrative level, the management of the affairs of town and villages, the achievements of the West Bankers are no less impressive. Municipal councils and mayors have developed their own ways of running their affairs efficiently, a case of the self-contained unit acting as a prop for the bigger whole. The refusal of the Israelis to allow West Bankers to run their affairs 'as a separate entity' has led to villages and towns assuming a greater share of the burden and their successful handling of their duties and the march towards self-sufficiency have undermined Israeli policy. In the words of a local mayor, 'If all the villages and towns are run well then the West Bank is being run well, each is a living part of the whole.'

In Bethlehem, Mayor Elias Freij works tirelessly with a myriad of civic and charitable organizations whose purpose is to keep the city alive and prosperous in the face of Israeli restrictions and the *intifada*-related drastic decline in the city's primary source of income, tourism. Freij's office is open to all groups, religious, commercial and civic and he has effected a remarkably successful measure of cooperation between normally competing entities. My survey of the town, deliberately without Freij's guidance, revealed that the olive presses are operating more efficiently, the local makers of handcrafts are finding outlets overseas to replace loss of local business and the pharmacies have settled for a lower profit because the local population is suffering financial pressures.

In my home town of Bethany, Mayor Hassan Shehadeh Al Khatib runs the community of nearly twenty thousand people with the help of two assistants. He settles local disputes, mostly over property, manages the collection of municipal bills (for electricity, water and telephone), oversees the activities of local schools, lends support to collections for the poor, and consoles the families of detained *intifada* children. All his activities are directly or indirectly aimed at functioning independently of the State of Israel and he is successful.

Even the Bedouins south of Bethlehem, the Sawahra, Ta'amra and Obediya, do a good job of managing their affairs with the minimum amount of Israeli involvement. Sheikh Nufan Al Obediya says proudly, 'Not a single intertribal dispute has reached the Israeli courts. We settle our disputes ourselves and on the odd occasion when we fail, we ask for the judgement of wise men from other villages and tribes. A brotherly spirit prevails everywhere and they are willing to help more than in the past – they think it is a common problem.'

And while success exists on the local level and the Israelis are opposed to activities on the West Bank level that might represent a challenge to their supremacy, there are groups and organizations that operate regularly or on an *ad hoc* basis whose work inevitably affects all the West Bank. The Association of Travel Agents works to coordinate the efforts of its members and with the villages and towns that have tourist potential. Its former chairman, the energetic Yussuf Awaidah, articulates the organization's efforts thus: 'a coincidence of interest which transcends the individual profit motive, either we float together or we die together. We are getting full cooperation from all the people involved.'

The Pharmacists' Syndicate issues regular bulletins telling members where to get much-needed antibiotics cheaply and the pharmacists accept its help and pass on the savings to the user. Many doctors devote a considerable amount of their time to treating poor people free of charge and some lawyers offer free legal advice. A crippling passing of the buck continues to exist among a considerable number of semi-educated people (see Chapter Thirteen) but this group is being assailed from above by the educated class, and from below by the younger generation, the *intifada*'s disciplined backbone.

To an expatriate like me with a frame of reference belonging to the past, there have been healthy grass-roots changes that don't mean much to an outsider and are missed by West Bankers who watch them evolve in small, imperceptible steps. These changes, important reflections of social maturity, are more prevalent among the young, but they have infected the older generation, who see fit to follow the lead of the youngsters. People stand in line for buses and taxis, help children cross the street, have a greater sense of time and its importance, are considerably more aware of the benefits of preventive medicine and are more communal and less individualistic and quarrelsome, all examples of behaviour unheard of during my youth. This is not to deny that wasteful, unconstructive complaining is still with us and a total sense of community has not been achieved, but it is a huge step forward.

The ability of West Bankers to manage their affairs doesn't stop at the obvious. There are a great many individual and communal attempts at innovation. Professor Jad Izhaq of Bethlehem University successfully channels the energy of many of his angry students into doing part-time community work. He has deservedly become a lighthouse for those looking for sane, constructive achievement. Samir Abu Huleileh, a thirty-two-year-old economist, spent weeks studying the effects of the Gulf crisis on the economy of the West Bank and produced a magnificent study, which he made available to one and all at a time when the local political leadership addressed itself to hollow and unconstructive exercises, neglecting this vital area. (The West Bank was more adversely affected than those countries that have received attention in this regard, namely Israel, Jordan, Egypt and Turkey.) Several professors (names withheld to protect them) who normally teach at universities that have been shut by orders of the Israeli military authorities tirelessly conduct seminars in their own homes and make themselves available to all students who need their help.

Beyond individual efforts, the West Bank is home to the best-run cigarette company in the Middle East. Thirty thousand people are employed in the manufacture of clothing, much of which finds its way to Europe directly or through Israeli exporters, and this activity is expanding. The handcrafts business throughout the West Bank is expanding despite the decline in tourism, because exports are booming. Canning fruit and vegetables is a highly sophisticated and growing industry. According to the UN's resident development officer Nikitas Nevrotis, 'All you have to do is show people how to do it better and they will; they learn fast.' I have met several civil engineers who have impressed me with their ability to design buildings that are functionally advanced yet ornate and ancient in their appearance, a balance between the new and the old Middle East. I have also experienced the efficiency with which West Bankers run service businesses (tourism, bus companies and shops), and develop new ones, as in the case of software for Arabic-language computer programs. These they have exported to the rest of the Middle East, having put in an extra effort because they are working for 'our own people'.

It is little wonder that the twenty-three-year-old military occupation has had scarce or no effect on the West Bankers' chosen way of life. The *intifada* is but one expression of the Arabs' determination to maintain their identity and, in spite of the Israeli sledgehammer approach, which has produced a heavy toll of dead, wounded, detained and traumatized, there are other important everyday aspects of this determination that are equally telling.

The Arab way of love, marriage, sorrow, death, respect for the elderly, their way of talking, walking and clicking their prayer beads, showing courage, appreciation of giving and receiving and the use of memory to alleviate the momentary wretchedness of being, all remain intact. As a matter of fact, the only Hebrew words to infiltrate the Arabic language have to do with roadblocks, curfews, rubber bullets and gas bombs.

This analysis, although considerably hampered and reduced by my inability to mention names and cite examples in order to protect the innocent and their work, nevertheless attests to the existence of a growing infrastructure that could still do with further help from the PLO, Arab countries and international organizations. It is all done without the involvement of the Israeli government. Even when West Bank hospitals are short of blood, as they unhappily often are, they buy it from the Israelis for cash. Nor have other organizations asked the Israeli government for help to which they are entitled. (The Israelis' lack of concern about what happens in the West Bank was the most shocking discovery of my three-month stay.)

I do not wish to minimize the problem of the Israeli settlements, which for the most part are eyesores, but the story of how the Arabs of the West Bank can manage their affairs is overdue and much more is possible. In short, the infrastructure of a Palestinian state is already in place and functioning, which means that an important question as to the viability of such a state has already been answered. At the same time, constant military raids and the taxation to support them are intrinsically counter-productive and will do nothing except strengthen the West Bankers' will to get rid of those responsible.

Conclusion
THE PATH TO A SANE FUTURE

The overriding purpose of this book has been to show the human cost of the situation in the West Bank. But I am also convinced that there is another way to use the discoveries I made during my three-month investigation. And that is to try to propose solutions to the appalling everyday problems and so maximize the potential for solving the bigger problem.

The end of the war in the Gulf and the shift of focus to the Palestinian situation make this task all the more pressing. But rather than offer sweeping solutions, I aim to identify who could solve specific problems, in some cases why they should, and occasionally how. If what I suggest falls short of a permanent remedy, it is because my main concern is to see an improvement in the everyday situation in the West Bank. These vital first steps may even play a part in determining the nature of the long-term solution.

The brutality of the Israeli occupation is beyond dispute, being attested to by dozens of reports compiled by humanitarian, religious, governmental and other organizations, and witnessed by me almost daily. The failure of the Israelis to subdue the *intifada* and other manifestations of unrest in the West Bank (such as non-payment of taxes) has led to the application of harsher measures when what is needed is a visionary long-term policy aimed at eliminating the root causes of Arab dissatisfaction. The frequency of acts of suppression by the Israeli security forces has escalated, but Israel lacks more than a policy to deal with Arab unrest: it has no coherent policy on the bigger problem of where it belongs in tomorrow's Middle East. Indeed its pride in its democratic system of government hasn't stopped it supporting reactionary Arab regimes and opposing progressive ones. This Israeli failure to develop sensible short and long-term policies implies a tacit acceptance of the present state of turmoil at the expense of the pursuit of peace. While this behaviour freezes the conflict and temporarily eases the pressure on Israel, it inevitably contributes towards the perpetuation of the problem.

A dangerous ghetto mentality exists in Israel and the resultant thinking says that all outsiders are anti-Jewish and anti-Israeli and this includes staunchly pro-Israeli countries such as the United States. Everybody is accused of wanting to settle the Arab–Israeli problem at the expense of Israel. What is worse, this xenophobia makes Israel unlikely to listen to any outside advice at all.

On the Arab side old maladies continue to infect the older generation of people and the political leadership. For the most part, the older generation continues to lack a constructive sense of community and this undermines their unity of purpose and claim to nationhood. This generation is crippled by narrow notions of commitment to family and tribe. In addition, the political leadership is shallow, selfish and insensitive and for the most part asserts its position through a class system that threatens and impairs the just claims of the people it ostensibly represents.

Among the younger generation of Arabs the story is almost the opposite. The *intifada* is not only a rebellion against Israeli rule, it is also a revolt against the old, obsolete ways of the Arabs in general. The young believe in freedom, hence democracy, and have a remarkable sense of discipline and community. Not only are they most unlikely to succumb to Israel's punitive policies, they are too sophisticated and aware to accept the dictates or misguided policies of Arab leaders.

Despite obvious shortcomings, the Palestinians are the most educated and productive people in the Arab world. The attitude of the *intifida* youth and the existence of a committed class of young ideologues, particularly among Christian Palestinians, together promise healthy development of the infrastructure already in place in the West Bank. The older, ineffective generation is disappearing and the young, constructive one is taking its place.

However, in a major and disturbing way the Arab attitude in the West Bank resembles that of the Israelis. The results of war in the Gulf and the world's refusal to treat the Palestinian problem with the same urgency it applied to the occupation of Kuwait has led Palestinian Arabs young and old to believe everyone is against them. They are paranoid, as crippled by fear as the Israelis. Both sides are the victims of their history.

On the face of it, there is little that augurs well for the future.

Arab acceptance of Israel as a conquering power is not possible, and Israel has shown scant acceptance of Arab claims to equality. Even at the lowest level of contact, dialogue between the two sides is stifled and, in spite of noises to the contrary, the peace advocates on both sides have failed, mostly because of the lack of courage and foresight. The violence of the past three years has produced rigid attitudes that militate against the emergence of healthy local developments that could in turn improve the broader situation.

The economic plight of the West Bankers threatens to exacerbate an already tragic situation. The four major sources of income, tourism, remittances from Palestinians working in the oil-producing countries, payments from the PLO and income from work in pre-1967 Israel have all at the same time dried up as a result of the war in the Gulf. The absence of efforts to ease the West Bankers' economic circumstances can only make things worse.

The gloomy, fluid background casts doubt on the possibility of remedial action. However, considering that things in the West Bank are getting worse and the rest of the world, which rushed aid to several countries affected by the Gulf situation, has indeed been neglectful, any help must be welcomed. Dozens of journalists, the International Red Cross, the United Nations, Amnesty International and the Commission of International Jurists among others have documented Israeli abuse of human rights and claim the violations are getting worse. Israeli claims to have crushed the *intifada*, repeated for the past three years, are untrue, as is attested to by the new harsher measures they continue to introduce. This response has in fact produced the opposite of what was intended, for violence is increasing on both sides. For both humanitarian and practical reasons, international pressure going beyond futile diplomatic reprimands must be applied to check Israel's policy of occupation. If the world is to escape accusations of using a double standard then it must deal with Israeli atrocities the way it responded to Iraqi behaviour in Kuwait. In this direction lie prospects for peace.

The Jews outside Israel, particularly those whose financial support is vital, namely the American Jewish community, are under a moral obligation to work against the xenophobia gripping Israel. The continuation and deepening of this feeling threaten the status of Jews everywhere and they will eventually have to answer the question of where their loyalties lie, with Israel or where they live. At the same time Israel must be told that it cannot rely on outside Jewish support to enforce policies that are damaging, unjustified and unacceptable, if not outright criminal.

Non-Israeli Jews, the United Nations and the world's leading powers must pressure Israel to articulate its long-term policy on its position in the Middle East. A negative policy that assumes the continued ability to dictate to the Arabs through military superiority and the indefinite continuation of the Arab–Israeli conflict must be replaced with a coherent long-term approach that defines Israel's national objectives in the area. Unless Israel takes steps to demonstrate a belief that its future lies in being part of the Middle East, the accusation that it is a proxy for American neocolonialism will stick. Inevitably, the present US policy of backing mostly corrupt regimes has already laid open both Israel and America to this widespread charge.

The Palestinian leadership must stop blaming all its problems on outside influences and must accept responsibility for educating its followers into shouldering part of the blame for their social ills, and tell them that they are self-inflicted. To avoid future political turmoil, the Palestinian leadership is under an obligation to be more responsive to conditions within the West Bank, and this should include replacing leaders whose ways do not reflect the thinking of the people. The average Palestinian should do all he can to pressure his leadership into adopting such policies.

The Arab countries must underwrite an economic aid programme aimed at alleviating conditions in the West Bank. They are easily capable of doing that (public perception that the cost of building one royal palace in Kuwait or Saudi Arabia is enough to make a material difference in conditions in the West Bank is indeed accurate) and international pressure on them to act is overdue. This would reduce the chances of further infectious radicalization of popular thinking, which threatens the stability of the whole Middle East. The risk of this happening has been exacerbated by the war in the Gulf, which produced an unhealthy alliance of convenience between the United States and the corrupt regimes of Saudi Arabia and the Gulf sheikdoms.

Palestinian leaders, the UN, Arab countries and all concerned parties must develop programmes to harness the constructive energy of the young people of the *intifada*. This could begin with efforts to provide them with higher and better education. Otherwise their sense of alienation will deepen and compel them to discard the PLO and its moderate policies in favour of more radical movements including uncompromising Muslim fundamentalist ones.

Above all, and as a first step, there must be an on-the-ground international presence to guard against violence and excesses. An international body of observers must be created immediately and it should be empowered to liaise with both Israel and the Arab community to stop the periodic explosions that retard and destroy whatever constructive steps are taken in the meantime. In addition, this neutral body should be entrusted with apportioning blame and the international community should be obliged to act on its recommendations. This would eliminate the wasteful cycle of claim and counter-claim between the parties concerned.

Israel is not listening to outside bodies or nations, and that includes the United States, without whose help it would not survive. Non-Israeli Jews concerned with Israel's future, instead of resorting to the idiotic glibness of 'she is not perfect but she's mine', would do well to use their influence on Israel more constructively. After all, they are more aware of worldwide developments and the rising tide of anti-Israeli sentiments than the Israelis. And Israel needs them and listens to them. A starting point would be to make the Israelis understand that their negative policies are harmful and counter-productive and that the world is unlikely to accept them for much longer.

Israel has failed to adopt or even consider developing long-term policies toward the Middle East. Its superior attitude to its neighbours and a short-sighted stance that assumes a lasting Arab military inferiority are but two examples of how wrong present policies are. The elimination of Iraq as a military threat confirms that Israel's survival is no longer an issue; rather that its future relationship with its neighbours is the priority. World Jewish leaders should act like the family of an estranged husband or wife and tell Israel, 'we love you very much but we're no substitute for the real thing', namely peaceful co-existence with the Arab countries of the Middle East.

The time has come for the PLO leadership to expand its efforts in areas not exclusively political. The Palestinians suffer from serious social ills and to pretend they do not exist and blame every problem on outside influences does nothing but perpetuate a destructive habit of buck-passing and augurs poorly for a much-needed political maturity. The PLO's admirable achievements in the areas of education and health care must be expanded and a massive self-help programme is needed that can augment gains in these and other areas. Specifically, the already successful development of an infrastructure that demonstrates the Palestinians' ability to run their own affairs efficiently, should be further encouraged and supported.

On another vital front, the PLO must take immediate steps

to stop the cynical exploitation of the Palestinian people by the bourgeoisie. Yasser Arafat has the stature and ability to effect such a radical change. Failure to take this corrective action does nothing except lend weight to Israeli allegations that the Palestinians are not ready for self-rule at the expense of the just claims of the Palestinians.

The Arab countries must stop their old practice of buying leaders' loyalties and must direct their aid programmes towards improving the economic and social infrastructure of the West Bank. There are Palestinian organizations in the West Bank through which such aid could be channelled and these have been successfully, if only partly, used for this purpose. Aid money of this type is needed to avoid a descent into poverty and political chaos. Furthermore, the amount needed is affordable.

The children of the *intifada* are a remarkable group of people who hold the key to the future. They are hungry for education, socially aware, energetic and have an attachment to the idea of freedom that is lacking in their elders. With a little guidance and help, real improvement in the level of education can be attained. Beyond this, work can be provided that capitalizes on their wish to contribute – from assisting with literacy programmes to providing help for the poor and aged and teaching better hygienic practices. Such programmes are easy to implement and relatively cheap to undertake and would give young people a much-needed sense of purpose.

The declarations of the UN and other international bodies calling for Israel to stop its violations of the Geneva and other conventions protecting the human rights of West Bankers must, as was done in dealing with Iraq, be enforced in a way that reflects the will of the countries who vote for them. The member states of the UN, the United States in particular, must cease to treat Israel like a spoiled relation. The new order in international politics that came into being with the Gulf crisis and its aftermath cannot absolve Israel. Indeed that country's continuation of its present policies should be met with a prohibitive response by the world community.

All the above comments make it clear that the people in power, the Israeli government, influential outside bodies and governments, and, until recently, the PLO, have failed to take the necessary steps to pave the way for peace. While this may be so, Israel still occupies the West Bank, holds most of the cards and can do much more than others. Given half a chance, the *intifada*'s children would force changes on the PLO that would make it a more sensible, responsive entity. And the Palestinians as a whole, who against all odds created something that resembles a functioning state in the West Bank, would turn their attention to making it viable and politically acceptable. But this cannot happen unless Israel changes its policies to include unconditional acceptance of the Palestinian right of self-determination.

I am aware that my view of the steps that need to be taken to avoid disaster in the West Bank are so simple as to border on the naïve. Each step is obvious and requires a change in thinking by the people, organizations and governments concerned. Even then this change would affect only the little things in life. I am settling for that because I believe that people must learn to walk before they can run and in this case walking means adopting immediate measures to solve the small everyday problems that produce pain and suffering. If these small measures are effected, then peace will follow. Humankind, including flawed Arabs and Israelis, is inherently progressive and the futility of the way of the gun must by now be apparent to all concerned.

ABOUT THE BOOK AND AUTHOR

Cry Palestine provides a unique perspective, a glimpse into the world behind the *intifada* from both the Palestinian and Israeli points of view.

Saïd K. Aburish was born in the West Bank village of Bethany and lived there until he was fifteen. He has a large number of relatives and friends who still live on the West Bank, many of whom, since the *intifada* began, have been victims of Israeli police methods and law. At the same time, Aburish has maintained a close relationship with many Israelis, who tell him of a nation constantly under threat by hostile Arab states. Palestinians, in contrast, tell of schools that are shut down, children beaten, and villagers' land and homes expropriated.

In its sympathy and broad understanding, *Cry Palestine* is a unique document, essential reading for anyone who wishes to comprehend fully the complexities of the Palestinian question.

Saïd K. Aburish was born in the West Bank in 1935. He attended university in the United States and subsequently worked as a consultant to several Arab governments and as Middle East correspondent for Radio Free Europe and the *Daily Mail.* He is now a journalist and author and has written for, among others, the *Independent,* the *Washington Post,* and *Liberation.* His books include *Pay-Off: Wheeling and Dealing in the Arab World, The St. George Hotel Bar* (published in paperback as *Beirut Spy*), and *Children of Bethany.* He lives in London.